MEMOIRS OF A BAD BOY

A true story of a young man's struggles, incarceration, and redemption

REGINALD J. TULL

Copyright © 2022 Reginald J. Tull
All rights reserved. No part of this publication may be reproduced, stored in a retrieval system or transmitted, in any form or by any means, electronic, mechanical, recording or otherwise (except brief passages for purposes of review) without the prior permission of the author.

Cover Designer: Sogbola Isaiah
Designer : Jonathan Relph
Copyeditor and Proofreading: Christopher Cameron

For my three heartbeats: Israel, Josiah, and Semaiah

CONTENTS

Introduction   1

1. Murder in the Second Degree   3
2. The Parents I Never Knew   21
3. No Good in the Hood   33
4. The Great Escape   54
5. The Suicide Attempt   70
6. Welcome to the System   81
7. Bronson Detention Centre   91
8. The Joyride   100
9. Innes Detention Centre   108
10. One Shot of Brandy Was Enough   125
11. Good Girls Love Bad Boys   134
12. Teenage Thug Life   152
13. Victim of My Environment   172
14. The Toronto Don Jail   177
15. The New Heavy on the Cell Block   186
16. Violence in the Don   194
17. United We Stood   202
18. The Final Court Appearance   215
19. Redemption Draweth Nigh   221

Acknowledgements   246

INTRODUCTION

In this memoir you will read about violence, sex, abuse, drugs and alcohol, and the redemptive power of the Most High. This is not a tell-all book, or a book of confessions, nor was it written by any means to glorify or justify any crime or sin that I have committed. You will read about my struggles as a kid growing up and how I learned to deal with life both on the streets and in the home. If you live in Toronto or have never been here, you will be enthralled by what you read about the mosaic city. While writing these chronicles, I have laughed, cried, gotten angry, bored, discouraged, and motivated. It took many years to conclude. I have written different parts of my story from North America, South America, Asia, Europe, and the Caribbean. When describing certain criminal scenes, I have changed some names, especially with crimes that have not been solved and are still open cases. My purpose for writing this book is to tell my own story, because it is a story that must be told, and there is no one who can tell it best but me. I am hoping that *Memoirs of a Bad Boy* will motivate young people to do something positive with their lives and not go down the path of destruction that I found myself on throughout the years. Many of my friends never made it out, but some have. My wish for you as you read through these pages, is that you will aspire to become a better kid, a better parent, a better role model, a better person.

CHAPTER ONE

MURDER IN THE SECOND DEGREE

May 24, 1993

"I saw who stabbed him! I saw who stabbed him!" my friend Winston kept repeating in the midst of the chaos and confusion. I stood frozen to the pavement as the young man lay on his back in front of me – lifeless. *What happened to him?* I didn't see any blood. Did someone stab him, or was he lying dead from the blow that I'd given him across the head with his own cane? How did I ever get myself into this situation?

The day had started off great. I had woken up next to my beautiful Hungarian queen, Bobbie. The sun shone through our bedroom window as a crisp morning breeze made its way in and filled the air with the fresh scent of spring. Bobbie and I were staying on the third floor of a four-bedroom townhouse, where we rented a room from Lenny, a family friend on my mom's side. Bobbie and I had plans to visit her sister in the West End for dinner since it was the Victoria Day holiday Monday, and neither of us were working.

Bobbie's sister was the only one in her family who knew that we lived together. Bobbie had done an exceptional job at hiding our two-year relationship from her prejudiced parents and older brother. They were a traditional family and opposed interracial relationships. But her sister was different; she accepted me with no qualms.

As we showered, dressed, and got ready for the day ahead, I received a call from my friend, Tony, whom I had grown up with in the projects of Regent Park in downtown Toronto. He told me that the crew was meeting up at Eglinton West subway station and then heading to Ontario Place for the Victoria Day fireworks.

I was now torn between hanging out with the boys or spending a quiet day with my girlfriend, her sister, and her sister's boring husband. The choice was simple – I decided to meet up with my unmannered, wannabe gang-banging homeboys.

Bobbie was peeved when I told her. "Why do you always do this shit? Whenever we have plans and one of your friends calls, you change our plans to go hang out with them. I can't believe you. My sister is preparing dinner for us, and now you're just not going to show up? Why can't you just tell your 'boys' that you're going out with your girlfriend? Are you too afraid they're going to think you're whipped?"

"Oh please," I responded, searching for the right words to say to cool her down and persuade her to believe that my decision was a good one. "That has nothing to do with it. I'm just going downtown for a bit because I want to see the fireworks. We can meet up later."

"You just want to see the fireworks? Yeah, and I was born yesterday. You just want to go down there to pick up girls, smoke weed and drink with your so-called homies. Don't worry about seeing me later. I'll just stay at my sister's tonight."

"Ok fine, if that's what you want to do, do it, but I would like to see you later, if you change your mind and stop being so upset for no reason."

As soon as Bobbie left I called Richie to tell him where and when we were meeting. Richie was one of the ringleaders of our crew, always instigating trouble. He was like an older brother to me and a big cousin to the others. Richie was always excited whenever we all got together, and with him there was never a dull moment. I called him the chief taxer. He took advantage of any opportunity to snatch a baseball cap off a white boy's head and put it on his own, and then look him straight in the eye and say, "Taxed!" as if daring him to take it back. It didn't matter where we were, on the subway, on the bus, on the street, or in a mall, Richie was taxing white boys who dressed in black urban clothes, left, right and centre. Sometimes he'd snatch a hat and say, "Gimme that! You ain't black!" in his Grenadian accent. It was always an adventure with Richie. But on this particular day, he wasn't gung-ho about hanging out.

"What's up, Richie?" I said after he picked up the phone.

"Nothin' man, I'm cool," he answered.

I got straight to it. "Hey man, everyone's meeting at Eglinton West subway station later and we're going to Ontario Place."

"OK, have fun bro," he replied.

"What, aren't you coming? Everyone's going to be there."

"Not me. I'm just gonna chill out here at home and rub my girl's belly, drink some Guinness and watch TV."

I realized that whenever Richie got something new, his priorities changed. When he got his new car, he no longer wanted to come bike riding through the city with us. When I would call to invite him, he would reply, "No, I got a car now. I don't want to go bike riding." We still hung out, but only when Richie was driving. Now that his girlfriend was pregnant, he didn't want to hang out with the boys. I was upset, bothered that I had cancelled my plans with Bobbie, and he didn't even want to leave his girl's side. I couldn't fathom why he felt obligated to stay home and babysit his unborn baby. The first one in our crew to get a girl pregnant had been Tony, and even after the kid was born nothing had changed, he was still out and about with us, on the streets and in the clubs.

"Man, your baby is gonna be there when you get back. She won't even know you're gone," I said, in a last attempt to persuade him.

"I'm not going. I'm good," he said in a more direct tone.

"What's up, your woman won't let you out of the house? You pussy whipped bitch!"

"F*ck you, Junior. Say whatever you want. You the f*ckin' pussy," he answered back slightly irritated, then hung up the phone.

To me it was unusual that he wanted to stay home on a holiday with a girl he lived with and saw every day, but after the phone call I didn't care. That was usually how we ended disagreements: *pussy and bitch* were like words of endearment in the world we came from, unless somebody outside of our circle said it, then they were meant as fighting words. Richie was his own man and I always respected that. He was almost five years older than me and had more responsibilities. He also wasn't one to have his arm twisted by anyone, unless he was being arrested by the police. Then he had no choice.

I got off of the subway at Eglinton West and took the escalator up to the main level of the station, where I met up with Tony and the others as planned. There were more guys than I had expected: thirteen strong. I'd seen most of them around, but I only knew a few. The guys I knew, I paid respect to with our own street style hand shake and one arm hug. A dap and head nod were used as a form of respect to the dudes I didn't know.

Tony and I had known each other since kindergarten. We had grown up together downtown, just a short walking distance from the Eaton

Centre, Toronto's largest mall. Denier was also a part of the downtown crew, although he hadn't grown up in the city. He was from St. Lucia and had only been in Canada for a few years. I had met Denier nearly two years prior. We called him Pork Dread because he wore his hair in dreadlocks and ate pepperoni pizza. To real Rastafarians, Pork Dread was an offensive term, but we said it for fun because Denier was a fashion dread, not a real Rasta.

Other than Richie, Tony and Denier were my closest friends. We hung out all the time. We went everywhere and did everything together. Our favourite pastime was picking up girls. It was always a competition to see who could pick up the most girls in one day, and it was a game I loved to play. I used my charm and good looks to my advantage. The others were good looking too, but Tony and Denier were more on the shy side. Richie, he was too aggressive, and that turned the girls off. I read what the ladies liked by their response and gave it to them. If they liked nice guys, I became Mr. Nice. If they liked to hear compliments, I became a sweet talker. If they liked bad boys, it was a done deal. I had finesse and confidence and approached females as the opportunity came. If it was not an opportune time, I created one, some way or another. As a hustler, I knew the law of averages: the more girls I approached, the more phone numbers I would get. My strategy gained me the victory all the time. The only problem I had with my success was remembering who was who the next day, and finding a hiding spot to put the numbers so Bobbie couldn't find them.

Locksley and his younger brother Winston lived within walking distance of Eglinton West station. I had known the brothers for almost two years. Locksley was the connection between the downtown crew and his Eglinton West crew. I mostly saw them on Tuesday nights, also known as "N*gger Night," because that's when all the black youths got together for half-price movies at the malls throughout the city, specifically the Eaton Centre, Fairview, or the Scarborough Town Centre. The Eaton Centre was the most exciting place to be though. The ballers drove up and down Yonge Street in their souped-up Nissan Maximas or Honda Accords, blasting their music for everyone to hear and acknowledge their presence. The young bucks like us, or the men who didn't have cars, hung out in front of the Eaton Centre or walked the busy downtown streets on the prowl for girls with no dates. We never paid for a movie; our entertainment was in front of the mall, where the thugs and wannabe gangsters spent their

Tuesday evenings acting hard. That was us, and that was how I'd met the brothers, Locksley and Winston.

When everyone arrived, we made our way to the back of the crowded bus, rudely jostling people as we passed. It was evident that some of the passengers were intimidated and others were annoyed by our aggressive and obnoxious behaviour. One black man who looked to be in his eighties shook his head in disapproval as if to imply that he was ashamed of our conduct. I felt a bit embarrassed and became conscious of my behaviour at that point, even though I wasn't acting inappropriately or loud. Other passengers made an assertive effort to turn their heads and look out the window or down to the ground. When we reached the back of the bus, a homosexual couple gave up their seats and moved to the front. "Battyman fi dead," Locksley muttered as they slipped by him.

There was an instantaneous connection between us, a bond formed like Jesus and his disciples, except *we* were up to no good. From the outside looking in, one would think that we had all grown up together. In most cases, we were similar. We were all a minority. We all came from single-parent, low-income homes. We were all familiar with the street's code of conduct. We all wanted to be gangsters. And we all believed the same lie: We had to rob, steal, pimp, or sell drugs to make it in life. Our similarities and mindset united and strengthened the friendship among us. Even though I had given up selling drugs and gotten out of the game after serving some time in jail, I still thrived when hanging out with my street soldiers, who were like-minded and loyal like me. Sitting at the back of the bus generated a sense of power and confidence. I felt strong and untouchable. I had a crew that would fight for me, even kill if necessary. We were all from the hood and knew how to survive on our own, but that day, we were travelling in a pack, and we were meeting more at our final destination – Ontario Place.

The thing that stood out to me the most about that thirty-five-minute bus ride was the six-inch kitchen knife that Greg was brandishing. He sat next to me, holding the knife down between his legs, turning it from side to side, showing off the sharp, pointy blade. He boasted that we were going to be the biggest crew down there, and if anyone f*cked with us, he would send them straight to their death. I had just met Greg that day, so I didn't know if he was serious or just showing off. I wondered why he would bring a knife when there were already so many of us, but I didn't care. When Greg had finished showing off his weapon, he wrapped it in a small kitchen cloth and put it on the side of his hip in his jeans. As the sharp object disappeared, it vanished from my mind.

We arrived at the gates to Ontario Place in the late afternoon and hung around in the parking lot with what appeared to be a thousand other black youths representing their hoods from across Toronto. None of us paid the entrance fee to go into the park. We didn't have to, because all the action was in the parking lot in front of the Ontario Place entrance. Reggae, Hip Hop, and R & B played from vehicles throughout the lot. We stuck together as we walked through the crowd, occasionally splitting up as we stopped to collect girls' phone numbers.

As evening approached, we were all enjoying the inner-city action. It was warm, with a cool breeze coming in from Lake Ontario. We had connected with a few more guys from Locksley's crew, none of whom I knew. There were about twenty of us at that point, but it was hard to determine if we were the largest posse there as Greg had predicted, because there were countless cliques that came out, and they were all represented in large numbers.

As the sun began to set, the crowd got more rowdy. A few youngsters started shooting Roman candle fireworks across the parking lot at each other, resulting in a mini firearms battle with different-coloured fireballs flying in every direction. The game didn't appeal to me. I couldn't see the fun in shooting fireworks into a crowded area and hitting the wrong person. There were too many gangs and too many bad boys – hit the wrong one and it wouldn't be fireworks coming back at you – it would be gunfire. The tension was building as more people got involved. I was close enough to hear one man say to his friend, "Bredren, if any a dem pussyhole lick mi with dat blood clot shit, mi a bust a shot inna em ross." His comment was confirmation that I wanted nothing to do with that sport.

It only took a few minutes for the game to take a twist. Thirty police officers stood along the west perimeter of the parking lot, some on horses and some on foot, watching the growing chaos from a hundred yards away, as if anticipating a violent outbreak. One individual decided to shoot fireworks at them, and by the time his second shot had landed, there was a barrage of fireballs coming from different angles, hitting the ground and some officers. The crowd had joined in on the attack, forcing the cops to retreat and separate. The ones on horses were most vulnerable, and they were the first to leave the area. At that point my mischievous nature kicked in, and I couldn't resist the temptation to join. I asked the guy next to me for one of his fireworks, which he happily gave me, along with a lighter and a mischievous smile. I lit the string, aimed it straight in front of me, and BANG, a flaming ball blasted out directly toward the area where the remaining police officers stood. After the third shot was fired, before I was able to see where it had landed, I felt someone wrap their arms around me, grabbing me from behind. My tube fell, shooting out the remaining flames along the ground, spinning in circles after each blast. I thought it was a cop that had grabbed me, but it was an Ontario Place security guard trying to bring me into the front gate to arrest me. Another security guard grabbed my arm to assist in the arrest as I struggled to break free, but a gang of riled up kids surrounded and outnumbered them. After some quick thinking, they released me and ran through the front gate in fear for their own safety. By then, the police had completely abandoned the area. The fireworks game had come to an end, but the mayhem continued.

After the sun fully set, only the dim parking lot lights hanging from the poles, the fireworks show in the sky, and the waxing crescent of the moon lit the grounds. Music played, coming from different vehicles parked in the lot. Every person within view was either black or thug white from one hood or another. Some guys danced, others canvassed the area for girls, and others looked for trouble. There was a tense aura, a feeling that a stare too long in the wrong direction could get you into a fight. It was no longer the safe family environment that the daylight hours of Ontario Place provided. The parking lot was in a state of rowdy disorder. The guys who rode the Dickie Dee bicycles selling ice cream and popsicles were robbed of both money and snacks. Innocent people were mugged for being white as they left the amusement park and walked through the parking lot with their families. Cars presumed to belong to Caucasians were vandalized. I saw a small group of teenagers about to break into a grey Jaguar until they heard a man with a Jamaican accent shout, "Yo a fi mi car dat, don't boda touch it." They quickly backed off and went on to the next car. In the Ontario Place parking lot, lawlessness prevailed and there was no sign of when the anarchy would cease, as the crowd was being led by a nefarious spirit.

Eventually, the inevitable happened. A fight broke out. Through the crowd I saw a stoutly built dark-skinned guy, my age, holding a walking stick in his right hand. It was evident that the cane was not an aid to help him get around, and although it was common for pimps to use canes to add to their snazzy appearance, his demeanour showed no indication that it was for style either. I continued to observe him indignantly pursue this much smaller young man who backed away in fear. I didn't think too much of it; it was just another fight. After all, I had seen a hundred of them at similar events.

I didn't recognize the two men involved in the confrontation at first glance, but when I had a better look, I noticed that the kid who was about to be attacked was Tony. I had to do something. I wasn't the type to stand by and watch a friend get beat down, even if the odds were against us. Impulsively I went up behind the assailant and snatched the weapon from his hand in an attempt to diffuse the situation. It didn't work. He turned to me as if he were the black Incredible Hulk, fearless and enraged. "You took it, now you better use it!" he said, and came after me instead. Tony had disappeared into the crowd, and now, here I was, facing this heavyweight on my own. Where were my friends? Where was our big posse now that I needed them?

He stepped toward me, closing the gap even as I backed away. It hadn't occurred to me how intimidating this guy was until I found myself on the defensive. I firmly held on to the weapon, hoping that I wouldn't have to use it. But he was intent – first Tony, now me – and he was not backing down. There was no talking my way out of this one.

Crack! I swung the cane as hard as I could as he came within range, clobbering him across the left side of the head. The impact was of such force that the cane broke in half, one piece flying into the air, and the other remaining in my clenched fist. The blow didn't impede him or slow him down in the slightest way. It only fuelled his indignation. He rushed at me, catching me off guard with a forward kick to the stomach, followed by a punch to my face. I fought back, but he gained the upper hand. The fight ended up on the ground with me on my back squirming and struggling to avoid his blows. I had always been a good fighter and was able to defend myself, but I had no chance against him. He was like an angry Mike Tyson on steroids. I feared for my life as spectators eagerly watched us battle like two wild animals. I was expecting his whole gang to jump in and pulverize me and the crowd of cheering bystanders to leave me there for dead. I heard a lot of voices, but none were familiar. The crowd appeared like a spinning strobe light as I looked up and saw all the angry shouting faces. I felt the presence of the angel of death hovering over the parking lot, waiting to snatch one of our lives. It was left to fate to decide whether I were to live or be murdered. I was alone and defeated.

Suddenly, in a split second, he was gone. The hundred-and-ninety-pound Goliath had disappeared from on top of me and I didn't know where he went. I got up as quickly as I could. It took me a few seconds to shake it off and figure out what was happening. When I regained awareness, I saw the crowd fleeing to the east side of the parking lot in a blind panic. Some shouted, "He has a gun!" I wasn't worried about a gun or who had it. I was just glad to be back on my feet, but common sense told me to run with everyone else. I ran and got lost in the crowd. The chaos had saved me. I was just another black face immersed in the hundreds. The mob then began to slow down and walk back to where the fight had occurred. A circle formed around a man lying on his back. He hadn't been shot because there were no gunshots fired. I squeezed through the onlookers to catch a glimpse for myself. It was him. It was the guy I had hit over the head with the cane.

I stood in shock, as I looked at his lifeless body, lying on the pavement. *Oh my God, what did I do?* The world and everything around me came to a halt. *I just killed a man.* At that point, I felt as if I had died with him. Every negative emotion flowed through my mind and soul – fear, worry, sadness, and loneliness permeated my entire being. Frozen, I stared down at him wondering what was next. *Will I spend the rest of my life in prison? Will I live on the run as a fugitive?* I was only eighteen – he and I were the same age. My life flashed before me – it had changed.

I was awakened by the words "I saw who stabbed him! I saw who stabbed him! Yo I saw that f*ckin shit, man!" Winston walked through the growing noise and hostility, boasting to everyone he knew about what he had witnessed.

I followed him and asked, "Who did it?" He wouldn't answer. He didn't want to say it right there and then. He just wanted the crew to know that he knew. He kept proudly repeating the same thing in an excited whisper to the others. At that moment I was only thinking of myself. I didn't care who did the stabbing, and I didn't care about the kid lying a few feet away from me. I just wanted to confirm that indeed he had been stabbed and I was off the hook for his death. After a few more attempts to get information from Winston, I stopped asking and continued to observe. As the young man lay on the ground, people shoved their way through to get a peek. It didn't seem as if many were too concerned as to whether he lived or died, just as long as they quenched their curiosity. A few more of his friends had joined in to help keep the crowd back, but the curious spectators were overwhelmingly forceful. The paramedics took over twenty minutes to arrive. They had to work their way through the congested Lakeshore traffic as hundreds of families left Ontario Place in their vehicles after the Victoria Day celebration. When they arrived at the entrance of the parking lot, they were met with yet another obstacle. A group of rebels, with no regard for the emergency situation, began firing a storm of fireworks at the ambulance. They were forced to reroute, causing a greater delay. When the paramedics finally arrived on the scene, they lifted the man onto a stretcher and slid him into the back of the ambulance. I still didn't see any blood. I was not convinced of what Winston said he had seen.

    I had to leave the area before the police arrived and started questioning everyone, so I slipped away without telling any of my friends. I headed across the bridge that led to another parking lot and walked until I got to King Street West, where I hopped onto a jam-packed streetcar bound for Broadview station. The streetcar was filled with happy passengers leaving Ontario Place. They talked loudly with excitement after a fun-filled day. The noise was too much for me. Everyone's energy was too much. I was relieved to arrive at Broadview and caught the eastbound train to Woodbine. The ride was much quieter, because the subway only had a handful of passengers. Free from the commotion, I was able to sit down and think. My mind replayed the traumatic event over and over. I couldn't understand how quickly things had led to that point. I never wanted to fight, much less kill someone. I was afraid. I was confused. I felt like crying. I felt like running. I wanted to disappear and end up in another part of the world with a new life and a new identity. My mind was all over the place. My world had just shattered and I had to face it. But what was I going to do? I couldn't turn myself in to the police because they wouldn't understand, and they wouldn't believe me. That would be suicide. I'd be killing my entire future. I knew that first-degree murder carried a sentence of 25 years to life, and second-degree was 10 to life – but this was not murder. I was protecting a friend and defending myself. If Winston was right, I was free; if not, I was going to have to explain to a jury why I shouldn't spend the rest of my life in prison.

    I got to Woodbine station a little after ten thirty and used the pay phone across the street to call Bobbie.

    "Hello," she answered.

The moment I heard her voice, everything I had been holding in, came pouring out. Tears streamed down my face before words could make their way out of my mouth. I sobbed loudly and she listened quietly, knowing that something very bad had just happened.

"Junior, are you okay? What happened?" she asked, breaking the silence on her end.

I didn't know how to break it to her. Should I simply tell her that I'd just committed murder and if I was lucky I'd be released from prison before we turned thirty, and then we could continue our lives from where we left off? Another minute passed. This time in complete silence on both ends.

In a low dismal tone, I let it out. "I just killed someone."

There was another moment of silence.

"Junior ... are you serious?" Her voice cracked as she fought back tears to avoid questioning from her sister. "Where are you now?"

"I'm at Woodbine station," I answered

"I'm coming. Wait for me, and don't go anywhere. I'm leaving now."

When I hung up the phone, I called Richie and told him that I had killed someone. "What the f*ck, Junior? You killed someone?"

I could hear Sharon in the background. "See Richie, what did I tell you about your friends when they get together. It's a good thing you didn't go down there. It's a good thing."

I had an hour before Bobbie would arrive. I found a bar on Danforth Avenue. It was a quiet pub. There were only three other patrons. One couple sat at a table off in the far corner talking amongst themselves. Across the bar from where I sat was a man in his mid-sixties, drinking his sorrows away as he watched the muted television set and listened to the soft country music playing from an old radio behind the bar. It was the perfect environment for me. I ordered a shot of tequila and a Labatt Ice to chase it. I downed the first shot and ordered a double, which I also chugged. I felt the burn in my throat and chest as the alcohol entered my body and settled in my system. I drank seven shots in total, but took my time with the other four. I sipped them, enjoying the effect of the strong Mexican liquor as my frontal lobe became numb and I started to feel more relaxed and tipsy. I was now calm enough to ponder the situation at hand and think about how the chain of events had unfolded, but it was still a mystery to me whether this guy had died from being stabbed or being hit across the head with the walking stick.

Bobbie met me at the corner of Woodbine and Danforth. I greeted her with a hug and kiss. There was no one else who I wanted to see more than her. There was no other person I could have confided in about what I was going through. Bobbie was my first real love. We had started dating when I was sixteen, and after two years in our relationship we were still head over heels for each other. If I had not seen her for a few days because of an argument or because her parents were visiting and she had to stay at her sister's, I would always get little butterflies when we reunited. Although I had other girls on the side, none of them could compare to her. I thought she was the most beautiful girl in the world, with her mild Hungarian accent, long light brown hair, and gorgeous smile. She was quiet and shy but had a body that would magnetically draw men's eyes toward her and demand their attention. Her tanned silky legs looked absolutely provocative in shorts or a skirt, causing men to lust and women to covet. I didn't mind other men looking at my woman. I felt proud when they did. I always liked being envied for having the finer things in life – and fine she was.

During the twenty-minute walk to our place, I told her the entire story. I told her about the fight and also about hearing Winston say that he saw who stabbed the guy. When we arrived, I was still describing the incident. I paused briefly as we passed by the living room where Lenny and his girlfriend were sitting on the couch watching a movie. Bobbie and I both said goodnight to them and headed straight upstairs to our room. I stripped down to my underwear and Bobbie changed into her nightgown. We continued talking about the event. I explained it over and over as if subconsciously trying to put all of the pieces together and make sense of the whole thing. But no matter how many times I explained it, it still didn't make sense.

We lay down on the bed next to each other in silence. I wished I had hung out with Bobbie instead of going downtown with my friends. At that moment I wished a lot of things. All I needed was a genie to grant me my wishes and turn my life back to normal. But there was one thing I didn't have to wish for, because I had her right next to me – the most amazing girl in the world. I placed my hand on top of her outer thigh as she lay on her side, and rubbed her through her silk nightgown. I struggled to keep my mind in the room and away from the incident. I wanted to block it out, even if only for a few minutes so I could make love. I began kissing the side of her neck and cheek as I lifted my hand along her body and toward her small but perfectly formed breasts. I gently turned her on her back as I climbed on top of her, putting my lips against hers. Silent tears made their way down the side of her angelic face. I wiped them away and replaced them with soft kisses, which said, "Don't worry, everything is going to be okay." She cried and held me tight as we made love. Neither one of us were into the sex, but I figured, if I was going to jail, I was going to have sex at least one last time.

We didn't sleep. Bobbie cried for the majority of the night, and I stayed awake pondering life. I expected the cops to bust down the door at any time.

Early in morning Bobbie scurried to the convenience store when it opened and bought a newspaper. We went through it, looking to see if anything had been written about the incident. The Toronto Star read:

Stabbed teen dies at fireworks

Metro homicide investigators are appealing for witnesses today after a youth who accidentally jostled someone in a crowd was fatally stabbed during a Victoria Day fireworks display.
Police say Mathew Anthony Smith, 18, of Flemington Rd. in North York, was among about 700 people who gathered in the Ontario Place parking lot last night so they could watch the fireworks without having to pay admission.
The crowd became apprehensive shortly before 10 p.m. when some people in the parking lot began to set off their own fireworks. Others started moving aside to avoid being hit.
Smith was among those who moved and he "pressed against a male person who took exception," a Metro police sergeant said.
"A short argument ensued," and Smith was stabbed, the sergeant said. As the youth fell to the ground, several people ran for help to nearby Ontario Provincial Police officers, who were assisting with crowd control at the massive annual event.
"(Smith) had friends in the crowd but I don't know what they were doing," said the Toronto police spokesperson.
First aid workers for Ontario Place desperately tried to help the teenager until an ambulance forced its way through a heavy traffic jam along Lake Shore Blvd. W.
The death is Metro's 25th homicide of the year.

I was sorry that a young man had died, but at the same time, relieved to know that it wasn't me who killed him. A thousand-pound weight had been lifted off my shoulders, but I wasn't completely stress-free. Although

I was now clear on how he was murdered, I knew this was far from over. Hundreds of people saw me fighting with this guy. I was in danger. It would be just a matter of time before the police came searching for me to name me an accomplice to murder. I also had to worry about the posse from Jungle, where Mathew was from. I knew they would be out gunning for me as well. I took the day off work at Toys 'R' Us and began my own investigation in pursuit of closure.

My first stop was South Regent Park – Tony's place.

Tony opened the door. "JUNIOR, DID YOU SEE THE NEWS, MAN?" he asked, extremely excited, appearing even proud. "Yo, it's all over the TV! And I saw the whole thing! Greg went right up behind the man and stabbed him in the back! The dude takes three steps forward and then drops, BAM, on his back! Holy f*ck man, Greg killed the guy!"

The news was still on in the background with the sports commentator talking about the Blue Jays' recent win against the Minnesota Twins as Tony continued to describe the event in vivid detail. He demonstrated repeatedly the way Greg had stabbed Mathew in the back. I listened and waited a few minutes for Tony to throw on a shirt, then we headed out.

Our next destination was George Harvey Collegiate Institute in the west end of the city, where we met up with Denier, Locksley, Winston, and Lloyd, who all attended the high school. In the school stairwell we talked about the murder. Denier and I didn't say much. We were the only ones who seemed to absorb the magnitude and seriousness of it all. The others laughed and joked as they described the incident from their individual perspectives. They explained it as if they were depicting something out of a comedy or action movie. Lloyd noticed that Denier and I were more disturbed than excited about the conversation and he started clowning on us.

"What's wrong with you two? Why do you look so worried? You never saw anyone get killed before?" he laughed, before taking on a slightly more serious tone. "Don't feel bad, man. That nigga had it coming to em! Them niggas from Jungle think they gonna f*ck around with our crew and live? They better think again!"

How many people have you seen get killed? I wondered, thinking about Lloyd's statement. Denier stood directly across from me as I sat on the stairs. A quick glance at each other confirmed that we were both on the same page – we were locked into something that we did not choose to be a part of. I just wanted to leave. I didn't want anything to do with Lloyd or his crew, and I definitely did not want anything to do with the beef they had with Jungle. I was not there to celebrate a victory. My probe into the murder of Mathew Smith had come to an end. I had gathered up enough information to protect myself. I was done, done with the stairwell meeting, done with hearing them boast about their crimes, done with them – period. With the exception of Tony and Denier, I had no interest in seeing those guys ever again. My plan was not to inform the police or rat out the killer – that was not my style. Hey, maybe he'd saved my life.

The following day, another article surfaced in the Toronto Star with a picture of Mathew Smith:

Slain teen tried to stop fight friend says

A Metro teen thought he was being a peacemaker when he was fatally stabbed in the back while trying to break up an argument at a Victoria Day fireworks display, Desmond Beckford, a friend of the victim says. Mathew Smith, 18, of Flemington Rd. in North York, was among the 700 people gathered Monday night at an Ontario Place parking lot, hoping to see the fireworks without having to pay admission.
The crowd became jittery around 10 p.m., after some spectators in the parking lot started setting off their own fireworks.
One of Smith's friends accidentally bumped into another man and they began to argue, said a family friend.
Smith tried to break up the argument and was walking away when he was stabbed in the kidney area, Beckford said.
"It's hard to believe that just a bump could trigger something like that," Beckford said.
Smith, a weightlifter who was almost 6 feet tall and weighed about 190 pounds, did not carry a knife, Beckford said.
"He didn't need one," he added.
The death is Metro's 25th homicide of the year.

The article was a complete fabrication. Mathew Smith was not a peacemaker in this case. It was true that he didn't have a knife, as Desmond Beckford had said, but he failed to mention that he didn't need it because he had a cane. Mathew didn't try to break up an argument, and he wasn't walking away from a fight. He injected himself into the conflict with the intentions of intimidating and hurting whoever he felt disrespected anyone in his posse. His actions added fuel to the fire that only came back to burn

17

him. In my brief encounter with Mr. Smith, my only memory of peace was when he was lying on the ground – dead.

As each day passed, we checked the newspapers and watched the news to see if there were any updates about the murder. Just a few days later, on May 28, another article circulated. The police came out with a description of the suspect:

> **Teenager sought in fireworks slaying**
>
> Police have released a description of a suspect sought in the fatal stabbing of a teen at Ontario Place on Victoria Day.
> Friends of Mathew Smith, 18, of Flemington Rd., North York, say he was trying to break up a fight when he was knifed in the back.
> One of Smith's friends accidentally bumped someone at the crowded Ontario Place parking lot during a fireworks display. An argument ensued and Smith tried to break it up, a friend said.
> He was stabbed while walking away, the friend said.
> Police are looking for a light-skinned black, 16 to 18, about 5 feet 5 inches, 130 pounds. His hair is dark with dreadlocks 5 centimetres (2 inches) long on top. He has a faint moustache and a goatee.

The description that was given matched Denier's appearance without a doubt. It was never clear how Denier's description got out, but everybody knew that it wasn't him who killed Mathew. As far as I knew, Denier wasn't even involved in the fight. The police and the media were off track with all of their facts. They were narrowing in on our crew, but they were misinformed. I didn't know where the authorities were getting their information, but we all knew who the killer was, and we all knew who he wasn't. He was not light-skinned; he was taller than five feet, five inches; he weighed more than a hundred and thirty pounds; and he definitely did not have dreadlocks. They were pointing to Denier and I was worried about him.

I called Denier that day. He had already read the article. His voice was low. The enthusiasm and excitement that usually resonated through his tone when he greeted me was not there. I was talking to a different Denier.

"Hey brother, you see that bullshit they got out in the newspaper?" I asked him.

"Yeah, I saw it. Why would they have my description? I didn't even do anything."

"I don't know, man, but that's really messed up. I guess we have to just wait around and see what happens. It'll be OK. This whole thing will soon be over." I tried to cheer him up but didn't know what to say. I could only imagine how he felt.

"Yeah, not soon enough. I'm going to lay low for a while. I'm not going downtown or hanging out until this stuff is cleared up."

"I feel you, bro. We'll talk."

"All right. Later," he said, and we hung up.

Denier was one to carry his emotions on his sleeve. It was never difficult to read him. Denier was Denier. He always kept things real. He was also one of the nicer guys in our crew. He didn't act like a bad ass like Richie and I. He was always the one trying to calm things down, or prevent us from smashing someone's face in. I was genuinely concerned for Denier and I didn't want anything to happen to him.

It was mid-June. Three weeks had passed since the murder. I hadn't seen any of the guys from the West End since our meeting in the stairwell. No new articles had surfaced. I figured this thing would altogether be forgotten and we could move on with our lives. That's all I wanted. I had too many things going on to be caught up in senseless crap. I had a summer job at Toys 'R' Us, a nice place to live, and a girlfriend who supported everything I did. Unlike any other time in my life, I had plans and goals for the future. I wasn't on probation, I wasn't in a group home, and I wasn't in a detention centre. I was on track. I had recently acquired my driver's license and had saved up a thousand dollars to put down on my first car. I was beginning to realize that success wasn't out of my reach, and that I could actually accomplish things without breaking the law.

I was super excited about the summer. I woke up early and eager to go to work. I showed the bus driver my bus pass and walked to the back of the bus, thinking, *this is the last bus pass I'm ever going to need*. I only needed two more paycheques to pay off my car and drive it off the lot. Gazing out of the window, I couldn't stop thinking about all the things I was going to do and the places I was going to go. *Soon I will have my own car, and I will be a free man this summer.*

I arrived at work a little early. I wasn't in the store long when I noticed two men in suits and ties walking from the front of the store to the back. They turned and headed in my direction. I didn't think much of it, just a couple guys from the head office visiting the store. I continued walking to the bicycle section. When they got closer, the shorter man said, "Hey, how are you?"

I stopped and answered, "I'm good."

"Are you Junior?" he continued.

Now I was feeling proud that someone from head office knew my name. My first thought was that they were going to tell me what a good job I was doing and hire me fulltime, as I was only on an eight-week placement program. I smiled from ear to ear and said, "Yes, I'm Junior."

My smile quickly faded when I saw the taller man shake his head. Right then, I knew who they were. They showed me their badges, and the detective's tone got serious when he said, "You are under arrest for the murder of Mathew Smith."

CHAPTER TWO

THE PARENTS I NEVER KNEW

She was a white French girl born in the frigid north. Snow, ice, slush. She was accustomed to the freezing winter days in New Liskeard, Ontario, Canada. He was dark-skinned and grew up under the sweltering sun. White sand, salt water, breathtaking sunsets by the sea. A small island in the Caribbean where tourists flocked from around the world for a taste of paradise in Barbados. Remarkable opposites.

My mother was the fourth eldest of thirteen children, with nine brothers and three sisters. Born in 1955, weighing in at a fragile three pounds. She was in the hospital so long that it was the nuns and hospital staff that named her. Jocelyn, they agreed to call her. They must have been English because they left out the *e* at the end of her name. Not long after her parents brought her home, they decided to move the family to Quebec. A small community in Baie Simard, Deschênes. It was there that she resided, on the French side of the Ottawa River, until the age of ten. She attended a Catholic school with her older sister, Diane. The school was divided, with the boys on one side and the girls on the other. Jocelyn enjoyed her time with Diane – those were happy days. The sisters walked back and forth from school together, through a path in the midst of the woods, always stopping to admire the Cave of the Virgin Mary (*La Grotte de la Sainte-Vierge*). There was a day Jocelyn had to walk that path alone. She was flunking in math and she'd had to stay after school. When the teacher finally released her from detention, she was walking past the large rock, and a figure jumped out from behind it. When she broke out of her startled state, she saw that it was Carol, her older brother's friend. She was relieved to see a familiar person. At her young age she was apprehensive about walking home by herself that late. She now felt comfortable to have company along the way, an older kid, five years older than her, and much bigger. She felt safe under his protection. That was until he shoved her to

21

the ground and forced himself on top of her. She ran all the way home, but not until he was finished huffing and puffing and drooling and rubbing himself against her. She told her mother what had happened, but nothing was said until the next day. The following morning Jocelyn was called into the principal's office to find her mom, Carol, and the Mother Superior there. She was questioned about the incident, but not believed. Carol stood there, glancing at his little nine-year-old prey with a smug look on his face. The look of a predator that thought he could get away with violating the weak. The matter was dismissed without anything further to be said – as the saying goes, it's easier to *sweep things under the carpet*. Mrs. Miron left the office with a disappointed look. Life went on.

After that, Jocelyn found herself in hot water more times than she cared to remember. One day on her way from school she stopped off at her neighbour's front yard where they had puppies that they were selling. They were the cutest little things, and without a second thought, she stuffed one up her shirt. Later that day she was forced to return it, humiliated by her actions.

Summer came and went. The family was busy preparing to move back to New Liskeard. The monotony of the five-hour-and-forty-minute journey was broken from time to time by sipping on bottles of Coca Cola, which was a real treat back then. Jocelyn was surprised to see how far apart the houses were when the family arrived. If you yelled at the top of your lungs, your closest neighbour *might* hear you, but there was no way you could drive a golf ball into their window, even if your name was Ben Hogan. It was real country.

Jocelyn would scrub her siblings' dirty cloth diapers outside using water that dripped from the eavestrough into a barrel, because the house was not yet equipped with inside plumbing. She noticed from a distance that there was movement coming from the bushes, as if she was being spied on. This went on for days, until her older brothers found out that it was just their little curious neighbours who lived at the top of the hill. She was relieved that it was not the Indians coming to take over their land.

The first day of school was exciting for the kids. Jocelyn, Diane, and three of their brothers, after posing for a picture for Dad, hopped on the yellow school bus. They had been accustomed to walking to school and back home for lunch; this was an adventure. But Jocelyn stopped enjoying school when she was held back from the fifth grade because she had to take English lessons. The rebellion began. Since they flunked her because she needed to learn English, the best thing to do was befriend Pauline and Paulette, the English twins. She even adopted the name Joyce. The girls caused enough trouble together that their parents forbade them from hanging out, which was impossible. They skipped school and caught rides along the highway and into town, where they hung out in the local pool hall.

When they were fourteen, the country and the small town of New Liskeard were not enough to satisfy the needs of these three young thrill seekers. One of the twins suggested that they go to Toronto, where the *real* action was. The day they were supposed to go, the twins chickened out, but that didn't stop Joyce. She made her way to the Husky gas station and hitched a ride with a trucker who happened to be going to Kitchener and would have to pass through the capital city of Ontario. It worked out perfectly for the underaged runaway girl. Along the way the trucker bought her sandwiches and allowed her to sleep in the bunk at the back of the seats. When she reached Toronto, it was still early, the sun was barely peeping out of the east. She wandered about in the streets until the city came to life. She stopped in the fast-food joints to use the bathrooms and sit in the booths. She begged people to buy her a drink or something to eat. She met up with hippies and was introduced to grass. She was a social butterfly, and within no time she was making friends. Her first buddy was a redheaded nineteen-year-old boy. Face full of freckles. Joey and Joyce became good friends. She knew about his terrible addiction to liquid LSD, but didn't care, he was a nice guy, and good company for her as she ventured the streets. He asked her a few times if she wanted to try the drug; she always refused, but still helped him to tighten the belt around his arm, as she watched him insert the needle into his veins and shoot up.

Joyce found any way to survive, even if it meant breaking into cars to sleep at night or removing window screens from low rise apartments and crawling inside to raid the fridge while the residents were at work. She scoped out some apartments and kept track of their ins and outs. Those were the places she broke into on a regular basis.

This specific day while she was in an apartment, she heard the rattling of keys coming from outside of the door. The couple came back home unexpectedly. She dashed to the room and hid herself underneath the bed. She could hear them talking as they got ready to call it a night. The pregnant lady and her husband slid between the sheets while Joyce lay frozen on the floor under them. There was a rap on the front door. It was the police. A neighbour had reported seeing someone break in. Joyce was found and taken to jail for the night. Of course she gave the cops a phony name and age. She was brought to the Salvation Army facility for girls. She ran away but wasn't on the run for long before getting apprehended again. The police had discovered that she was a missing child and contacted her parents. The following day she was brought to juvenile court for the Break and Enter charge. The detectives who arrested her were there, and to her surprise, so were her parents. She was sent to a reform school in the west end of Toronto, where she found herself in more hot water. Not only was she causing trouble on her own, but she was inciting the other girls to rebel against the authorities. This landed her in the solitary confinement room. While she was in solitary, her mind passed on one of her school mates who suffered from epilepsy. During a baseball game, Joyce had seen her fall into a seizure. This fascinated her. She decided to pull one to get the attention of the nuns who ran the facility. As a result, she ended up at St. Michael's Hospital. The doctors ran a bunch of tests on her but were unable to find anything wrong. When they were going to send her back to the reform school, she faked another, and another. The reform school did not want to take on the responsibility of treating an epileptic – they decided that it would be best for her to go home to be with her family.

While in the hospital, she met a nineteen-year-old young man named Boisey who worked as the elevator liftman. She kept him company riding the elevator all day. She shared a room with a few ladies, and once when Boisey was visiting, a flower guy came in and dropped off flowers for one of the ladies. She thought the flowers were beautiful. Boisey took note, and the next day, flowers were delivered to her. From that day, all she wanted to do was spend her time with him. She was discharged and sent home to New Liskeard. She was there for three long days before hitting the road back to Toronto, where she moved in with Boisey, her new boyfriend.

Joyce wandered around in awe of the bustling city streets while Boisey was at work. She was a butterfly emerging from her cocoon, about to live life the way her young mind imagined it should be lived.

Growing up was not happy, nor was it fun for my father. At the age of six, Reginald had some fond memories of being with his mom and great grandmother, but those were short-lasting, interrupted by the transition to live with his grandfather, grandmother, and dad. They lived only a few hundred yards away, but it was a completely different environment for the youngster. Reg was forced to work hard, with little time to play with friends. In the morning before school, he did his chores. When he came home for lunch, he watered the dry grass. When school let out, all he wanted to do was stay back and play cricket with the other kids. Occasionally he was able to, but most of the time, he angrily walked home, quietly rebelling in his mind, hating the fact that he had to cut grass, feed the cows, pigs, sheep, chickens, and ducks, before doing whatever else was waiting for him. He even grew sugar cane and corn with his grandfather.

Reg had a close relationship with his grandfather, which induced jealousy in his own dad. Reg's dad felt that his father showed more love toward Reg than toward him. He grew resentful of his son, and treated him aloof, at times even straight-up mean.

Elementary school was over. Reg was fifteen years old and ready to start high school. There was a problem though. Although he graduated one of the top in his class, his dad refused to send him to secondary school. He was never sure of the reason why he was held back. He speculated that his dad never wanted him to succeed past the level of him. Instead of busting the books and getting an education, Reg walked the beach every day for a year. People spent tons of money to fly in from all over the world just to get a taste of the beaches in Barbados, but Reg, he only wanted to go to school. When he turned sixteen, he started an apprenticeship at the Barbados Foundry in Bridgetown, where he worked during the day, learning how to mold metal and make engine parts. In the evening he bartended at a hotel. He even applied to take the police course, but he couldn't take them shouting in his face and giving him orders. It didn't take long to drop out. He was a big but timid guy who shunned violence and outward aggression. He continued working at the foundry until his dad caught him taking a nap past his break time and told the boss. He was fired on the spot, after five years of service. He believed his dad wanted him out of the way. He didn't have many options for an income and began working at the hotel full-time. He was tired of his job, in fact, he was tired of his life in Barbados and applied for a visa to enter *The True North Strong and Free*. His application was accepted, and he was granted entry into Canada.

Reg didn't have a clue as to what to expect when he touched down at YYZ. He had a couple of cousins and a few friends from Barbados who would show him around. Within no time he found his own place and landed a job. He rented an attic in a house for twelve dollars a week, a short walk to the world-famous bargain centre, Honest Ed's, where he shopped for all the things he needed for his new place. He began with the cookware: pots, pans, plates, cutlery, and all the things he needed for what he loved the most (other than women), cooking. Two Jamaican girls stayed on the second floor. He rarely, if ever, saw the people living on the first floor; he had no idea where in the world they were from. He was told about Canada Manpower, a government agency that provided job training, job placement, and school enrolment. His first job was working as janitor in a factory in Scarborough. It was an easy job. He did the bare minimum and spent the rest of the time hiding in the bathroom, while the machine workers and packagers busted their behinds to earn their wages. He didn't have the same supervision, nor did the production of the factory depend on his duties. So what the heck, he didn't care. If he got paid by the hour just for being there, he was happy. After all, he had done enough free labour in Barbados; this was owed to him.

He worked for a few months until he got settled in and became more familiar with his new world. He picked up a job at a foundry for a short period as well, something he was acquainted with. That didn't last long. The place was small, hot, dusty, and miserable: way below Reg's standards. He decided that he would enroll at George Brown College, in the culinary arts. He coveted the position of executive chef. He thrived at the idea of having the power to be able to boss people around. He had endured enough of it back home, and now it was his turn to dish it out. He never made it into the program, it was full. He wound up taking a baker pastry chef course and landed a job at Eaton's as production supervisor in the bakery section. Finally, a job he enjoyed doing.

It was that era when Reg saw Joyce. She was still fourteen years old and he was in his mid-twenties: an eleven-year difference to be exact. He kept a close eye on this free-spirited girl, full of life and more than eager to try new things. He followed her. A year had passed before the first words were exchanged. Joyce was impressed with his vocabulary. He told her that he was *overwhelmed* by her. She didn't know what the word meant, but it sounded flattering – from there he had her. She was now following him, walking him part way to school before cutting back to her original destination after a few blocks of chit-chat. Reg knew that she had a boyfriend, but that didn't stop him from pursuing. Shortly after, Joyce and Boisey moved out of the rooming house and into a bigger place on Euclid Avenue. In a city filled with millions of people, what were the chances that her next-door neighbour would end up being the big black guy from Barbados?

When Joyce turned sixteen, she and Reg started dating. She was still going out with Boisey, but she broke it off, because in her mind Boisey was a boy and Reg was a man. They moved in together on a street directly behind Honest Ed's.

The Toronto landmark discount store became her favourite place to shop. The lights and eye-opening displays in the windows never ceased to lure her in. As she walked up the stairs, she couldn't help but be in awe of the bargains, and the temptations that hung on the wall. So much so that she would accompany her friend, Debbie, to go shopping, even when she herself had no *dinero*. Once Joyce tagged along with Debbie to Honest Ed's. Debbie was shopping and Joyce was just looking around. Unbeknownst to Debbie, Joyce was stealing, and she wasn't only stuffing her own pockets, she was slipping the odd thing here and there into her friend's coat pockets. At the cash register Debbie had paid for the items she had in her basket, but both girls were stopped at the door on their way out. Debbie was taken aback but had an idea that Joyce had been up to mischief by the way she was acting, continually going into different aisles to look at random things. They were led to the security office. They asked Joyce to empty her pockets first. Both security guards were stunned to see baby clothes, a tin of Penaten, and a pacifier land on the table. *How could such a young girl be pregnant?*

When it was Debbie's turn, she stood up as proud as a peacock. "I never took anything, that's on her," she claimed, pointing an angry finger at Joyce. But when she placed the unexpected items from the cosmetic department on the table, her feathers dropped. Joyce was let go because she was a desperate expectant mother. Debbie was detained.

Life was tough for both Joyce and Reg. She was too young to be tamed but mature beyond her time – a wild child in a big city. Life was nothing but black boys and parties. For him, he couldn't control his womanizing hormones and jealous ways. He was ready to settle down, but not with just one woman – he wanted them all.

One time he jokingly mentioned that he wouldn't mind pimping her and broke out like it was the funniest thing ever. If there was any truth behind it, they lived in the perfect area, a few blocks from Jarvis and College, Toronto's prostitute capital. She shot him down as fast as he spoke it.

There was a night when Reg was acting like a gentleman and offered to walk Debbie home because it was late. She only lived five minutes away, but it took him over twenty to return. Joyce thought it would be clever to stress him out, and at the same time get some much-needed attention, as he was always giving it to other girls while depriving her. Before he entered the house, she lay on the floor as if she had fainted due to her pregnancy. He rushed in without closing the door to attend to his six-month pregnant girlfriend. His concern, despite how genuine, was not enough to keep her around. The next day Debbie told her that Reg made an advance at her, reaching in for a kiss. This prompted Joyce to move out and stay with Debbie, which turned out to be for the rest of her pregnancy.

Debbie accompanied Joyce to the hospital and supported her as she gave birth to a baby girl. A beautiful brown sugar and cinnamon doll. Reg never visited for the week that she was there. Nevertheless, she went back to him. She was a young mom, with no one to guide her, proudly parading with her baby, not realizing the scorn on people's faces at the sight of this teenage girl with a black baby. (*Black* was not the word they used.)

Reg came home tipsy one night when Leisa was two weeks old. He crawled into bed with sex on his mind. Joyce told him that the visiting nurse (who was appointed to her because of her age) said that it was too early to have sex because she was still bleeding. He claimed to have seen her in a car with another guy that day and told her, "If you could be with another man during the day, you can be with me now." He forced himself on her, impregnating her again.

Leisa was six weeks old when Joyce found out that she was four weeks pregnant. She didn't know what was going on with her body when Debbie just happened to pop in to check on her. She saw that Joyce wasn't doing too well and felt her forehead. "You're so hot, I can fry an egg on your head." And she immediately called 911. Joyce was in a delirious state when she entered the ambulance. She refused to leave without her baby, so the paramedics allowed Debbie to sit in the back with Leisa. At the hospital they told her that she'd suffered from a hemorrhage, but never told her that she had a miscarriage. She found out a couple of days later when the nurse discovered her balled up on her bed crying. The nurse asked what was wrong. Fighting through the painful lump in her throat from excessive lamenting, she told her that she wanted her baby, referring to her little girl at home with Debbie.

"Don't worry, Dear, you'll have more babies."

Boom! It hit her. She had just lost a baby.

She moved out and took Leisa with her. They lived by themselves on Bathurst Street. Diane came to visit, seeing the baby for the first time. Joyce's sister was successful at convincing her to go back with her to New Liskeard so their parents could meet the baby. They took the Via Rail and arrived at the house at five in the morning. They first went to the boys' room in the basement and woke them all up. As the siblings sat and talked, the boys were admiring the baby, when a little voice came from behind, "Yew, she's all dirty." Joyce nearly fell out of her seat as she burst out in laughter. She explained to Sylvain, her five-year-old brother, that she wasn't dirty, that was her colour.

When Joyce mustered up enough courage to knock on her parents' bedroom door, her mother said, *"Rentre."* When she opened the door and stepped in with her three-month-old baby, her mom's face dropped. She tapped her husband sleeping next to her to wake him up.

"Joycelyn," he said groggily.

She walked over to the bed and placed Leisa between them both, introducing her as their grandchild. "If you don't accept her now, you will never see her again."

Mr. Miron cried as he fell in love with her at that moment. But the little brown baby remained a hush-hush chapter, never to be seen by the New Liskeard locals. Over the years their humiliation at being seen with a mulatto kid in public would mellow. The first trip was a bittersweet experience for Joyce. At one point when she was changing Leisa on the bed, she heard a voice from behind her, "Well, look at that. A little n*gger baby."

"What? Isn't she beautiful?" Joyce turned and retorted.

Her aunt, realizing the inappropriate comment she'd vomited out of her mouth, turned and hightailed back to the car to wait for her husband. That was how Leisa was introduced to that part of the world.

Joyce was sitting inside a West Indian restaurant on College Street sipping on a cold drink when she met Sheila, who was working as a waitress. Sheila's shift was ending, and she was getting bags of groceries together that she had purchased on her lunch break. Joyce offered to help her, and from there they hit it off. Sheila was born the same year as Reg, and the two would become archrivals, as would Joyce with Sheila's boyfriend, Brutus.

Leisa was fourteen months old when her aunt Diane came again to visit. By this time, Reg, Joyce, and the baby were living on Pape, in the east end. While Diane was sleeping on the living room couch, Reg entered and lay next to her. He rested his head on her breasts and commented on how soft they were. The following day when Reg had left for George Brown College, Joyce's sister told her what had happened during the night. Joyce went into a rage and cut up all of Reg's clothes and covered the wall with nasty words written in red lipstick. Diane went back up north to New Liskeard, and Joyce went to stay with Leisa's babysitter, her husband, and their two little girls, who lived a short distance from where she left the man she now despised. She kept her first job at the laundromat, steaming clothes for ten cents a press. Reg knew where they were staying, but whenever he came knocking, they told him that Joyce was not there. Shortly thereafter, the family moved to Winnipeg. Joyce picked up and took her daughter on the long Via Rail ride with them, where she lived in a city that she hated for ten months.

When she returned to Toronto, she found Reg in the same flat and moved back in with him. He was leaving for Barbados in a few days. He had won a ticket on some radio station that he called into. When he returned from his short trip they got married, and within a month Joyce was pregnant with her third child. The marriage did not help the relationship though. Too much damage had been done on both ends – it was at the end of its rope. She took Leisa and her pregnant belly, and moved into a flat on Brock Street, on the other end of town. This was where she lived when Reginald Junior came into the world, weighing in at a solid seven pounds, two ounces, peeing in the nurse's face as she raised him above her. He was ready to take on the universe.

Junior was eighteen months old when Joyce and Sheila had found an apartment together on Cowan Avenue in Parkdale. Brutus was a professional wrestler and was away in Japan. During that time Joyce started seeing a guy named Danny. They met at a club where Sheila worked. It didn't take long for her to fall in love with him. He treated her with respect and showed her a good time.

Junior was an energetic little boy who enjoyed playing on the balcony with his tractor and was fascinated by the view from the third floor. Joyce left him to get something in the kitchen. She wasn't gone for long, but Junior was a fast toddler. He continued to play while Mom was away, standing on his Tonka truck, reaching over the rail, until he plummeted to the ground. Joyce returned, but her son was not there. There was commotion coming from below. She looked down and saw her baby lying helpless on the grass, just a few feet from the pavement. She rushed down the stairs, heart racing in her chest, but the only thing she could do when she got to him was wait. She and several bystanders waited by his screaming side until the ambulance arrived and carried him off to Sick Kids Hospital, where he spent a week in observation.

Brutus returned three months later and moved in with Sheila, Joyce, and her two kids. A taxi driver from the area told Brutus that the ladies were running a brothel. They gave one party, had friends over to smoke joints and drink alcohol, and a whorehouse was his conclusion. The rumour didn't sit well with Brutus, which added extra stress on his already strained relationship with Sheila and his negative perception of Joyce. The final straw came when Brutus and Sheila were arguing in their bedroom. Joyce had had enough of the fighting and cursing around her two kids. She busted into the room and told him to stop yelling at her. Sheila's hands were up in front of her face, afraid to be struck by this powerful man spewing profanities at her. Sheila excused herself to go to the bathroom, which was down by the kitchen where the back door was. She left and never returned.

Joyce moved to Scarborough, close to the Bluffs. Her name was on the list for Ontario Housing, and it couldn't have been called quick enough. Rent was expensive and she had no financial support from Reg. She also had constant issues with one of her neighbours, who got off on calling her kids n*ggers, and her a n*gger lover. This woman who lived in the next building caught Joyce on the wrong day. She was coming home with little Junior and Leisa from grabbing McDonald's take-out, when Junior got to the building, being the little man that he was, ran ahead to open it for his mom and sister. The woman on the other end of the glass door pushed it hard enough to send Junior flying with a bump on his forehead. Imagine Mom's rage. Their apartment was on the ground floor. She brought the kids in, set them up to eat their lunch, and flew out the door to give that bitch what she deserved. Joyce grabbed her in the headlock and dragged her to her own building. "You like to taunt my kids. I bet you'll will never f*ck with them again after today." She rammed her head into the brick wall of the building, dropped her, and left her on the ground. Her brother saw everything and yelled out of the window. She rushed to her apartment, grabbed the meat cleaver hanging in the kitchen, and returned. Before the brother reached the bottom of the stairs, Joyce was there. "One more step and I'll chop your f*ckin knee off." He ran back upstairs and called the police. The ambulance arrived before the cops. Joyce was arrested, charged with assault, and released with a promise to appear. The woman never showed up for the trial and the charges were dropped.

Joyce left the area and moved into a tiny two-bedroom flat on the second floor of a house that belonged to a Pakistani family who had a nephew visiting from back home. She had not unpacked yet because she was expecting to move into Ontario Housing soon. One night when she was asleep, she felt something crawling up her inner thigh. She opened her eyes, startled to discover the grinning fool staring at her. She yelled, "You motherf*cker! You're going to die tonight!" She reached for the small pistol she had in her nightstand and chased him outside. He ran around the block as Joyce fired at him. This happened at least four times; every time he came around to come inside, she fired a round and told him to keep running. The Pakistani pervert would have been shot to death had the gun not been a starter pistol that only fired blanks.

She called Danny from the landlord's phone. Danny arrived all the way from Whitby with his friend Milton to confront the guy. Nervously picking the front of his teeth with a toothpick until they bled, the landlord denied knowing where his nephew was.

She informed Ontario Housing of her living situation and what had happened; within two weeks they found her a permanent place: 15 Belshaw Place, Apartment 603 – South Regent Park.

CHAPTER THREE
NO GOOD IN THE HOOD

Regent Park was the oldest and largest housing project in Canada. Located in east downtown Toronto, it housed over ten thousand residents. The perimeters were Gerrard Street East to the north, Shuter Street to the south, Parliament Street to the west, and River Street to the east. Dundas Street East divided the north part from the south part. South Regent Park had five high-rise buildings reaching thirteen stories, along with several townhouses cluttered on each side. North Regent had mainly low-rise buildings and townhouses. Across the Don River sat the Toronto Don Jail. Regent Park was originally designed to alleviate that part of the city's substandard housing and crime problems. However, the changes to the Canadian immigration system in the 1960s led to an inflow of multiethnic immigrants, mainly from Jamaica, China, India, and Pakistan. The influx changed the racial composition of the neighbourhood from a low-income white project to a multicultural community where all races blended. However, while most of the whites and blacks mixed and mingled, the Chinese, Indians and Pakistanis stuck to themselves. All the convenience stores were owned by Chinese families living in the higher-end houses north of Regent Park, in the area called Cabbagetown. The Pakistanis and Indians were shunned by the whites and blacks because of distinct differences in culture, language and religion. The downtown project was also home to a large number of black Nova Scotians. With the introduction of crack cocaine in the mid-1980s, Regent Park became well known for its violence and crime, driven mainly by the Jamaicans and Nova Scotians, but not exclusive to them.

My early memories of life were not those of an average kindergartener or preteen. I lived in the most violent, crime-ridden and drug-infested projects in the country. Day in and day out, I was surrounded by corruption and illegal activity. I was accustomed to the sound of gunshots that went off every so often in front of my building while I lay awake at night. I was used to seeing the gambling in front of the convenience store whenever I was sent to buy a pack of Du Maurier Regular cigarettes for my mother. I was also familiar with the arguing and fighting that occasionally led to someone getting stabbed or chased away with a broken beer bottle when the Jamaicans disagreed about whether the ball was in or out of bounds during their street soccer game. At the age of six, I observed how the hood ran and who ran it, and by age eleven I had seen more crime than the average person sees in an entire lifetime. The things I'd seen, heard, and experienced as a child seemed nothing but normal to me because it was all I knew. The violence, the crime, and the toughness of the streets became embedded in my mind, and I later used these as a guide for solving my own problems.

In our projects we had neighbourhood role models, the hustlers who hung out all day and night, gambling and selling drugs in the front and back of the Root & Burger. They always flashed wads of money as they rolled dice. They were the ones who made us feel safe. The things that scared us were not the shootings, stabbings or muggings that took place in the Park. We were afraid of the things we heard that took place in the *pleasant* neighbourhoods nearby, like Rosedale and Forest Hill. Stories of female joggers getting raped by perverts jumping out of the bushes as they ran by, or little kids getting abducted and never returning home. These were the stories that frightened us. To the outsider, Regent Park was a violent and vile place, full of drugs and criminal activity, but to us it was home, our safe haven. The average person didn't come to our hood uninvited or unescorted; they were too afraid, and for this reason, we felt protected from all the outside predators.

Like most kids in my neighbourhood, I grew up without a father. I didn't even know mine. I didn't know how he looked. I didn't know how he dressed. I didn't know the sound of his voice. I knew nothing about him. On the very rare occasions that I did hear about my father, it would be in a derogatory manner by my mom or older sister, Leisa. They would describe him as the sperm donor or refer to him as a loser or jerk. I was too young to understand all of the pent-up anger and hatred they had towards my dad. I never asked about him, because if I did the conversation would only be short and negative. It didn't bother me that my father wasn't around. It was normal, as normal as waking up and going to school in the morning. There was only one kid I knew who lived with his dad, a kid in my Grade Five class named Linky, whom I envied for that one reason. We both went to Regent Park/Duke of York Public School, but he was from the projects on the southwest side of Regent Park called Moss Park. Moss Park was similar to Regent Park, with the crackheads, drug dealers, and prostitutes. The only noticeable difference was that Moss Park had a large population of winos that slept on the park benches or on the sidewalks all day and night. You couldn't walk through Moss Park without seeing homeless people at every turn. As a kid it was a scary place to walk through at night. I definitely wasn't jealous of the neighbourhood Linky lived in, and although I admired the Ralph Lauren Polo shirts and Reebok sneakers that he wore to school, it wasn't his attire I coveted either. I envied Linky because he had someone to call Daddy. He had the gift that every fatherless boy yearned for – the love of a father.

Though my dad was not in my life, I did have two male examples to learn from: two men who mom brought home with hopes that I would look up to them as father figures. The first was Danny, a light-skinned tall Jamaican man with short hair. He was a playful type of guy who would chase us around the apartment for fun. Danny came over quite often. Mom liked him a lot, and I guess that's why they spent most of their time locked in the bedroom while I watched television or played outside. He was a decent guy who worked as an electrician and made an honest living. My mom encouraged Leisa and I to call him Daddy, which was awkward because he wasn't my dad, and I wasn't used to using that word. He was just a guy who came around to see my mom. He was nice, but he was not a father to us. He never took us places, helped us with our homework, bought us clothes for school, or said I love you. As much as Mom wanted us to have a father and thought he would be the perfect one, the reality was, their relationship was merely an extramarital fling for him. Danny promised her plenty of things throughout their five-year affair, but leaving his wife was not a promise he made good on. So things changed during his extended vacation with his family to Jamaica. She had more than a month to reflect on all of the lies and broken promises. When he returned, the relationship was over.

After Danny came Keston. They met in the building lobby where we lived. A few months later he moved in with us, and after a year of living together they had a baby boy and named him Andrew.

Other than the fact that Keston and Danny were both from Jamaica, the two men were opposites. Keston was slim, short, and dark-skinned, with a neatly kept afro. Keston loved his Calvin Klein jeans and leather jackets. He was serious and soft spoken. Although Keston and my mom never got married, he was like a stepfather to Leisa and me. He helped out financially and tried his best to be there for us. His sincerity was seen through his rare laugh or smile. His genuineness was demonstrated by his long lectures whenever I got into a fight at school. The smell of whisky came from his breath in the middle of the day, as he scolded me in his thick Jamaican accent. "Yuh kno, Junia, yuh cyaa win every fight. There's always guh be sum'ady out there bigga an badda dan yuh. Dem cya tek up a knife an tab yuh inna yuh back or shot yuh. Yuh haffi learn fe waak away from trouble."

His accent was so strong, most of the time I couldn't understand half of what he was saying. I would simply nod and say yes, hoping that it would shut him up so I could go outside and hang out with my friends. At times I liked hearing him talk. It made me laugh whenever he said the word film because he pronounced it as *flim*.

Keston was a hard worker and generous with his money. He worked any job he could in order to make a living, whether it was sitting in a taxi driving people around the city all day or working in construction under the hot sun. And because he mainly got paid cash, he regularly had a pocket full of money. He gave me money whenever I asked him, except I never asked him directly; I was too shy. When I got home from school and my mother wasn't home I would let Keston know what I wanted without actually asking him directly. "Hi, Keston, is my mom home?" I'd ask, knowing clearly that she was not.

"No, Junia, she guh up di street fi get sup'm. She soon come," he would answer, and then ask, "Wah yuh need?"

"Oh, I was going to ask her for a dollar," I'd answer.

"Here, Junia, tek dis." And like always, he would reach into his pocket and give me more than what I asked for.

"Thank you," I'd say with a big smile, then take off to the Root & Burger to play Crystal Castle, my favourite video game, and eat French fries with gravy, ketchup, and salt and pepper with the five dollars.

On the flip side of Keston's quiet exterior and gentle demeanour, he had a bad temper and at times acted aggressively. One night as I lay sound asleep on my bed, I was suddenly awakened to the sound of smashing dishes coming from the kitchen right next to my bedroom. It took me a moment to realize that I was not dreaming. I came out of my room and peeped into the kitchen to see what all of the ruckus was about. I saw the floor covered with shattered glass and broken pottery. I stood in shock for a few seconds, watching Keston take glasses, cups, and ceramic plates out of the cupboard and hurl them to the ground as he cursed to himself something about that *bitch* and her friends. Traumatized by the sight in the kitchen and worried that he might see me, I made my way back into my room, closed the door, and sat on my bed. I wanted Mom to hurry up and get home. While I sat on my bed listening to the violent noise coming from the kitchen, my sister quietly crept into my room from upstairs. We waited together, occasionally peeking out to see what he was going to do next while Andrew slept peacefully in his crib upstairs in Mom and Keston's room.

We were still awake when Mom arrived home in the wee hours of the morning. In her drunken state, she stumbled through the door as she usually did after partying. Keston was sitting on the couch in the living room. When she saw the state of the kitchen, a full-fledged war broke out in our small apartment. Leisa and I watched the confrontation unfold through the crack in my door set slightly ajar. We didn't want to miss anything. They yelled profanities back and forth until Keston stood up and flung over the glass coffee table with such force that the glass shattered and covered half of the living room floor. My mother was just as violent and defensive as they came. In retaliation, she heaved the solid two-pound marble ashtray sitting on the dining room table at Keston, skimming his 'fro. If he had not ducked, the ashtray would have hit him square in the forehead and probably would have fractured his skull, or worse. He charged at her, grabbed her by the collar and slammed her against the wall. Unable to handle the sight, I ran into the kitchen and grabbed a butcher knife to help my mom. Keston let go. Leisa and Mom grabbed me and took the knife out of my hand. Keston headed for the door and left the apartment, cursing as he slammed the door behind him. Mom spent the rest of the dark morning hours cleaning the mess and crying as she picked up each piece of broken pottery and swept the glass.

A few days later, Keston returned. It seemed as if they had patched things up and everything was back to normal.

One afternoon on my way home from school for the lunch-hour break, I stopped in the Root & Burger to watch the older kids play Crystal Castle. I didn't have any money to play but watching was almost as fun. When I arrived home, I knew that Keston was angry about something. When I got downstairs, he approached me and asked if I took twenty dollars out of his wallet. I told the truth and said no.

"Den wah yuh a come home suh late from school?"

"Because I was in the Root & Burger watching video games."

"Wah yuh nuh tell di truut?" he asked, moving nearer to me.

"I am telling the truth. I didn't take your money."

He grabbed me by my collar and put me against the wall with both of his hands and demanded that I tell him the truth. Keston had never acted aggressive toward me before. In fact, no man had. I didn't know what to do or say. I looked to my mom for help, pleading with my eyes to make him stop. She looked away, unsure if I was guilty or not, and said nothing. The mother who was supposed to be there to protect me watched in silence as I was being draped up and accused of something I didn't do. I wasn't hurt physically, but I was bruised emotionally.

Leisa was the one who had stolen Keston's twenty dollars that day. Unknown to him, she had helped herself into his pockets on previous occasions.

Other than the regular rifts in our family and the fact that my sister and I fought like lions and hyenas, we had some good times in Regent Park. Our apartment was cozy and always clean. Mom played records when she scrubbed the place to the point where you could eat off the floor, but no matter how clean she kept it, the roaches still passed through.

Of the music that Mom played, my favourites were *everything* by Michael Jackson, *Karma Chameleon* and *Do You Really Want to Hurt Me* by Boy George, *Candy Girl* by New Edition, and of course the one-hit wonder *Pass the Dutchie* by Musical Youth. For the songs we didn't have, we recorded them on a cassette from the ghetto blaster waiting on pause until I'd almost trip and fall on my face to unpause it when they played Chaka Khan's *I Feel For You*. At times I was too late and miss the first part of the song, or I'd forget that it was recording and get five minutes of commercials at the end. Music always made me feel good, and Mom played a lot of it.

Leisa was a tough girl. She was bigger than the average boy her age, and she could fight. Not too many people at school messed with me because they knew my sister. My friend Jerome and I were play fighting on the grass in front of the school when the bell rang and we were let out for the day. He had me down in the headlock in a submission hold. I struggled to break free instead of tapping out. My sister saw what was going on from a distance, and came running to my aid, kicking Jerome in the stomach and punching him anywhere her fists would connect. Jerome cried out for me to tell her that we were only playing, but I couldn't speak because I was on the ground in tears laughing at him trying to get away from her like someone trying to escape an angry pit bull. And I was able to relate to that as well; we had an over-protective Doberman who we called Doucette. Everyone in the hood was afraid of her. One of the older cats was jogging past me as I walked with Mom, Leisa, and Doucette, who was next to us but off the leash. He gave me a friendly tap on the back and said *hey bud*, without stopping. The dog chased him down and almost grabbed him by the leg, but we all screamed for her to stop.

As tough as Leisa was, as Keston always told me, there's always someone bigger and badder than you. And this big bad butch was no joke. Leisa mouthed off to the wrong person, and Lisa gave Leisa a whooping one day after school. My sister kept crying out to me, "Junior, go get Mommy! Go get Mommy!" Lisa was relentless with the blows to the face, grabbing her hair and swinging her around like a rag doll. This was the first time I had ever seen Leisa get beat. I didn't know what to do; I didn't want to leave my sister there. If I ran home it would have taken at least seven minutes, including the elevator ride up to the sixth floor. That would have been almost fifteen minutes of this girl pounding away mercilessly at her. If I stuck around maybe she would feel sorry for me and stop beating on my sister.

In front of the Root & Burger parking lot, I had gotten into a fight, and I was getting my ass kicked, until I saw my mother coming. I noticed her first. That's when I started spazzing out on the guy, screaming and swinging my fists in every direction until she noticed me and ran over. Everyone knew Joyce, and she was the craziest white woman you could come across, especially if you messed with her kids. When the other kid saw my mom coming, the fight was over. He took off behind the Root & Burger and never bothered me again. My mom gave me trouble on the way home because I was fighting with a Freezie in my mouth. "Why would you fight with that stupid thing in your mouth? Next time throw it away and fight properly!"

It was in Grade Three that I was almost suspended for bringing nunchucks to school. We were just getting ready to go out for lunch when I decided to show my Nigerian friend, Sunday, my nunchucks, which were hidden in my winter jacket that hung outside of our classroom on the coat rack. Unable to keep a secret, Sunday blabbed to the teacher as he walked by us on his way to the teachers' lounge.

"Mr. Spencer, Junior has nunchucks," he shouted.

"Mmm, sounds delicious," Mr. Spencer said, rubbing his belly as he continued on his way to the teacher's lounge. He obviously had no idea what nunchucks were.

"Those things are deadly!" Sunday exclaimed, more dramatically than the first time.

It was now obvious that he was not talking about food. Mr. Spencer stopped in his tracks, turned around, and came to see what had caused Sunday such concern. When he saw the black wooden martial arts weapon I had concealed in my coat, I was taken to the office and my nunchucks were confiscated.

I couldn't understand why Sunday would tell the teacher on me. The way he acted was as if I had intended to use them against him. I wanted to punch Sunday in the eye. The problem was, he was bigger than me, and I knew I couldn't take him. My mom had just bought me the nunchucks that week from a secondhand store, and I brought them to school only to show my friends. We were all into Bruce Lee, ninjas, and martial arts, and having a pair of nunchucks was a real cool thing.

Grade Three was discouraging for me in different ways. I was sent to take some tests at the guidance counsellor's office because I was having difficulty reading. I had to look at blobs of ink and describe to him what it was that I was seeing. He told me to say the alphabet. The only way I could remember it was by singing it aloud. I began. "I told you to say it, not sing it!" I was abruptly interrupted. Afraid and intimidated, I started again. The teacher told my mother that I needed to practice reading aloud for fifteen minutes a day. Her impatience did little to help improve my reading. "Come Clifford, come," I tried to read from the book *Clifford the Big Red Dog*. I was confused with the *e* at the end, thinking that it was supposed to make the vowel before it long. After mispronouncing it three times, I was yelled at. "How many times do I have to tell you how to say that word, what's wrong with you?" For years to come I shied away from reading in front of people.

Tony, James, and Jerome were my best friends. Tony was light-skinned like me. He had a twin sister, who I thought was pretty, and a little brother named Todd. His mother was white, and his non-existent father was black – he was a fatherless mulatto, also like me. Out of all of my friends he was the closest. We both lived in 15 Belshaw; I lived on the sixth floor and Tony lived on the third. We went to the same daycare, preschool and elementary school. Our mothers were friends and spent time playing cards or chatting outside during the summer while Tony and I played in the park. James and Jerome were Nova Scotian and had accents, but nothing like their mothers'. Jerome was my age but a little taller, and James was a few years older but a little shorter. My mom was friends with James's mom, but not with Jerome's. Jerome lived at 63 Belshaw Place, the building on the other side of the Root & Burger and two convenience stores. The two buildings were perpendicular, so I could look off my balcony and see the front of his building – who went in and who came out. Tony and James's mothers were nice, but Jerome's mom, everyone was afraid of her. She was mean and unpleasant. None of our moms would hesitate to beat us if we did something wrong, but Jerome's mom was extreme. There were times when we went to Jerome's door to call on him to play outside, but when we got there, we already knew the answer. We'd hear Jerome screaming and pleading for her to stop, along with the sound of the lashes from whatever she was using. She yelled in fury, all of the bad words that we were forbidden to say. We listened for a while and chuckled outside the door, glad that it wasn't us getting the licks.

The four of us hung out as much as our moms would allow us. Sometimes we would be banned from hanging out together when we got ourselves into trouble, but we still did, separating and going in different directions the closer we got to our buildings. I was usually the one who got blamed for things. One day Tony and I went to Jerome's place and his mother answered the door.

"Hi boys, how ya'll doin?" she asked in her Scotian accent.

"Fine," we answered, simultaneously.

"Is Jerome here?" I asked.

"Yeah, what ya'll got planned today?"

"I don't know," I answered, a little surprised with the question. Since the years that I had known Jerome she had never said more than hi to me. "We're probably going to play marbles behind 15 Belshaw or something."

"Well you know last time ya'll went out together ya'll got yourselves into trouble." She stepped out into the hallway and continued. "Now I don't mind if Jerome comes out here in the hall and ya'll talk for a bit, but he's not allowed to play with you outside, Junior. I heard that you were the baddest kid in Regent Park, so I don't want him goin' out and g'ttin' himself into no trouble. And besides, he's grounded, but wait here, I'll go get 'im." She went inside and closed the door.

It felt kind of good to be called the *baddest* kid in Regent Park, but at the same time my feelings were hurt because of the way she meant it. She wasn't calling me a badass, she was calling me a bad kid, and there was a big difference between the two. I wasn't a bad kid; at least I didn't see it that way. I was just like all the other kids in our neighbourhood – misled and misguided. We wanted to fit in, but stand out. We wanted to be the best baseball player in the park. We wanted to be the best hockey player on the ice. We wanted to be the best soccer player in the school yard. And we wanted to be the toughest kid in the hood. When we went out to cause trouble, we even took that to another level. We didn't knock on the doors when we played *Nicky Nicky Nine Doors*, we kicked the door with our heel from behind as hard as we could, sometimes busting the latch, causing the door to fly open. Then we'd run away laughing our asses off all the way down the staircase. When we went to North Regent to throw rocks at the windows of the low-rises, we didn't throw pebbles, we hurled stones the size of baseballs to see which one of us could shatter our target first. No matter what we did, we did it with all of our hearts and always had fun. In our crew there wasn't any bullying or peer pressure. When we got together, we came up with ideas, and whoever had the best one, we all went along with it. We probably tried everything there was to try. We collected beer bottles and lined them up in the street car tracks because we liked the sound of them smashing as the street car passed along Dundas. Sometimes we put stones or steel objects in the tracks to see if they would derail the street car. We went to other neighbourhoods to beat up kids for the fun of it. We stole the coins out of the wishing well in the Eaton Centre. We did whatever seemed like the most exciting thing to do at the time. We were simply kids having fun. But we didn't only cause trouble to entertain ourselves, we played ball hockey in the hallway of our buildings, went swimming in the outdoor pool in North Regent, and in the winter we enjoyed the slopes of Riverdale Park where we went tobogganing. Shoot, we were even hustlers. In the summer we made money by collecting pop bottles at construction sites when the workers were gone home; during the holiday season we went door to door singing Christmas carols in the upper end townhouses just south of Shuter. We were never short of things to do.

Jerome came out of his apartment a few minutes later and sat on the hallway floor with us.

"Did my mom say that you were the baddest kid in Regent Park?" he asked me.

"Yeah, but why would she say that? That's not true," I said.

"I know," Tony commented. "Gumbo is the baddest kid in Regent Park."

"No, I think DJ is the baddest. He's always doing something bad to someone," Jerome said.

"Yeah, I agree with Jerome. DJ's the baddest kid," I said. "I don't like him. I think Gumbo can kick his ass. DJ only acts tough because he's always picking on the younger kids. I think I can beat him if we got into a fight."

"Yeah right, you can't beat up DJ," Jerome said in disbelief. "Tony, you think Junior can beat up DJ?"

"I don't know. I think it would be a tie."

Tony and I stayed for a few more minutes talking about all of the trouble that Gumbo and DJ caused in the neighbourhood. Both boys were Caucasian. They were older than us by a few years, but Gumbo was taller and broader, and DJ was short for his age, making him about the same height as us. I respected Gumbo, as did everyone in South Regent Park, because he didn't bother anyone unless he had an issue with them. He certainly had the confidence, and he acted like it. If he wasn't the toughest, he was at least one of the most feared and respected white boys that we knew. He certainly had the confidence, and he acted like it. He was considered a bad boy because of the illegal activity he was involved in. It wouldn't be a surprise to hear that Gumbo was arrested and led off in handcuffs by the police. DJ was different, he was a bully by nature. He was a mean kid who bullied and intimidated anyone who appeared weak. At times we were his target. One time he tried bullying James into giving him his chocolate bar after we were walking home from the convenient store, but that day we weren't having it. We fought back. James had DJ on the ground in the headlock and I kicked him a few times in his head. The fight didn't last long. DJ was stronger than what I had given him credit for. When it looked like DJ was breaking free from James's grip, I stepped back to avoid him from grabbing me. James yelled for my help just before letting DJ loose and taking off. We both ran away. DJ gave chase for a few seconds, shouting, "I'm going to f*ckin kill you when I see you!" DJ lived on the ground floor of my building, near the staircase exit next to the Root & Burger and the two convenient stores. The same staircase I used to exit the building. Over the next few days I took the stairs on the other end to avoid him, and went around the back of the building instead. DJ couldn't be trusted. He always had to win, even if it meant using a weapon.

We had been outside in the hallway for not more than ten minutes when Jerome's mom was already calling him to come back inside. Tony and I left. We went to play marbles behind our building, but after bumping into Nathan, we decided to go home and get our trunks and towels and head to John Innes Recreational Centre in Moss Park to swim in the indoor pool. Along the way we saw Linky riding around the front of his building on a bicycle, probably stolen, like the different-coloured polo shirts, Roots jogging pants, and Reebok sneakers he wore to school. All along I thought it was his dad who bought him those clothes, until he bragged to me that he went to the Eaton Centre almost every weekend to shoplift. Nathan didn't know Linky because he went to Park Public School, not Regent Park/Duke of York. After a few minutes of chatting we went on our way.

After swimming we were hungry, and it was common for us to satisfy our hunger by stopping off at the convenience store on Parliament and Queen, where the donuts were kept at the back of the store by the door; the cash register was at the front. One of us held the door open while the rest snuck in, grabbed a few variety packs, and ran out, as the Chinese man yelled for us to come back with his donuts. We finished them all before we got home.

One time I did this when I was by myself. It didn't turn out good. I grabbed the pack of donuts and sprinted across the street through the red light without looking in either direction because the store owner was coming after me. *Bang!* I was hit in my shoulder by the handlebars of a motorcycle traveling through the intersection. I was knocked violently to the ground. I got up and continued east on Queen with the motorcyclist shouting at me with genuine concern to come back. The Chinese man picked up his donuts and went back into the store. I walked the rest of the way home with the most throbbing headache I had ever experienced.

The last time we went to get donuts, they were moved to an aisle closer to the cash register. We changed our minds.

Another friend of mine was Chris. I thought it was cool that his dad was a professional wrestler. We were all into Hulk Hogan, Andre the Giant, and Superfly Jimmy Snuka. We never missed a match on WWF; except when I found out that they weren't fighting for real, then I stopped watching it. Chris knew his father and saw him every now and again. I'd seen him from a distance when he came to pick up his son, but I had never met Brutus due to the ongoing feud with him and my mother. My friendship with Chris was born from default as opposed to personality or character attraction. We hung out because our mothers were friends. We were like cousins who either liked hanging out or abhorred each other's presence. In a family you can't choose your siblings or cousins, and in our case, we didn't choose our friendship. He came to my place with his mom, Sheila, and other times I went to his apartment with my mother, since around the time Chris was born, they had lived at 605 Whiteside Place, the high-rise building behind mine. There wasn't a lot to do there; Chris was an only child and didn't own any board games or video games, and by then we were too old to play with toys but too young to smoke weed with our moms. The only thing I enjoyed about visiting was the view from the thirteenth floor. Their balcony faced south, providing a view of South Regent and Lake Ontario. It was hard to imagine that the blue body of water that appeared so clear and drinkable from that distance was in fact too contaminated to even swim in. The scenery from Chris's bedroom always put me in awe. It faced north, with a view of all the five boroughs of Toronto. I could gaze out of the window all day and not get tired of watching the city in motion. The cars looked like Hot Wheels and the trucks like Tonkas from being up that high. I liked spitting and watching it split up in different directions as it fell to the ground. It was also cool to see birds fly past the window at such an altitude. But you couldn't see the CN Tower; my building blocked the view. I only lived on the sixth floor, but I could see it clearly from where my balcony was. Both views took you out of the hood, but whenever you left the apartment, the smell of urine that stunk up the elevators, the occasional smell of human feces that filled the staircases, or the junkie scratching their arm in the lobby brought you right back to reality.

Neither my friends or I liked having Chris around when we went to cause trouble. He was either complaining because he was afraid of something or annoying us with his stupid jokes until I slapped him in the back of his head or kicked him in his ass for talking too much. If I made him cry I'd have to make it up to him before we got back home because he took forever to stop bawling. I usually took the long way back to buy time for him to calm down. He was also chunky and couldn't run fast enough to keep up, and if he got caught, I got caught, not because he would necessarily tell on me, but because our moms knew we were together.

I remember one summer day our moms kicked us out because it was a nice day, and they figured we should be playing outside instead of being indoors. I'm sure it didn't only have to do with the weather. I reckon they wanted their privacy to gossip and smoke their weed without a couple of kids around.

"Why don't you boys go play outside?" Sheila said.

"Yeah, get out," my mom agreed.

And out we went. Tony was up in Barrie visiting family. No one was at the baseball diamond or the park. We didn't have a plan, so we wandered around aimlessly until I decided we should go up to Riverdale Farm. We walked through Cabbagetown to our destination. Behind the farm was the steep hill that led to two baseball diamonds, much bigger than the ones in our neighbourhood. When they were covered with fresh snow, the hills were perfect for sledding, probably the best in Toronto. On the east side was another hill, almost as big. We never went over there. That's where the uppity white kids from the Broadview and Danforth area played. We didn't know them, but that's what we referred to them as. We were separated by a footbridge. Underneath the bridge cars raced north and south along the Don Valley Parkway, and parallel to that, murky river water flowed south into Lake Ontario. The Don Jail could be seen clearly from our side of the hill.

We started our tour through the farm, visiting the horses first, but we'd seen them a thousand times. We checked out the peacocks, the roosters, the chickens, and that was boring too. I had to urinate pretty bad so I thought I would humour Chris by pissing on a chicken that was locked up in a cage. It worked. When Chris turned around and saw me urinating on the chicken, he too almost pissed his pants laughing. At nine and ten years old we thought every stupid thing we did was funny. We continued through the farm until we got to the barn that housed the goats. We were the only ones in the barn. I noticed that the billy goat and the ram were in the same stall but separated by a wooden gate. I wondered if they would fight if I put them together. Without a second thought, I unlatched the gate that separated them. They kept their distance from each other, as if hesitant to invade each other's space. The billy goat was bigger than the ram but the ram had much thicker and longer horns that curled around the side of his head. The billy goat had little horns that looked more like two lumps in the middle of his forehead covered with a bit of skin and fur. The ram was within my reach. I leaned over the fence, grabbed one of its horns firmly, and pulled him toward the billy goat to see if we'd get some action. He resisted, but I insisted, and kept pulling. When they got within two feet of each other, they went at it. They both stood on their hind legs, then came down full force, clashing their horns against one another's. They bucked heads several times, but when the billy goat realized that he could not match the power of the ram, he retreated to his corner. It was cool to see them, but I felt a little bad because the billy goat's head was bleeding a bit.

When the farm closed at 5:00 p.m., we collected a few rocks, each of them about the size of an adult's fist and headed to the top of the bridge. Not once did it dawn on either of us that what we were doing could have tragic results for an innocent person. I lunged the first and only rock down at a pick-up truck travelling northbound on the Don Valley Parkway at about a hundred kilometres an hour in the left passing lane. The rock landed directly in the centre of the windshield and shattered it. The truck swerved across the centre and right lanes and came to an abrupt stop on the shoulder of the Parkway. The driver, a medium-built white man, ran out of the truck to the yellow emergency phone connected to a pole on the side of the highway. We didn't stick around to see him call the cops. Chris and I bolted back toward the farm. The gate at the bottom of the hill was locked, and it would have taken too long to run around the farm and up the hill. We had to scale the six-foot fence and get out of there. I helped Chris's fat ass over the fence and then climbed it myself. Half way up the hill I had to turn around and yell at Chris to hurry up. By then, he was walking and gasping for air. We finally reached the Simpson House at the top of the hill where the main exit was. It was a relief to see that the exit gate was still open. The last thing I wanted was to ask one of the staff to let us out, and I wasn't in the mood to assist Chris over another fence.

We casually walked out through the gate and back home as if nothing had happened.

Returning to school after the summer was always exciting, at least for the first week of September. It felt nice wearing the new shoes and clothes that my mom bought me. They weren't Ralph Lauren or Adidas like what Linky wore, but they were new.

School for me was stimulating in the schoolyard but boring in the classroom. My perception of education was inordinately warped. I didn't know what we needed an education for, I just knew that I had to learn the things that the teacher taught, and I wasn't good at it. Within my sphere, it was more important to be the toughest in the class than the smartest. Winning a fight meant more than winning a scholastic award, and the logo on our shirt meant more than the numbers on our report cards. How would I know that the purpose of education was to advance in life? I didn't know anyone who finished school. The only successful people I knew were the drug dealers and criminals that I saw every day. At Regent Park/Duke of York Public School, proving how tough you were or how good you were at sports was what earned you respect. I got into fights often during recess or lunch break, and if it got broken up because a teacher was coming, the fight would continue after school. Word got out about who would be fighting, and there would be a group of spectators waiting outside once the bell rang. I always had something to prove, and I was more afraid of being perceived as a coward than I was of losing a fight. So, I never backed down from anyone, except once. Another kid and I got into a small scuffle and exchange of words during recess. He was a kid in my Grade Five class. We were scheduled to finish the fight after school in front of the east doors were the Regent Park kids exited. Pretty much all the kids in our grade knew about the fight, including the kids from Moss Park, who were supposed to exit through the west doors.

During the afternoon I watched as this kid cut popsicle sticks into sharp points with a pair of scissors, occasionally glancing in my direction to make sure I was watching. At the end of class, he taped them tightly to the top of his hands, with the popsicle sticks sticking out at least two inches. *I didn't want to get punched in the eye with those.* I exited through the front doors nearest to the office and bolted across the street, down a side road toward my building. One of the older kids saw me fleeing and gave chase. He caught up to me on the walkway behind the townhouses and told me that I had to come back and fight. I was adamant about not going back, even when he assured me that he would take the weapons away from the other kid. Failing to convince me to return and fight, he let me go, and I went home. I didn't care what anybody thought. The next day the popsicle stick kid never bothered me. I guess he felt that he'd won by scaring me into running away, or maybe he didn't want to fight a fair fight with me.

Regent Park/Duke of York was a fun school to attend when we weren't fighting or encouraging negativity. The most exciting extracurricular activity I participated in was the talent show. I was on the breakdance crew with Sunday and Raheem. Sunday was considered the best break-dancer in the school, and he was the leader of the crew. Raheem and I were tied for second best, according to Sunday. It was a pleasure to stay after school and practice our routine as opposed to staying behind for detention. On the evening of the talent show we were all very excited to perform to the classic *Rocket*, by Herbie Hancock. I looked up to my sister and was feeling good about showing off my moves on the stage as she watched on in the audience, only to be saddened to see that she wasn't there. She had better things to do, like hang out with her friends in the hallway outside of the auditorium.

Raheem and I were both friends and foes. One week we'd be playing sports, the next week we were on the ground throwing punches. We competed over everything: who was the toughest, who was the fastest, who was the best break-dancer. But regardless of how much we fought, we always ended up friends again.

Spring and summer were the best times of the year, whether it was before school let out for the break, or after. There was always a lot to do in the inner city. On our way home from school when tomato season arrived, it was customary for us to stop by the backyard of the Chinaman's house, who lived in one of the townhouses across the street from our school. He grew tomatoes in his garden, and we would reach over the fence, grab at least two tomatoes each, and dash them at his window, causing them to splatter. Then we'd all take off to the Root & Burger and play Crystal Castle. Life for us was one big game.

One day when I arrived to class in the morning, I was called down to the principal's office. I had no idea why I was being summoned. *What did I do this time?* I entered the reception area, and, through the slightly ajar door, I saw an Oriental man talking with the principal.

"Have a seat, Junior! Mr. Burksworth will be out momentarily," the office administrator told me.

I sat down, wondering what I had done. I knew I didn't do anything that I should've been worried about, at least not that week. I didn't recognize the man speaking to the principal, but one thing was certain – he was furious. After only a few minutes of sitting on the bench, my anxiety began to build and I just wanted to know why I was there. I had never been called to the office for my good behaviour, so I knew I wasn't there to receive an award. Finally, Mr. Burksworth opened the door and called me in.

"Do you know why you are here, Junior?"

"No Sir!"

"Well, Mr. Yeung here, tells me that yesterday after school, you and a couple of your friends threw stones at his window and broke it."

"It wasn't me, Sir!" I said. "I wasn't even around his house yesterday." I was innocent of *that* offence, but at the same time I'd put my foot in my mouth.

"Oh, you weren't around his house yesterday? Tell me something, Junior, do you know Mr. Yeung?"

"No."

"Ok, well if you don't know him, how do you know where he lives?"

I knew exactly where Mr. Burksworth was going with this. "I don't know Mr. Yeung and I didn't break his window. I'm not lying."

I thought it might have been Tony, but of course I didn't say it. Nonetheless, my reputation as a mischievous kid preceded me. I was suspended for three days.

Getting suspended from school, at times, had no punitive measure. I was suspended six times by the fifth grade. My mother would initially yell at me and tell me that I was grounded for a month, but that never lasted. Sometimes I would get a spanking, but it depended on how she felt at the time. By the second day, I would be sleeping in and then watching television all day. On day three, I was outside playing tag or marbles with my friends at the park when they returned from school. She was not consistent. Her form of discipline was a beating when she was fed up with my behaviour, which was always emotionally driven by her impatience with me. I was usually hit with the closest object she could get her hands on: a belt, a wire hanger on my bare bum, and even a hockey stick one time for swearing at Chris when he and Sheila were at our place. Once she even strangled me with a pair of thick fluorescent break-dance laces that I had bought at the Eaton Centre with the money I took from the wishing-well while playing hooky from school. She thought I had stolen them. Occasionally she would send me to stand in the corner for lesser offences, such as calling my sister names, or talking back to her.

Although I was horrified to be beaten by my mother, it never curbed my behaviour. One afternoon during lunch, Tony and I went to Mr. Tasty's on Parliament, right across from Moss Park, to get a milkshake. On our way back to school, while passing an autobody shop, I suddenly got the urge to climb up onto the top of the car parked in front. I jumped up and down as Tony stood there sipping his milkshake, laughing with the straw in his mouth. By the time one of the employees ran out from hearing the noise, the entire roof of the car was dented in. I jumped off and we both darted to school. We were late returning from lunch, so I tried to walk into my classroom as inconspicuously as possible, but to no avail. The teacher spotted me. After a few minutes, I was called down to the principal's office, and I knew exactly what it was for. The owner of the body shop had come to the school and reported the incident. My mother was notified, and I was suspended. The principal handed me the phone to talk to her. She blasted me and told me what to expect when I got home. Fearful of my mother's wrath and choice words, I decided not to go home.

I ran away, but I didn't go far. I didn't have many options. The only people I knew lived in Regent Park or Moss Park, and there was no way they were going to harbour a ten-year-old runaway. When it got dark, I set out looking for a place to sleep. I had never been out this late by myself. I wandered through the projects for hours until I got tired. All of the kids my age were tucked in bed, sleeping. I avoided going in front of the Root & Burger because the big guys sold their drugs there when the restaurant was closed. I knew they would question me about being out this late. Besides, I didn't want them telling my mom if they saw her the next day. I walked behind it instead, on my way to Park Public School to scout out a place to lay my head. Congo spotted me. "Junior, what are you doing out here so late, bwoy?"

"I'm going to my friend's house," I answered, and quickly went on my way before he was able to ask another question. He watched me walk off into the dark as he continued leaning up against the brick wall, inhaling the smoke from his joint in the cool of the night.

When I got to Park School, I climbed up onto the lower roof in the back of the school. It had rained earlier that evening, and the roof was still damp. I searched for a place to sleep. The driest part of the roof was a little spot in the corner. I curled up, closed my eyes, and tried to sleep. The damp, hard ground was my mattress, the chilly spring breeze was my sheet, and the clouds above were my blanket. I couldn't stop shivering. I was hungry and tired, but couldn't sleep. I hadn't even made it through the first night, and I was already thinking about what I was going to do tomorrow, and the night after that. *How could homeless people live like this?*

I couldn't take the cold any longer. I climbed down and aimlessly walked around the hood, hoping that the sun would rise and a new day would dawn. I didn't leave the perimeters of Regent Park; I was too afraid of being kidnapped by a child molester. I went into 63 Belshaw Place to warm up in the lobby. I could see my balcony through the front lobby window. Congo had moved from the back of the Root & Burger. I could see him and a few of the other hustlers directly in front of my building, slanging their dope to the neighbourhood feigns. It was a quiet night with not much going on. By now it was no longer the fear of a spanking that was preventing me from going home – it was pride. I ran away, now I had to prove that I could stay away and make it on my own. As much as I wanted to go home and sleep in my warm bed, I wasn't a quitter. I fought against my fatigue and loneliness. I didn't know what to do next. It was too cold to sleep outside, and the staircases in all the buildings were filled with the overwhelming stench of urine and infested with cockroaches. As I contemplated my next move, a security guard entered the lobby from the back door. Puzzled to see me standing there gazing outside, he asked, "Junior, what are you doing out at this time? Is everything alright?" It was Rex. All of the security guards knew me on a first- and last-name basis. He was one of the cool ones; he actually cared about the people who lived in the community.

"I'm just waiting to go home," I couldn't think of a better answer.

"Come on. I'll take you."

I didn't object. It was past two o'clock in the morning, and I desperately wanted my bed, even if it meant getting a spanking for what I had done at school. We both walked past the Root & Burger toward my building. Congo and the guys hanging out in front went through the lobby to the back as they always did when they saw security coming. Rex tapped gently on the door. Mom was fully awake. I expected her to be fuming when she saw me. On the contrary, she began crying as she embraced me with open arms, as if welcoming back her prodigal son. After she thanked Rex, she tucked me in bed and told me how much she was worried about me. The love was felt. It was comforting to hear her express her feelings. She kissed me on the forehead and quietly left the room. I fell fast asleep.

CHAPTER FOUR
THE GREAT ESCAPE

The move to Ottawa came as a bolt from the blue. It was mid-June and Keston had just left for his taxi shift late that morning, and my mom was acting unusual. She rushed to the window to watch him exit the building and drive away. She then got on the phone and called the South Regent Park maintenance office and said she needed the lock on the door changed immediately because she'd lost her key and had to leave. It took at most thirty minutes for the maintenance man to arrive and change the lock. Immediately after he left, she ran into my sister's room and pulled out a small suitcase from under the bed. The suitcase was already packed and ready to go. She then retrieved a locked wooden trunk the same size as the suitcase from her closet. "Junior," she told me, "go put on your shoes, take the suitcase and go press the elevator." I realized what was going on and did exactly what she said. She picked up my baby brother and took the trunk and off we went. We exited the front of the building and headed to Mary's place in North Regent Park.

As we crossed Dundas Street, Keston happened to be driving by and saw us with the luggage. My mother thought for sure he was going to stop and confront her, but he had a customer in the cab and continued driving.

We stayed two nights at Mary's apartment. My mom figured that would be enough time for Keston to cool down and accept the news that she was leaving him. The two days at Mary's were super fun. I hung out with her two sons, Jason and Patrick, who were both in their early teens. We played Donkey Kong, Pacman, and a host of other video games on their Atari system. They even taught me how to "roll bums." It was a thing they did at the end of every month after the welfare cases had cashed their cheques. We went out along Parliament Street looking for drunken sleeping bums on the street to pickpocket. In less than an hour we made over a hundred dollars. I didn't actually do any of the pickpocketing; I just kept watch. They gave me ten dollars for my part and for me that was a lot of money, so I was happy.

During the time that we were in North Regent Park my mom had visited Sheila and had noticed some of Keston's things in the corner near the couch. When she questioned Sheila she learned that he had been staying there because he had nowhere else to go. On another visit, Keston happened to be there. They spoke, and Mom confirmed that it was so, we were moving to Ottawa in a couple of weeks. She also let him come back to stay in the apartment for the rest of the time that we would be there. They didn't talk to each other much during the two weeks. Mom was busy packing and Keston was busy working and drinking. They argued almost every day but nothing that escalated past a door being slammed or a cuss word being thrown out.

My mom's main reasons for moving to Ottawa were to escape the trap that Regent Park was setting for me, and to get away from Keston and his drinking. I was eleven and a half years old, and a lot of boys only a year or two older than me were already smoking weed and selling crack and heroin. Some of them even carried a gun in their backpack. I wasn't far behind. I liked what I saw. The life of guns, drugs, and money was exciting – like cops and robbers. I was being prepped for that type of life in Regent Park and my mother could see it, but she wasn't going to let it happen.

Two of my uncles came down from Ottawa to help us move. They rented a moving truck and began packing it up. Keston sat and watched them carry out everything belonging to us. "Hey, Keston, you wanna give us a hand wit' some of this stuff, eh?" My uncle, Léo, asked in his French accent.

"If she wa fi move to Ottawa, gwan go move, but mi nuh help with nuttin," Keston rudely replied.

When the truck was packed my uncles drove it to Ottawa, and we went to the bus terminal where we took a Greyhound.

It was a bittersweet experience. I loved Regent Park, but I was excited to explore another part of the world. Starting a new school didn't make a difference to me. I had failed the fifth grade, and I had gotten in enough trouble at Regent Park/Duke of York that they were not accepting me back in September anyway. I was registered to start Dundas Street Public School, which was across the Dundas Bridge, right next to the Don Mount Court projects. I hated that part of town. I was not looking forward to leaving my hood to go into another hood for school.

It was the middle of the afternoon when we boarded the Greyhound. The weather was great, a perfect summer day. The bus drove from the Bay Street terminal to the Don Valley Parkway along Dundas Street. We passed by Regent Park for what I thought would be the last time. My sister and I waved to our old building and said goodbye. We could see some kids riding their bicycles. The Jamaicans were playing keep-up with a hacky sack on the street in front of the building. It was a good time to leave the Park; nine years was enough. My mother told us that the security guards had a pop and chip party in the security office in celebration to our departure from Regent Park. I never knew I gave them *that* much trouble.

We settled into Ottawa nicely. We started in Vanier, the lowest income section of the city, although nowhere near the level of where we were coming from. The area was safe but there wasn't much to do and I didn't have any friends. We lived near Beechwood Avenue on a backstreet called Barrette Street. We rented a small upper-level apartment in a house, which Mom hated because the people who lived downstairs would steal her mail. My mom's room was on the main floor between the kitchen and the living room. There were two tiny rooms in the attic. I shared one with Andrew, and Leisa was directly across from us. It was smaller than our apartment in Regent Park, but it would suffice for a short-term stay. I did a lot of walking and exploring, so I learned the area rather quickly. To me it never seemed like a low-income part of town; I liked it, and I never considered us to be poor, even when there was no food in the fridge and my mother had to wait until her government baby bonus arrived in the mail in order to go grocery shopping. She always found a way to feed and clothe us and maintain a roof over our heads. When the extra money from her baby bonus did come, we lived the high life. Mom took us to the movies, bought us ice-cream, and if my shoes had holes in the soles, we went to Zellers and she bought me a new pair.

In September, my sister and I started school at Robert E. Wilson Public School. It was a small building on McArthur Avenue. I got off to a good start and made a lot of friends from the jump. Leisa, however, was more standoffish and less social; it took her longer to make friends. At the dinner table after our first day of school, Mom asked about our day. I had all good things to say. We talked about who we met and what we did. There was one girl in particular who stood out among the rest.

"Did you see the tall black girl?" I asked Leisa.

"Yeah, her name is Rose, she's in my class. I don't like her."

"Why not?"

"She thinks she's all that. She acts like she's better than everyone else."

"Did you talk to her?" Mom asked.

"No, but you can see how she is by her attitude. I don't have to talk to her, I just don't like her."

Leisa always prejudged people before getting to know them. She judged their clothes, hairstyle, makeup, shoes, and all their exterior parts first. If she didn't like a person's nose or how they were dressed, she didn't like *them*. If someone was well dressed and had no physical flaws to criticize, their attitude became the next target of judgment. And *her* opinion was the only one that mattered. If you said something good about someone she didn't like, she brought up every piece of dirt about that person until she made you feel the same way she did. If you didn't end up agreeing with her, you definitely walked away second-guessing the person. She was usually wrong about people. It was *her* insecurities that caused her to think that self-confidence meant that you were conceited, or if you had a positive outlook at life, you thought you were better than everyone else, and anyone who dressed outside of Leisa's fashion schema was out of style.

Interestingly, within a month of us being at Robert E. Wilson, Leisa and Rose became best friends. They were inseparable. They hung out at school, after school, at the mall, and they even began going to the night clubs in Hull, Quebec, although they were underage. Anywhere you saw one, you saw the other.

At school there was a girl that I liked, a very pretty light-skinned girl named Andrea. I had been going to the school for over a month but she hadn't noticed me once. I tried walking in front of her. I would dribble the basketball in the hallway and show off hoping to get her attention or make eye contact. Every day when I saw her in the schoolyard I admired her beauty and the way she carried herself. I always wore my best clothes to school and combed my hair neatly just in case she noticed that I existed. Nothing I did got her attention.

It was Friday, October 31. When I woke up for school I realized I had no costume to wear for Halloween, so Leisa suggested that I dress up as a woman. When I didn't object right away, she enthusiastically took me by the hand and led me to the bathroom without giving me a chance to say no.

"Mom, we're gonna to dress Junior up like a girl for Halloween."

Of course Mom thought it was a great idea, so I gave in and went along with it. They were excited to paint my face with makeup and lipstick and dress me up in a dress. They put a bra on me and stuffed it with toilet paper. I had pantyhose, high heels, a wig that belonged to my mom, and the whole nine yards. When we were on the city bus on the way to school, a little girl said to her mom, "Mommy, look at that woman." Her mom looked over to see who her daughter was referring to, and saw me. I smiled, proud of the good job my mom and sister had done.

"That's my brother, he's just dressed like that for Halloween," my sister said to the mother. The lady smiled and turned back around in her seat. When I got to school everyone thought that I had the coolest Halloween outfit. I was getting compliments from my friends, other students, and teachers, as I walked around in high heels. I felt pretty cool. What made that day the best day of the school year was that Andrea finally noticed me. We talked all day. We spent morning recess together, lunch break, afternoon recess, and we even talked after school while I waited for the bus. She gave me her phone number, and by Monday she was my girlfriend.

During the winter I learned from the local kids in the area how to "bunk." It became my favourite winter pastime. It was similar to what my friends and I used to do in Toronto, just not as dangerous. When we went bunking, we would wait at a stop sign for a car to stop, then run up behind it and grab onto the bumper and have it pull us along the snow. In Toronto we would jump on the back of trucks, especially the mail trucks and go for a ride. I was with my friend Roddey one time, and we jumped on the back of a Canada Post truck heading east on Dundas. After the truck crossed the Dundas Street East bridge, over the Don River, it suddenly made a right onto the DVP ramp. The speed of the truck increased dramatically. Roddey got scared and jumped off. I watched him roll on the pavement several times, protecting his head and face with his hands and arms as he was being flung by the velocity. It looked very painful, and by the time it was my turn to jump, the truck was going way too fast – I don't think I would have made it out with bruises, bumps, and scraped up skin like Roddey. I banged on the back door until the driver came to an almost complete stop, then I jumped off and caught up to Roddey. He looked a mess.

The following year we ended up moving out of that shithole apartment (as my mom referred to it) and into a two-bedroom apartment a few blocks away. There weren't many fond memories of living on Barrette Street. In fact, the strongest memory I have of that place was when my mother went into a rage and beat my sister over the head with a hairspray aerosol can until her head busted open and blood came streaming out. Mom was holding her and hitting her continuously, yelling, "You want to go on like a big woman and disrespect me, you little bitch?" At the same time Leisa was yelling at me to call the police. This was the worst abuse I've ever seen from my mother. I'd been whipped with an iron hanger, hit with a hockey stick, and strangled with shoelaces, but the indignation that I saw that day exceeded it all. Leisa ended up being sent to a group home, and Mom, Andrew, and I moved into a new apartment on Genest Street.

I liked it on Genest Street. We lived across the street from a park where I rode my skateboard and practiced stunts with other kids in the neighbourhood. One of the best things about living in that area was that there was a convenience store not far up the street that rented out VHS movies. We had just gotten a VCR and we rented movies every weekend. Each cassette rental was for three days, so I watched the movies I liked at least two or three times before returning them. That was pretty much how my first year in Ottawa was spent.

The following September when I returned to school I met Robin. We ended up becoming best friends. He lived not too far down the street from the school. His mother was mulatto and his father was Caucasian, although he too never knew his father. We were together just as much as Leisa and Rose, except we were evidently too young to go to the clubs or hang out downtown. We usually spent our time at each other's place, talking about things we wanted to do and places we wanted to go, or we were outside throwing snowballs at the stop signs. Robin and I even decided to become *blood brothers*. One day when we were at my place we poked our thumbs with a knife until they bled, joined them together, and declared ourselves blood brothers.

During the school year the Boys and Girls Club across the street from the school had Friday night dances for teens and preteens. Robin and I went every week. It was fun to dress up, go out with friends, and slow dance with the girls. The dance floor never had many people on it until a slow song played. Most of the kids were either sitting on the portable bleachers watching the few that were dancing, or out in the main area socializing. Whitney Houston's *You Give Good Love* and Elton John's *Can You Feel the Love Tonight* always filled the dance floor and the bleachers. The guys sat at one end looking across at the girls as we tried to muster up enough courage to ask one to dance. The girls waited at the other end, hoping that the guy they liked would take them by the hand, lead them onto the dance floor, and sweep them off their feet. I was nervous to ask a girl to dance if I didn't know her, but the desire to have her in my arms and hold her close to me as we moved to the music was stronger than my fear of rejection. I regularly targeted the girl I thought was the most attractive, then waited a few moments to build up enough courage. At times I missed the first song because I wasn't prepared for the approach, but thankfully the DJ played at least three or four love songs in a row, which gave me enough time to get my game right. Once I got my words in order and prepped myself for the approach, I fixed my baseball cap and walked around the perimeter of the gym. I preferred the pop-up approach as opposed to walking directly towards her. I didn't want her to see me coming, nor did I want everyone to see me ask her. I thought it would be smoother if I just ended up by her side and whispered the question in her ear: "Would you like to dance?" And if she said no, at least the entire club wouldn't see me get rejected. However, it never happened. My game became so tight that none of the girls ever turned down my offer to dance. It was cool to be able to dance with all the girls, and my friends admired my ability to get along well with the ladies. Robin was good at it too. Every slow song we were out there with a different girl, smiling at each other from a few feet away as we tried to lower our hands from the waist to the butt, hoping that she wouldn't pull them back up. It was one thing to dance with them, but if they let you feel their ass, you were the man. Other than playing humping tag in Regent Park – where the boys would give the girls ten seconds to get away, and then chase them, and the one they caught, they got to hump on the slide for ten seconds – The Boys' and Girls' Club dance was my second physical experience with girls, and my introduction to the game. It was sweet and innocent.

When school was out for the summer my mother sent me to a summer camp just outside of Ottawa for a week. I didn't stand out much at that camp, except for my skin tone. I was the only person of colour, and for the first time in my life I felt different. Growing up in Toronto I'd never felt out of place because of the colour of my skin. At Regent Park/Duke of York Public School I was made fun of and called zebra because I was a half-breed, but that didn't bother me because it was either a black kid or another mulatto kid saying it. At the end of the day, they were only heckling me and there were no real feelings behind it. But at this particular camp full of white kids from Ottawa, Pembroke, and the surrounding areas, I felt isolated. They didn't have to say anything to me, I felt it, and I didn't like it. However I tried to fit in, I still felt like I didn't completely belong.

There was one time when I felt as if I was a part of the group. On the last Saturday night there was a camp dance in the main hall. I was hanging out with the five other boys from my cabin. It was a warm night and the stars could be seen clearly in the sky. None of us really danced except for a few slow songs with some of the girls. We spent most of the evening outside of the hall. At the end of the dance, unknown to me, there was a tradition where the guys picked a girl they liked and they French kissed. I didn't have anyone in particular in mind. One girl named Janet was pretty, but I wasn't about to jump in front of everyone and have my pick first. I didn't even know if any of the girls wanted to kiss me; none of them showed interest. I waited for the others to choose. It was like picking teams for a soccer game. Once a girl was picked, they both went around to the back of the hall and found a semi-private spot to make out. At the end, surprisingly, Janet was left. She was one of the best-looking girls in the lineup but no one chose her. This was possibly because she didn't let off any vibes or hints that she was interested in any of them, and the last thing a guy wanted was to be rejected, especially when there was a handful of other chicks anxiously waiting to be picked. Janet and I were the last ones standing there; we looked at each other. She walked towards me and I met her halfway. I knew it was on; the chemistry was there, and my heart was racing. I was about to have my first French kiss. Before we were able to make our way behind the back of the hall, one of the assistant directors came out yelling that the dance was over and we had ten minutes to return to our cabins. I saw the guys grab their girls and bolt into the forest away from the counsellors and other campers. Janet and I did the same. We found our own private spot just off the path that led to the boys' cabins under a large oak tree. That's where it happened. She leaned toward me and I followed her lead. The feeling of her soft tongue twirling around mine sent a sensation throughout my body that I had never felt before, and my eyes closed automatically – I felt as if I were in love. I didn't know Janet very well. I had just met her at the camp, and even throughout the week she never spoke to me much. None of the girls spoke to me; I was just the brown kid who hung out with the cool kids from Cabin Three. But I didn't feel that way anymore; now I was just as cool as the rest of the boys from my cabin – at least for that moment while I was kissing Janet. It was obvious that she had experience and knew what she was doing. The way she did everything made me feel like clay in the hands of a potter. I was in love with Janet. No, I was in love with the feeling of being with her. I didn't know what I was in love with, all I knew was at that moment I was hooked. Girls became the most potent drug to me. All I wanted was to kiss them, feel them, smell them, and be around them. At thirteen years old I was being brewed to become a serial philanderer.

When all of the guys arrived back at the cabin we spent most of the night talking about the girls we were with and how the kiss went. That night, there was no coloured kid in the room; it was just a cabin full of excited boys talking about their favourite topic – girls.

The next morning was the last day of camp. We all packed up and headed to the outdoor picnic tables for breakfast at the sound of the bell. I was looking forward to seeing Janet. The guys went ahead of me as I packed the last few things into my bag. After lining up to get my boiled eggs, toast, and cereal, I saw that the others were already seated. The boys usually all sat together as did the girls. But the last morning of camp, after our special night, the guys were sitting with the girls they had kissed. Janet was sitting in the middle of the table. There was no room for me so I sat at the one next to it with a few guys from another cabin. I was hoping that she would come over and sit next to me. She didn't. In fact, she didn't even look up at me to say hi. I sensed that they had been talking about me prior to me arriving for breakfast because at times some of the girls looked in my direction then quickly dropped their eyes. They were all acting indifferent. Janet even appeared uncomfortable as she engaged in conversation, occasionally forging a laugh at something that was said. When breakfast was over, all the campers hung around outside the hall sitting on the picnic tables conversing and enjoying the last few hours that we were going to be together. Janet walked off with the rest of the girls from her cabin, with still not a word or a single look in my direction.

"What's up with Janet?" I asked the guys that were sitting at her table.

"Dude, why would you lie about frenching her?" Taylor asked.

"I didn't lie. Why would you say I lied?"

"You told us last night that you frenched her. Remember? When you said it was so good you couldn't even keep your eyes open." He continued. "She said you're a liar."

"I'm not lying," I said, embarrassed and hurt by the conversation at this point.

"Yeah right. I know Janet, and she doesn't even like black guys. Why would she kiss you?" Taylor walked away, and the others followed.

I didn't have anything else to say, nor did I have anything to prove. For the next hour I sat around by myself while everyone else continued to chat, play cards or hit the tether ball around the pole. Once the big yellow school buses arrived onsite, I was the first one to grab my bag and enter the bus with the sign that read Ottawa. I never wanted to return to that camp again; I'd rather spend the entire summer doing nothing than be around those people.

The rest of the summer was pretty eventful for me. Shortly after returning home from camp I got myself into trouble with the law. I was charged with stealing a bicycle. I didn't actually steal the bike, nor did I try to; I was only up to my usual mischief. In Regent Park we took other kids' bikes all the time and rode around teasing them as they chased us, screaming, "Give me my bike!" When we'd had enough we'd ride really fast and jump off, letting the bicycle continue to go without anyone on it until it came to a crashing stop. This case was no different. I took one of the kids' bikes as he was playing on the playground with a few other kids. He immediately began chasing me, yelling for me to get off of his bicycle. I didn't like his tone or his choice of words, so I took his bike and rode it into some broken glass that happened to be on the ground, with the intent to flatten his tires. I left the bicycle on the grass at the other end of the park with his tires still intact, but by then it was too late. The kid left the park to tell his mother that I had stolen his bike. She called the police and they came and charged me with theft under a thousand dollars. That was my first – but far from my last – criminal charge.

It had been a little over a year since we had moved out of Toronto, and Regent Park had already gone to hell. I was in the kitchen when my mom found a disturbing article in the newspaper and read it to me. A schoolmate of mine, Kelly Mombourquette, had been brutally murdered. She was severely beaten in the head, her neck was slashed, and her naked body was dumped in a parking lot behind a building in another part of the city. The news was confirmation that my mom had done the right thing by moving us out of that godforsaken place. When we had left, the projects were being taken over by crack cocaine; only a year later it had become a huge epidemic. Kelly Mombourquette was proof that the crack problem in Regent Park was out of control. Kelly was only a year and a half older than me. According to different sources she had started using drugs at age eleven and shortly thereafter became addicted to crack. She did anything to feed her addiction, and prostitution was no exception.

The newspaper read:

> Kelly Mombourquette went missing from a Rexdale group home on Warrendale Court in Etobicoke on October 3, 1987. On Monday, October 29, Kelly's nude body was discovered in the parking lot of 300 Yorkland Boulevard in North York by a woman on her way to work. The 4'10" 82-pound girl died from a knife wound to the neck and had been severely beaten about the head.
>
> At the time, police said that Kelly spent time in the downtown and Regent Park areas. Due to an absence of blood at the scene on Yorkland Boulevard, police also said that it was likely she had been murdered somewhere else, with her body later being disposed of at this scene.
>
> Kelly had been sentenced to time at the group home instead of a jail after a recent brush with the law, but had run away after two days. Several of Kelly's friends and acquaintances spoken to by the press said she began to get into drugs when she was only 11, becoming addicted to cocaine and crack and prostituting herself to feed her addictions.

The news about Kelly was difficult to assimilate. I remembered her as fun and full of life. I never knew she'd started doing drugs. I began to think about what else was going on in my old neighbourhood. Who else was involved in drugs? I came to grips with the fact that it wasn't my problem. Whatever went on in Regent Park wouldn't affect me. I lived in Ottawa.

My dad came to visit that summer. It was the first time I had seen him since I was a toddler, and I had no memories of him at all. I was under the direct influence of my mother and older sister, and they had nothing positive to say about him. My perception of him was one-sided and biased from all the negative things I'd heard about him growing up.

My sister and I were in my room while my dad spoke with my mother in the kitchen. Leisa was telling me that she wasn't going out there to talk to him and didn't want to see him at all. Although, deep down in my heart I wanted to see him and get to know him, I followed suit with Leisa and refused to leave the room. I took on my sister's views without knowing any of the facts that transpired throughout the years. I should have gone out voluntarily to see him – it was rude and disrespectful of me not to. My mother called me out into the kitchen, and I went.

"Hi Junior," my dad said.

"Hi," I responded with my head down.

"How are things?" He continued, trying to get a little more out of me.

"Fine."

The conversation only lasted for a few minutes and didn't get beyond the question-and-answer stage. He ended up leaving without ever seeing Leisa.

That summer we also moved. Mom had been working hard over the past two years. She had taken courses for word processing and data entry and began working for an agency as a secretary. I admired my mother's work ethic and dedication. After two years of hard work and no support from any of our fathers, she was able to move us into a nice three-bedroom condominium on Jasmine Crescent in the east end of Ottawa. It was a lot bigger than the other places we had lived, and I had my own room with a cool view of the Queensway. We lived on the ninth floor. There was a pool and a hot tub on the main floor of the building that I took advantage of often. Leisa was back and forth from Toronto and Ottawa. She didn't know what she wanted. She was fifteen years old, running around and doing whatever felt good at the time.

Chris came to visit me for a few days near the end of the summer. His mom sent him up by himself on the Greyhound. We didn't do much; I just showed him around downtown and took him to different malls. On our way back to my place from the Rideau Centre, we were sitting at the back of the bus. There was a black man sitting across from us, probably in his mid-twenties. He overheard us talking about Regent Park and joined in on the conversation. "You guys are not from Regent Park," he said. Chris and I started throwing out names of the older cats that ran around Regent. He still didn't believe us, and said that we just heard of those guys but didn't know them. I'm not sure if he truly didn't believe us, or if he was messing with us. Either way, we brushed him off. He obviously didn't know anything about Regent Park except that it was a bad neighbourhood.

I had started Grade Seven at a new school on St. Laurent Boulevard, called Queen Elizabeth Public School. I was put in a special education class for kids with learning disabilities or behavioural problems. I was embarrassed to be placed in Special Ed, but I ended up liking my class. There were about six students, and the teacher, Mr. B., he was the best. He taught us how to play chess. We played every day as if it were a part of the curriculum, and we became pretty good at it. I didn't socialize with too many of the kids outside of my Special Ed class, except for lunch time, when we bolted to the arcade to play Super Sprint, a race car video game. It was everyone's favourite, and there was always a line up to play.

Every day I took the big yellow bus to school and back home, until I got permanently kicked off for something I did. I realized quickly that in Ottawa they weren't going to give me a lot of chances. At my first school, the French teacher put me at a small wooden cubicle desk facing the wall away from the rest of the class for touching the girl's hair who sat in front of me. I was sentenced to that desk for the entire school year, while the teacher's favourite student was continually praised for all the *smart* things he said. I didn't know why she was so bitter towards me. Was it because I was the only black kid in the class, or because my mother was French Canadian, like her, and I couldn't form a single French sentence? After living in Ottawa for two years I learned prejudice first-hand, and regardless of what the teacher's prejudice was, it just seemed like she hated me from day one. Each day I spent the entire hour of French class drawing on the desk walls; needless to say, I didn't learn a word of French. Now at my new school, Queen Elizabeth, I was kicked off of the bus for a few minor incidents. The punishment, however, worked out well for me. The school issued me an OC Transpo bus pass to take the city bus instead. I preferred taking the OC Transpo, but I wasn't expecting the school to give me a bus pass each month. I thought they would take it away from me on the weekends. They didn't. I used the bus pass to go touring the city, exploring Ottawa from one end of the city to the other and back every weekend. I enjoyed sitting on the bus with the window opened, looking outside at the buildings, the people, and the cars. Getting kicked off the school bus was worth it all. The bus pass came in handy for my mom as well. Each day after school I took the bus to pick up my brother from daycare downtown. She was happy that she didn't have to pay and I was happy to be travelling.

Coming home to the condo was always nice, whether it was from being at school or just out and about on the weekend. I loved the pool and the hot tub that were shared by the residents. I even made a few friends. One time we were hanging out in the hot tub talking and joking around. I liked one of the girls, but they were all into the other guy. There were three girls and only the two of us boys, and all three girls wanted the same guy. None of them paid any attention to me, and for the first time in my life, I wanted to be white. White guys got all the girls in this city, I thought. This changed one night when my mother brought me to one of the night clubs in Hull, Quebec.

The club was called 747. My mom wanted to go out and I was her date. I was thirteen years old, but the bouncer didn't care. She paid for both of us to get in, and in we went. That was where I met the guys who I would be idolizing. The pimps with the Jheri curls, leather pants, gold chains, and Cadillacs. I was dazzled by their swag and ability to attract the ladies. The money they flashed and the style of their expensive clothes made me want to be like them. The biggest pimp in the city was a man named Jackson. Everyone respected him. He had it all. It was nothing for him to have girls around him at the club and another few working for him on the street. He was the essence of a pimp. Charming, smooth, stylish, and well built, just not that good looking. He was a businessman and knew all about the hustle. He even took the younger upcoming pimps under his wing and trained them. I stood in the club and watched in awe how he interacted with people. He was like a celebrity, everyone wanted to be around him. It was fascinating to see the number of white girls attracted to these guys who were my colour or darker. Never again did I wish to be white. I was happy in my own skin.

I met Orval, Jackson's younger brother, in an arcade on Rideau Street downtown, and he later introduced me to Layton. Orval called Layton "Bigga" as a nickname. These two brothers of Jackson changed my entire Ottawa experience. They became my best friends. Orval was seventeen and Layton was fifteen. They had recently moved up to Ottawa from Jamaica around the same time I had arrived there. They were exposed to much more than I was and therefore knew a lot more people. They were fascinated that I was able to understand *patois*. At first Layton didn't believe it. Orval put me to the test and told me, "Tump Bigga inna de head." When I lifted my hand to slap Layton in the back of the head, we all started laughing as he blocked my hand. We hung around the streets in the Clarence area or the Rideau Centre. Sometimes we jumped on the bus to St. Laurent Mall for a change, or after we got kicked out of the Rideau Centre, usually for loitering or being too rowdy. We were always fighting with either mall security or the skinheads. We even stole fish bonkers to use as billy clubs and small cans of hairspray to use as mace.

We almost used the fish bonkers once, while Layton was getting arrested by the Rideau Centre security. He'd been banned from entering the premises for a prior violation. One security guard spotted him as we walked through the mall. It only took a few minutes until he was surrounded by five of them. They held on to his arms and shirt as they pulled him through the doors to the back hallway leading to the security office. He struggled and fought back. We tried helping but there wasn't much we could do. "Gimme da fish bonka, gimme da fish bonka!" Layton yelled to me. I was wondering how he was going to use the fish bonker with so many security guards trying to restrain him and take him away. It would have been an impossible attempt at escape. I didn't give it to him. Later that week when he was released Layton made it known to me that he was mad that I didn't give him the fish bonker. I don't think he realized that I'd prevented him from picking up an assault with a weapon charge, for which he would not have been released so quickly. It was clearly a losing battle for us, and there was no point in me getting arrested as well. He got over it.

The skinheads – they just didn't like us and we didn't like them. The ones who wore the red laces in their boots were supposedly the racist skinheads and the others who wore the black laces were the antiracist skinheads. They all hung out outside of the Rideau Centre along Rideau Street. I didn't know why we hated each other. I guess it was because our cultures were so different; but it didn't matter why, they were just the enemy, and that was that. There was a time when we encountered a red laced skinhead by himself in the McDonald's across the street from the mall. I was walking in with Layton and Steph, and I decided that I would shout out to him to see if these guys were so tough when they were alone. "What's up punk?" I said. He shot up his two middle fingers at me and didn't say a word. I wasn't going to allow him to humiliate me in front of my homeboys. I walked over to him, pulled out the hunting knife that I had concealed along my waist. I saw the fear in his face as I got close. I sat next to him and put him in the headlock with my left arm, turned the knife upward away from him, and began beating him on top of the head with the bottom of the handle until he bled. In the process I cut my thumb with the blade of the knife so deep that I was able to see the bone. Steph tapped me on my shoulder. "Junior, that's enough man let's go."

We left McDonald's and walked across to the Rideau Centre food court to clean and bandage up my thumb. In the mall we bumped into Garret. Garret was cool. He was a few years older than me and I admired him because he was part of a rap group. I'd heard him rap one time at the popular all age dance club called Astro Light. He suggested that I put black pepper on the cut to stop the bleeding. He went and got a few packets from one of the food court restaurants and put it on my thumb. I thought it was unusual but went along with it anyway; all I wanted was for my thumb to stop bleeding. He enclosed the pepper by wrapping up my thumb with napkins, and to my surprise it worked and the bleeding stopped. I don't know what happened with the skinhead and his bleeding head, but we all had a good laugh about it.

Sadly, a few months later Garret ended up dying in a car crash after leaving a club in Hull, Quebec. There wasn't enough room in the car and so he opted to go into the trunk. The car smashed into an oncoming tractor trailer.

CHAPTER FIVE
THE SUICIDE ATTEMPT

It was our first visit back to Toronto since we had moved to Ottawa two years earlier. Stepping out of the Greyhound, downtown in my hometown, was awesome. I could feel the rush-hour energy of a city filled with over two million people. Everyone was going in different directions and doing their own thing. The fast pace and multiculturalism were what I loved the most; every block in every neighbourhood had its own unique feel. I was a proud Torontonian, and although I no longer lived in the mosaic city, Toronto still lived in me.

We hopped in a cab and headed to South Regent Park, where we would be staying with Sheila and Chris. The taxi driver wore a turban and spoke with a Pakistani accent. We had a hard time understanding him, but he understood us clearly and took us exactly where we wanted to go. The eight-minute ride along Dundas Street brought back fun memories of growing up downtown. We stopped at a red light at Parliament Street, which had always been a drug corner, and it was the entrance into Regent Park. I looked out the window as we waited for the light to change. It was evident that crack cocaine had taken a noticeable toll on the neighbourhood over the past couple of years. The streets were filled with crackheads who stood out with their dirty clothes, rotten teeth, and fiending dispositions, as did the drug dealers in their gold chains and brand new sneakers. I continued watching the people as the light turned green and the driver drove through the intersection. When we arrived at the building my mom paid the cabbie and left him with the change. We entered the lobby and I pressed the thirteenth floor. Only one of the two elevators was working. After a short wait, the elevator arrived and both of us had to step over a puddle of urine to get in. It was always nasty to see piss on the floor, but the smell of fresh urine in the elevator was not half as bad as the dry festering smell of human shit that sometimes lingered in the stairwells. It took only a minute to get to the top floor but I could see from the look on mom's face that she couldn't wait to get out of that elevator.

Sheila and Chris greeted us at the door and welcomed us inside. I put my bag in Chris's room and looked out of the window overlooking North Regent Park and Uptown Toronto. I had always loved the view from his window. If you put your head out and looked to the right, you could even see the Toronto Don Jail across the bridge. Sheila had prepared French fries and chicken fingers for dinner. When I had finished eating I said, "Thank you!" Her response was always the same, "Don't thank me, just thank God you got it!" We all stayed up late. Our moms played cards downstairs at the table, smoking and drinking Johnnie Walker, while Chris and I hung out in his room as he updated me on all the crazy things that had been going on in Regent Park since I had left. Kelly Mombourquette was murdered. Congo had become a crackhead. DJ had become the gun-toting neighbourhood bully who would later go on to kill his best friend and spend the rest of his life in prison. Mostly all the older teens had already started selling drugs and carrying guns. I thought I was missing out on the most exciting part of my life in the hood. I'd never really wanted to leave.

I was the first one up in the morning, and I went directly to the balcony, which faced South Regent. There were a few kids out playing in the park as their mothers sat on the bench smoking cigarettes and chatting away. I reminisced about when I used to play in that same park. Tag was our safest game, but we also played war. We chose teams, collected rocks, took cover, and then tried to ping each other off. The rules were that the rocks were only supposed to be the size of marbles, but as the game progressed, we got carried away and started pelting any size stone within our reach – you'd better make sure you took cover. It was always fun until somebody got hurt and went home bleeding. I was excited about seeing my friends. I wanted to see them all and hang out like old times. I was waiting for Sheila to wake up before having breakfast, because I wasn't comfortable helping myself in their fridge. My mother woke up from the couch when she heard me come in from the balcony.

"Hey bud, how'd you sleep?" she asked in a cracked sleepy voice as she sat up.

"I slept good. I'm just hungry."

"Have some cereal. There's Corn Flakes on top of the fridge."

Sheila had woken up as I was finishing my breakfast but Chris didn't wake up until almost noon. By that time I was already dressed and waiting to go outside.

My mother and I had gotten into an argument while I was waiting for Chris. It started off minor, but she had a habit of majoring in minors and blowing things up. She got heated to the point that she reached forward to hit me, yelling her famous words, "I brought you into this world, and I can take you out!"

I blocked her swing. By then I'd had enough of my mother's anger and quick temper lash-outs. I struck back, "F*CK OFF!" and left the apartment. It was the first time I'd ever sworn at my mother. I walked around the neighbourhood to cool off. I didn't know where I was going to sleep that night, but I knew that I would not be going back to where she was.

James and Tony were in front of 15 Belshaw Place hanging out. I spotted them immediately when I turned the corner. I was happy to see them, and by the greeting they gave me it was evident that the feeling was mutual. We talked for twenty minutes until Chris showed up.

It was a hot day and we decided to spend it at Centre Island. We walked for almost an hour to the docks where we boarded the big ferry. None of us had money, but it was easy to slip past the ticket collectors as they collected tickets from paying families and smiled, saying hello to all the little kids entering the gate. It was our first time at the park without our parents. We realized that it wasn't much fun not having money to go on any rides, especially since that was the purpose of visiting Centre Island; that and picnicking. So we found another way to enjoy the theme park and entertain ourselves.

The Lumber Log Ride was one of my favourite rides. We stepped over the single chain fence onto the restricted area where the log passed by carrying riders seated inside. We hid behind a bush in the perfect place for an ambush. The log moved along slowly in the flowing current of water with a group of four older kids. They were all white and were dressed in polo shirts and khaki shorts; they looked to be from the suburbs or uptown. We were going to get them before their log turned the corner and was carried up to the top like a roller coaster by a big conveyer belt, followed by a rapid descent which would cause a huge splash as it plunged to the bottom on the other side. The splash would drench anyone standing on the bridge in front of it, but those inside remained virtually dry. We were close enough to bend down and put our hands in the water. When the group of teenagers got close, we splashed them as hard as we could. They got soaked and began cursing at us but were not able to get off the ride until the end. We shot them the middle finger and said a few bad words back as we walked away, amused by their reaction.

Near the end of the day, on the ferry heading back to the mainland, we saw our new friends. They didn't appear impressed with the game we'd played. One of the guys looked a lot taller standing in front of us than when he was sitting in the Lumber Log Ride. The two girls appeared much more attractive from up close as well. The incident had happened over an hour ago and all four of them were fully dry from the hot sun, but that didn't cool down the taller kid, who was quite keen on fighting one of us. The ferry pulled up to the dock, and as we exited a few words were exchanged, a scuffle ensued between James and the bigger kid. James got pushed to the ground and when he got up he looked hesitant to continue fighting. I felt brave though. I knew there wasn't much of a chance of me beating this guy, especially with the size and age difference, but I was from the projects, and I always had to prove that I was bad. I went up to him with my fists in the air. I took my first swing, which was also my last. He dodged the punch and swung back with a right hook, hitting me in the face. I landed on my ass in humiliation. He turned his back and walked toward the exit gate like a high school jock who had just knocked down two nerds. He thought the fight was over. But in the streets where we came from, you don't turn your back on your opponents, especially after humiliating them the way he had. I went to Tony and told him to give me the knife that he had concealed in his front pocket. He handed it to me without hesitation and I ran up behind the suburban hero and stabbed him in the back of the shoulder. I pushed the handle of the knife up as I pierced his skin in order to avoid deep penetration. I didn't really want to hurt him – I only wanted to save face.

"He f*ckin' stabbed me!" he screamed.

The entire crowd had seen everything and people started to surround me. I wielded the knife, backing them up and making my way outside of the gate. There were too many of them to get through; they trapped me by the corner of the fence. Behind me was Lake Ontario. I had three choices: stab every one of them to death, try to climb the ten-foot steel fence behind me and swim back to Centre Island, or throw away the knife and wait until the police arrived. I chose the obvious. I kept the knife in my hand to protect myself in case anyone tried to hurt me. When I saw the police car approaching from a distance, I threw the blade over the fence into the lake to get rid of the evidence, not that it would have made any difference in court with the hundred witnesses against me. James, Tony and Chris had run away before the police came. I didn't have a problem with that; there was nothing they could have done to help my situation. We never believed in snitching, or that everybody should take the fall if some could get away.

The police took me to 52 Division where they charged me with aggravated assault. After the long booking process they transported me to the Youth Detention Centre at 311 Jarvis Street. I went through the administration process and then I was strip-searched for the first time in my life. I had to take off all of my clothes as an officer stood in front of me and went through everything. When he was finished searching my clothes, he told me to open my mouth and stick out my tongue. Then I had to turn around and bend over to make sure that I didn't have anything hidden in my anus. When I arrived on the unit, all the juvenile inmates were getting ready for lockup for the night. As they made their way to their rooms, they were becoming more boisterous. The detention centre was overcrowded, and I was put into a room with two other kids. In the room were a bunk bed and a desk with a chair fixed to the floor. Since I was the newcomer, I would be the one sleeping on the mattress on the floor.

It was an exciting night. The kids were kicking and pounding on the doors and yelling at the detention centre staff. They weren't angry at anything in particular, just letting off steam and having fun annoying the staff. I participated in the door-banging as well. All three of us took turns kicking the door as hard as we could, competing with the kids in the other rooms. The ruckus lasted for hours until each kid dropped asleep one by one. By one in the morning the place was quiet and everyone was sleeping.

In the morning we had breakfast. I thought we would all be in trouble because of the night before, but not a word was mentioned. I played Monopoly with one of the staff and two other kids while we waited to be called in for court. The 311 Jarvis Detention Centre was connected to the courthouse so we didn't have to take a paddy wagon.

When they called me for court, I was disappointed because I wanted to finish the board game. I reluctantly got up and went with the detention centre staff, who brought me to a court officer in a blue uniform. The officer handcuffed me and led me into a courtroom, where I was placed in an enclosed prisoner's box. The first person I noticed was my mother sitting by herself on one of the benches where other parents and spectators sat waiting to bail someone out. She didn't look happy, but I didn't care. Rarely was she ever happy with me. *What's she doing here?* I didn't want to go back home. I didn't even like Ottawa, and I hated being yelled at and called names by her. I hated being afraid that if I did something wrong she would go into a rage and grab the closest thing to her and hit me with it. I wanted to stay where I was for as long as I could. I felt safe there. It didn't even click to me that I was in a detention centre. All I knew was that I fit in, and the staff didn't hit you when they got angry – they didn't call you stupid.

My name was called. I stood up and faced the Justice of the Peace. I confirmed my name and date of birth for the record before they read out my charge. I felt like a bad ass as they read in detail the sequence of events, even though I knew it wasn't as serious as they made it sound; the kid probably only needed two stitches. My mom took the stand and vowed that if I was released, she would do her best to ensure that I didn't get into trouble again, and that I would attend all of my court appearances.

The Justice of the Peace addressed me. "Mr. Tull, do you understand the seriousness of the charge?"

"Yes," I lied. I was acting in the way that was expected of me – remorseful. I really didn't give a rat's ass about piercing this guy with the tip of the knife.

The Justice of the Peace continued. "If you breach any of your conditions, you will end up right back in here. And I know you don't want to be in here."

How the heck does this guy know what I want? I disagreed with him, but nodded and said "Yes" again. I wanted to tell him that I preferred to stay there, but the words wouldn't come out. I was released into the custody of my mother.

My mom and I arrived back in Ottawa in the early afternoon. She kept going on about sending me to live with my grandmother in Brooklyn, New York. I didn't have a problem with that. In fact, the thought of living in New York fascinated me. I've always loved The Big Apple. I didn't dare make it known that I was happy about what she was planning though. Her mind would change in an instant if she knew that her decision would be a reward for my misbehaviour. I played it off as if I were sad, but stayed clear of saying the slightest thing that might persuade her to change her mind. The more she talked about the idea, the more excited I got on the inside. Ever since I was a kid my mother had kept in touch with my grandmother, so to send me to New York City to live under her wing for my teenage years seemed like the best thing for me. She was a good woman who loved her grandkids. She had a hand in raising my cousins who were born in New York. I had never met her or anyone from my dad's side of the family, but her love for me was manifested through her words and affectionate tone when I spoke to her on the phone. I wasn't sure which excited me more, meeting my grandmother, cousins, aunts and uncles, or becoming a New Yorker.

My mother called my sister and told her what she was planning to do with me. I sat on the couch in silence as she spoke to Leisa on the kitchen phone. I was able to hear everything that was said on both ends.

"Hi Leisa, how are you?"

"I'm good. So what's going on with Junior?"

"Oh boy, this kid is stressing me out. I really don't know what to do with him anymore. I called Enid Tull in New York and told her about the situation. I suggested that maybe he live with her and go to school down there because he's not doing anything but getting into trouble up here. I'm really at the end of my rope, and I think it's the best thing to do at this point. I'm going to buy him a one-way Greyhound ticket and hope that things change for the better for all of us. She's all for the idea of him staying with her. I think it would be great for him to get to know his grandmother and the rest of his father's side of the family."

"Mom, I don't think that that's such a good idea."

"Why wouldn't it be a good idea? I can't handle him anymore. He's out of control. He doesn't respect me and he always wants to do whatever he wants to do with no limits. He's getting into trouble with the law up here. I mean look at what happened when we went to Toronto. He goes out with his friends and ends up getting an aggravated assault charge for stabbing someone. I didn't even want to bail him out. I'm seriously done. I can't tolerate this anymore. I just think he would respect Enid and start to change some of his ways."

"Yeah, but Mom, you have to think about where you are sending him. It's not necessarily who you're sending him to live with but where he would be living. New York, Mom. Brooklyn at that. I mean Regent Park wasn't the best neighbourhood, but think about how much more crime he would be exposed to living in Brooklyn. You already know his obsession with American gangster movies and his admiration for pimps, drug dealers and the fast life. Brooklyn would only be a place for him to live out his wannabe thug life. Don't send him to New York. Plus, with the charges he has, and already being on probation, I don't think he will even be allowed across the border."

It was disturbing hearing them go back and forth planning my life for me. I wished my sister would stay out of it and let Mom go ahead and send me to Brooklyn. Nothing hurt me more though than what my mother said next.

"Well, he can't stay here anymore. If he can't live with his grandmother for now, I'm going to have to put him in Children's Aid, where they can find him a suitable group home to live in for at least a year until he changes his ways. That boy has been…"

I couldn't listen anymore. I got up from the couch unnoticed and made my way to my bedroom, wiping the tear that was finding its way down my cheek. My heart sank and my throat burned as I fought against exploding into tears from the feeling of abandonment. The person who had nurtured and protected me was now throwing me into the world. I didn't know how to cope with the idea of living in a group home and being taken care of by strangers who didn't care about me. I knew that if I went to New York there would be family there to welcome me with love and open arms; but what would be waiting for me at a group home? I was afraid of the unknown. I would be alone with no mother or father.

I sat on my bed, and the feeling of isolation made me want to cease from existing. I saw no future ahead of me and no reason to live. No one was there to motivate me, encourage me, or tell me that I could make it. My mind was scarred with the words that my mother yelled at me when she was angry, and my heart was torn because she didn't want me anymore. Under her leadership and guidance I had become a broken product of society, and because she couldn't fix me, she was now handing me over to strangers to finish the job.

I got up and walked over to the window, which was always wide open because I liked the breeze and the view from the ninth floor. Directly below was a paved path that led from the fire exit door to the front and back of the building. There was a clear view of the highway a short distance away. I stood there and watched the cars race by in both directions as everyone went on with their busy lives, while I contemplated suicide.

I climbed up and put one foot on the outside ledge of the window while the other remained on the windowsill inside. I was halfway there.

The fate of my life was now in my own hands. I didn't want to make any mistakes; I didn't want a failed suicide attempt where I would end up paralyzed and in a wheelchair for life. My life was shitty enough, I didn't need that. I studied what was below me, looking for the best place to land. If I jumped too far forward I might land on the lawn on the other side of the concrete walkway, but if I dove straight down it would be mission accomplished. Then who would be the one hurting? I looked back up at the cars passing by on the highway. The movement and velocity of the vehicles generated an energy within me that caused me to ask myself, "Is this how I want to die?" The answer was a clear no. I was an adventurous thirteen-year-old kid, always seeking the next thrill, and there was nothing exciting about plummeting to my death from the ninth floor. The entire plan came to me as I sat with one foot still outside of the window, ready to jump – I would steal a car and go joyriding until the gas was low, then I would smash it into a brick wall at full speed or drive it off a cliff in Quebec. *That's how I'm going to go!*

    I climbed back down from the window. If my mother had come into the room and seen me sitting up on the ledge, I would have ended up on the other side of the window, and – even better – she could watch. I left my room and I could still hear her talking on the phone in the kitchen. I went into her room and took the twenty-dollar bill that I'd seen on her dresser earlier that day. Quickly and quietly I opened the door to the hallway next to the kitchen and left the apartment. I didn't want her coming after me so I took the fire exit and ran all the way down the stairs. I hopped onto the number two bus and went to the arcade near my school to play Super Sprint. I didn't usually get to play much at lunchtime because I didn't have a quarter every day, and the lineup was always long. This time no one was playing, and I had enough quarters to play to my heart's content. But I wasn't content, I still felt sad and lonely.

    When I'd had enough of Super Sprint I left the arcade in search of my car. It didn't take long to find a vehicle to steal. As I walked down Montreal Road I noticed a minivan parked in front of a convenience store just off the main street. The owners were in the store and had left their vehicle running. Novice car thief that I was, I suspiciously crept across the street and ran towards the van. I opened the door and hopped into the driver's seat, threw the vehicle into drive, and sped off. I was filled with a rush of adrenaline. I was laughing and yelling hysterically as if I had just won the lottery. On the passenger seat there was an Oh Henry chocolate bar. My favourite – I wasn't even dead yet and I was in heaven. *I will eat that later*, I thought. In the meantime, as a new driver, I had to concentrate on the road. I had learned to drive by sitting on my uncle Dennie's lap and steering the wheel as he pressed the gas and the brakes. This was my first time driving on my own. I felt good; I felt alive; and I felt free. I drove along the back streets in Vanier enjoying life. I wanted to live forever and see the world. Nothing could stop me now. Thoughts of suicide had vanished.

Ten minutes into my joyriding excursion I arrived at a three-way junction. I stopped at the stop sign and looked both ways when I noticed a car in my rearview mirror passing the vehicle directly behind me. *What an impatient idiot.* I waited a second for him to continue ahead of me and make his left turn, but he didn't. He stopped his car in the middle of the intersection to prevent me from turning left. The man came running out of his vehicle with a black handgun pointed at me through the windshield. Without thinking twice I spun the wheel right and stepped on the gas. I made another quick right into the cinema parking lot where people were exiting from the movies. The parking lot was almost full and I wasn't thinking straight. Instead of honking the horn, I drove toward the crowd at top speed in order to scare them out of my line of escape. It worked. The multitude of movie goers separated in either direction faster than Moses was able to part the Red Sea. I only had to make one last turn around the corner of the building before I was out of the parking lot and onto the street. I veered right, attempting to turn in a ninety-degree angle, but I was unsuccessful. I lost control of the van and smashed into the parked car in front of me. The velocity forced the car that I hit into the one parked beside it. Three vehicles were completely destroyed but I was okay. I wasn't thinking rationally. Instead of opening the door and fleeing, I tried climbing out of the half-open window. I just wanted to get away from the lunatic with the gun. *Where did he come from anyway?* My torso got stuck in the window, and the man caught up to me. He opened the door with me halfway out of the minivan. I cried and begged him, "Please don't shoot me! Please don't shoot me! I didn't mean to steal your van." He opened the window and pulled me out. He didn't have the gun in his hand.

"You are under arrest." It turned out that he wasn't an angry crazy man chasing me for stealing his van. He was a plainclothes police officer who had seen me enter the vehicle from his car while he was across the street. He'd followed me during my entire joyride.

I was handcuffed and taken to the police station. The cop ended up being a nice guy. He even charged me with a lesser crime of joyriding instead of car theft. My mom came down to the police station with Denise, a family friend but more like an aunt to me. I was released into the custody of my mother, with a promise to appear in court.

CHAPTER SIX
WELCOME TO THE SYSTEM

My mom had decided to put me in a foster home instead of a group home. It was the same one that my sister Leisa was in, so my mother thought that it would be a good fit for me as well. The house was owned and operated by a white middle-aged couple, Bob and Sandy. Bob was a pudgy man with a receding hairline and a pot belly – the white version of Uncle Phil from *The Fresh Prince of Belair*. Sandy was a tall, attractive lady with long black hair. She had an athletic body and boobs that were impossible to miss. The two worked well as a team, maintaining the house and making sure the kids who lived there were treated fairly and taken care of.

The house was beautiful, nicer than any house that I had ever been in. As you walked through the front door there was the open kitchen concept to the right, the living room straight ahead, and just past the kitchen to the left were the stairs leading to the second floor. It was a higher-end middle-class townhouse. I didn't know anything about classes of people; all I knew was that there were the rich, and then there was us, and of course the people who were starving in the Third World countries. But I had always counted myself to be fortunate, even when we had to stand in the line at a food bank. I was just happy that there was food available to eat. So to me this foster home was absolute luxury. The refrigerator was always filled with food, with all the things that I saw in the grocery store but couldn't have. If I did ask, Mom's answer was, "I can't afford that, Junior. Do you think money grows on trees?" Now I was able to indulge in frozen yogurt, cheesecake, and real fruit juice instead of the artificially flavoured crystal Kool-Aid that I grew up on. The best part was, there was no rule about what or when we could eat; the only kitchen rule was to clean up after yourself. And there were no sit-down meals together because everyone's schedule was different; for this reason we were all responsible for preparing our own meals. We ate a lot, and we ate well. My mom had done the best she could to provide for me and my siblings, but life just seemed better at Bob and Sandy's.

There were two other kids living in the house, both older than me, and both serving open custody sentences. Tyrone was seventeen and the other kid was already eighteen and about to finish his sentence and move out on his own. I shared a room with Tyrone, who was an outspoken, wild Jamaican kid who lived to party and do drugs. He was always fun to talk to. We would stay up late at night talking and laughing. Our laughter was loud enough that Bob or Sandy would have to come to our room and tell us to keep it down. The theme was usually about Sandy's tits. It was nice when she came to tell us to *hush*, because she came in with a different colour nightie each time.

Tyrone was rambunctious and energetic and never stopped talking. He rambled on and on: he was either excited about something, complaining about something, or voicing his opinion. I respected him like an older cousin. He was the toughest teenager that I knew and he wasn't afraid to flaunt it. He loved wrestling and sparring as much as I did, but I always regretted calling him on. He would hit me too hard and bend me up in ways that my body was not meant to be bent, and he took pleasure in making me yell for mercy. I was either determined to beat him or just a sucker for pain because I always went back for more.

I had been sentenced to a year of probation by the Ottawa courts for stealing the van, and I still had to deal with the aggravated assault charge in Toronto. The entire thing turned out to be a blessing in disguise for me. Bob was the type of man who enjoyed first-class convenience, especially off the government's coin, and since he was the one responsible for escorting me to court, I was able to partake of that lifestyle as well. We flew business class from Ottawa to Toronto and back. It was my first time on an airplane, and I loved it. To fly above the clouds and through the sky was breathtaking to say the least. None of my friends had ever flown in a plane, and there I was, flying first class. Life was teaching me that good things came from bad behaviour, a lesson that would require much pain and hardship to unlearn later on.

We landed at Toronto Pearson International Airport and took a black airport limousine to 311 Jarvis Street. I met with my Legal Aid lawyer and he told me that the Crown Attorney was willing to reduce the charge from aggravated assault to assault with a weapon, but I would have to return in two months for a guilty plea. *This thing just keeps getting better.* Another trip to Toronto in two months. I regretted nothing.

After court, Bob and I had a few hours to spare before our flight back to Ottawa, so I showed him around downtown. We grabbed a hot dog from the hot dog stand and walked along Yonge Street and through the Eaton Centre. I brought him along Queen Street where the freaks hung out, and I also offered to show him my old neighbourhood which was close by, but Bob refused to step foot in Regent Park. We saw a few more sights and then took a cab back to the airport.

The second trip to Toronto was much shorter than the first. Bob had booked both the arriving and returning flights within a close timespan so we would not have to spend all day there. We landed in Toronto, took a limo to the court, I pled guilty and received an eighteen-month probation sentence to run concurrent with the twelve months that I was already serving. Immediately after court we took a cab to the airport and flew back to Ottawa in time for lunch.

As much as I liked living at Bob and Sandy's, my time there was short lived. I got into an argument with the white kid, and although I didn't mean it, I threatened to stab him. Days had passed and I thought we had resolved the issue. I forgot all about it. To me it was nothing, but to Bob and Sandy it was a big deal. They told me that my social worker, Maria Buddhu, would be there in an hour because I was being transferred. I tried to explain that I wasn't serious, but after attending my court appearance in Toronto, Bob was afraid of what I was capable of.

Hillary House was a Children's Aid emergency group home used for housing kids for a short period of time until a permanent and suitable group home was available. The process could take several weeks or months, but for me the transfer never came. I accumulated over a dozen assault charges on both residence and staff during my four-month stay at Hillary House, which ultimately led to me being escorted away with a set of iron bracelets around my wrists. I had a lot of pent-up anger inside of me with no knowledge of how to channel it. Anger and resentment played an influential role in my day-to-day decision making and how I acted toward others. But although I was angry, small things made me happy, like a game of cards, or fixing my Jheri curls in the bathroom mirror. I adjusted quickly to Hillary House. After the number of times I had moved, I had a good ability to adapt to change. However, Rose was the main reason the transition was so easy for me. She was living there when I arrived. Every kid at Hillary House had their own troubling story for why they were there. Rose's story began with her abusive alcoholic father. Her mother had all that she could take from him and fled to Queens, New York, bringing Rose with her. Rose found the move to the United States difficult to deal with, especially being so far from her friends. After a few months she decided to go back to the place where she'd grown up. She packed her stuff and told her mom that she was going to visit Ottawa, although her mother knew that she would not be returning. They hugged, said good bye, and Rose left with her one-way ticket.

When she arrived in Ottawa she stayed with a friend for a few weeks until moving back in with her father, hoping that things would be better now that her mom wasn't in the house to be abused by him. But nothing had changed. The excessive drinking continued and the abuse escalated. After he threw an empty case of beer at her, Rose feared for her life. Every night she slept with a knife underneath her pillow to protect herself from the man she had once called Daddy.

Eventually, Mr. Rochester had enough of taking care of his teenage daughter and called the Children's Aid Society to come and pick her up. After hearing the conversation on the phone, Rose felt overwhelmed with feelings of fear and abandonment. Not wanting to be thrown in a group home, she went into the basement, opened a window to make it appear as if she had run away, but instead hid in an unplugged freezer. When the three social workers showed up to escort Rose to the emergency group home, her dad led them to the basement, where there was no sign of Rose, just a wide-open window sucking in the cold winter air.

"Well, Mr. Rochester, it looks like Rose ran away," Maria Budhoo, Rose's primary social worker said. Because of her many years of experience in these cases, she seemed aloof.

"Just take her stuff. You'll find her," Mr. Rochester replied.

Crouched down in the fetal position in the dark dry freezer, Rose heard everything. "I don't think so!" she shouted as she pushed open the door of the freezer and walked straight to her suitcase at the bottom of the stairs. "Leave my shit alone!"

"Rose, we don't want your things," Mrs. Budhoo explained. "But your dad has turned you over to the custody of the Children's Aid, so you will have to come with us for now. You can bring your belongings with you," she concluded with a half-smile to help ease the pain that Rose was experiencing.

Rose realized that she didn't have much of a choice. She couldn't fight the four of them and take her suitcase, and if she fled up the stairs and out the front door she would be losing all of her possessions. Makeup, hair products, and brand name clothes didn't come cheap to a fifteen-year-old girl who didn't have a job. Rose's only option was to cooperate and go with the social workers to her new home, the Hillary House emergency group home.

I looked up to Rose more than my own sister, literally and figuratively as she stood six feet one inch tall, towering over all of us. She was a dark-skinned attractive girl with a genuine personality and a loyalty to her friends and family.

Rose and I never fought or argued, like I did with my real sister. Leisa and I would fight all the time, and if Rose was around she would usually try to intervene. One time in the condo on Jasmine Crescent when Mom wasn't home, Leisa and I had gotten into an argument about something. Because Leisa had difficulty expressing herself verbally, arguing with her always resulted in some form of physical violence. She customarily lashed out with a punch, a kick, or she attacked the person with the closest weapon she could reach. This time she threw a cup at me while I was in the kitchen. The cup hit my leg and caused me to flare up in anger and attack her back. I grabbed the plastic broom and broke it over her shoulder. Rose was screaming for us to stop, but by then we were both too heated to hear anything. I reached for two kitchen knives in the drawer and chased her down the hall into my mother's room as she screamed to Rose for help. I had no intention of hurting my sister with the knives, but it was nice to watch the bully, who was bigger than me and beat me every time she got mad, run like a big coward. Regardless of why Leisa and I fought, Rose never took sides.

Rose made the group home a fun place for me to be, and if it wasn't for her, I don't know what I would have done. The place was often in a non-stop state of chaos, the complete opposite of Bob and Sandy's. I enjoyed the constant entertainment though, and often participated in it or created it.

The group home was full of rowdy teenagers who felt the same way as me – rejected by their parents and society. There were six of us living at Hillary House at the time. None of us ever talked about our problems or why we were there, except one kid, Guy. He was always desperate for acceptance and opened up to us no matter how often we laughed at him or made jokes. He was the oldest kid there and had the most issues. At the age of eighteen, he had the mind of a nine-year-old. I was never aware of his mental state or condition; had I known about the deep-rooted issues he had, I would never have pulled the type of pranks on him that I did. But I just thought that he was a stupid teenager who fell for anything. One time I pissed in the popsicle tray and put the urine in the freezer to make popsicles. After they froze I gave one to him, but he grew suspicious because I didn't offer any of them to anyone else, and all of us were standing around him in the kitchen waiting for him to put it in his lips. As Guy raised the apple-looking popsicle to his mouth we all started laughing too soon; he threw it in the sink and laughed along with us.

The pranks with Guy stopped when I had asked him about his mom. There was a rumour that Guy had been having sex with his mother. He admitted it to me with a smile on his face. I didn't know if he was smiling because he was uncomfortable or because he thought it was cool. Either way, I thought the whole thing was disgusting and that he was a sicko. But when he told me that it had been happening since he was six years old, my perspective changed. I saw Guy as a victim and felt sympathy for him. I respected him even more and always tried to be friendly to him after understanding where he was coming from. The pranks I played on him after that were all in clean fun. "Hey Guy, you lost your shoe," I'd say, pointing to the floor. He would look down and ask, "Where?" And we would both laugh when he realized they were on his feet.

There wasn't much to do at Hillary House except lounge around and watch television or listen to music in our rooms. We could use the phone in the basement next to the office at any time during the day; it even allowed for long distance calls. I called strangers in New York, Los Angeles, and all over the world. I dialed numbers not knowing which part of the globe I was calling. I loved hearing the different accents. We played the occasional board game or a few hands of cards, but other than that we found our enjoyment in escaping from the group home. During the daytime I hung out with Orval, Layton and the rest of the homeboys downtown at the Rideau Centre or the St. Laurent Shopping Mall.

The weekends were the best. It was our time to get away from the group home. Some of the kids went home to visit their parents. Rose went to the adult clubs in Hull or to Astro Light, the only all-age nightclub in

Ottawa. She would be gone every weekend, even if she was grounded. She would pack up her makeup bag and everything she needed and head out to a friend's house to get ready for the night. I didn't have anywhere to go to get ready. I showered at the group home, soaked up my Jheri curls with curl activator and moisturizer, got dressed, and found a way to leave. The staff knew when we were planning to go out, but there wasn't anything they could do to stop us. We either left through our bedroom window or walked out of the front door while they were on a phone call in the office.

I went to the clubs in Hull occasionally, but I never missed a chance to go to the all-nighters at Astro Light. I knew almost everyone in the club; they were either guys and girls I hung out with or friends of my sister and Rose. The atmosphere and vibe of Astro Light made me feel like I belonged. It was a place where I could be myself, dance, and mingle with the ladies. It was also a preying ground for the younger upcoming pimps. Because it was an all-age club there were many young girls who were vulnerable; girls who wanted to fit in and be accepted, and were willing to do whatever it took to earn that acceptance. The pimps took advantage of that and lured them in with their swag, money, and promise of a prosperous future.

Rose and I usually got grounded or lost privileges for staying out all night or past curfew, but we didn't care. It was always worth it. We stayed in our beds and slept most of the next day, played cards, or just stayed in our rooms and listened to music. If I wanted to go downtown, I would jump out of my bedroom window and go. An extra day of grounding didn't matter to me.

The staff at Hillary House were easygoing for the most part, except Scott. He was the jerk that none of the kids liked. He resembled Kenny Rogers with his white hair and beard, but his attitude resembled that of a dictating prison guard. We all dreaded whenever Scott showed up for a shift. He didn't feel as if he'd earned his day's pay unless he made our lives miserable. He had no problem overstepping his authority by sending us to our room for a time-out for the smallest things, knowing that we would probably object. And if we did refuse, face down on the ground we went, with one arm behind our back and an assault charge on our record. Scott targeted Rose and me the most because of our tough exteriors and quick tempers. But instead of reasoning with us as teenagers to show us a better way, he preferred to provoke us in order to get a reaction.

Rohan was the opposite. Rohan's background was Jamaican. He was in good shape and had a positive energy. Unlike Scott, Rohan listened to us and tried to solve conflicts without rushing to physically force us to the floor for disagreeing with him. Rohan enforced the rules, but did it with tact. Some of the times he let things slide, sometimes he gave us a talking to, and other times he sent us for a time-out or took away a privilege, but regardless of the outcome, he was fair.

Theresa was short with long hair. She wasn't very attractive but she was an overall nice person. Theresa rarely enforced a rule. She was the pushover that all the kids loved. Her weakness was that she acted too much like a friend, to the point that if she tried to be assertive and enforce a rule, no one respected her authority. She let us get away with a lot. Theresa was easy to talk to and fun to play cards with, but she strongly opposed violence and would be the one to call the police whenever we were physical toward another resident or staff.

We were all in the dining room joking and carrying on like the kids we were. I guess Scott didn't like one of the jokes that I made and ordered me to my room. The dining room grew quiet as we looked at each other wondering if Scott himself was joking, but we all knew that was impossible, because Scott never kidded about sending us to our room.

"Why do I have to go to my room?" I asked.

"Because you're being inappropriate," he replied.

"What did I say that was inappropriate?"

"You know exactly what you said. Now go to your room and stop talking back before things escalate."

As I continued to refuse, Scott became more and more adamant about me complying. He wasn't backing down, and neither was I. Everyone in the house knew where this was going. When he attempted to reach out to grab my arm, I pulled away.

"Don't touch me!" I said.

Theresa was already worried. "Junior, please just go to your room for fifteen minutes and this will all pass away," she pleaded.

The time-out was only for a short period, but I refused to be the subject of injustice. "Why doesn't *he* leave it alone and then it will all *pass away*?" I responded.

The rest of the kids started to get involved. "Why don't you leave him alone? He didn't do anything," they shouted. Rose was the most vocal.

Rohan was not on shift that day but the part-time male staff member that was on duty heard the commotion from the office and ran up to assist Scott. I tried backing away from them until my back was up against the wall. Now I had two grown men standing in front of me demanding that I cooperate. Scott continued to do what he did best and escalated the situation. "Listen, Junior, now you have thirty-minutes. Do you want to make it an hour? I have no problem doing that. Either way, you go on your own, or we're taking you," he said, in a stern, piercing voice.

"F*ck you, asshole!" I shot back.

They both grabbed me by my arms. Scott put his leg in front of my shins and they pushed me forward. I fell to the ground. Within no time Scott was sitting on my back and I had one arm twisted behind me. The other staff member held down my ankles to prevent me from using my legs.

Rose couldn't handle the sight of what these men were doing to me. "Get off of him!

You're hurting his arm, you f*ckin' jerks!" she shouted.

"Stay out of this, Rose!" Scott warned. "This is not your problem. Don't make it yours."

I squirmed and shouted as they dragged me toward my room. Rose followed, shouting at them to let me go. When we got to the door of my room, Rose reached out and grabbed Scott's shoulder to prevent him from getting me through the door. Scott let go of me and turned to Rose. I tried to get up but the other staffer shoved me into the room and closed the door.

It was my turn to help Rose. I heard the thump from the carpeted wooden floor as she went down. She cried out, yelling profanities at them. I could have opened my door and gone out in attack mode, but that's what they were expecting. I climbed out of my window and went in through the front. None of them saw me coming with a jump-kick to the side of the part-timer, knocking him off of Rose. The staff were not allowed to hit the kids back – lucky for us or Scott would have had a field day on both of our faces. They eventually subdued us and restrained us on the ground, but not without Rose getting a few body kicks in on her way down. Meanwhile, unknown to us, Theresa was in the office on the phone with the police.

After several minutes with our faces on the carpet and our arms behind our backs, Rose and I agreed to a fifteen-minute time-out. Immediately after the time-out dinner was being served. Everything had calmed down and we were all around the meal table eating our evening meal. There was a knock at the door. It was the good ole Ottawa police. They came in and arrested Rose on the spot. She was charged with two counts of assault. They charged me with the same thing, but I was able to stay at the group home. They hauled Rose off in handcuffs.

Rose returned to Hillary House the following day. A few months later, on her sixteenth birthday, she moved out permanently.

I couldn't wait to turn sixteen and move out and get my own apartment, but I had three more years to go.

I spent a couple more months at Hillary House and racked up thirteen assault charges in total. I even lost my virginity in the apartment building just down the street with a Jamaican girl who was a year older than me. As much as I disliked it at Hillary House, it was much better than my next destination – The Ottawa Youth Detention Centre, also known as Bronson Detention Centre.

CHAPTER SEVEN
BRONSON DETENTION CENTRE

The Ottawa Youth Detention Centre, popularly known as the Bronson Detention Centre, was built in the early 1960s as a residence for young people who had committed heinous crimes, such as truancy and petty theft. Under the Juvenile Delinquents Act (JDA), kids could be incarcerated for being incorrigible – there were very few remedies available to the court when young people went even mildly astray; the choices were pretty much either being placed back into the care of parents on probation or being sent to training schools. Bronson was presumably an intermediary step that provided a residential setting with structure and the consistent presence of a professional staff to help a kid get back on track.

With the introduction of the Young Offenders Act (YOA) in the mid-1980s, the court was given more options: extrajudicial measures, extrajudicial sanctions, probation, open custody and secure custody. The notions of prevention and diversion were strengthened under this legislation, and thus the list of impositions really represented a "menu" for judges. The focus was placed on "habilitation" of youth (teaching skills necessary to become contributing members of society) and holding the youth responsible for their actions. This was a different slant than what was offered by the JDA, where the focus was more on imposing adult-type restrictions on kids who had simply gone astray.

When the YOA caught on, a period of unprecedented youth incarceration began. At its height, Canada was locking up kids at rates that exceeded those of the United States – a country that values a "tough on crime" stance. The legislation allowed for kids who had breached probation to be held in detention and kids who had left open settings to be held in secure settings, all at the discretion of the Provincial Director – a ministry-appointed individual who was the gatekeeper for detention and custody facilities.

Bronson Detention Centre was entirely funded by the Ontario Ministry of Community and Social Services and was one of several facilities spread across the province to provide secure services to young offenders. The facility was staffed by ten full-time youth workers, three supervisors, an assistant superintendent, a superintendent, a secretary, and a cook. There were fifteen bedrooms – all lockable – but one was designated for secure isolation (when kids acted out and had to be contained), so it was only used when numbers exceeded fourteen. At times, the numbers soared and it was not unusual for there to be over 20 kids in the facility – many sleeping on mattresses in the games room. It was a very busy time.

There was a portable classroom situated in an enclosed yard at the rear of the building. The kids spent a good part of the day in that classroom and were offered the opportunity to earn high school credits while in secure custody. Kids who were sentenced to longer terms of secure custody were normally sent to St. John's School – a large centre in Uxbridge, Ontario that had access to resources that could not be matched at Bronson. In fact, in those days, kids were moved around the province with regularity for various reasons – sometimes it was necessary to separate co-accused, or to protect a youth who may have been a witness to a peer's criminal activities. Sometimes there were youth gang conflicts in a Toronto facility and rivals had to be separated. Sometimes it was simply to support facilities that were over capacity. All movement was managed out of the Central Provincial Director's Office in Toronto, and the staff had to be ready to move a kid on a moment's notice.

The building was past its prime by the mid-1980s. Staff asked if the ducts could be opened to allow more fresh air inside, as people were complaining of dryness and chronic coughs. The response was that there was so much dust and dirt accumulated in the system that it would be inadvisable to touch it, as the contaminants would be cast into the air!

The bedroom doors were solid wood and could withstand a serious beating; if they were kicked or rammed from inside, the wood would bend and absorb the punishment. The doors eventually began to fail and were replaced by cheaper models that consisted of a 2x6 wood frame filled with particle board that was then clad with quarter-inch plywood. The integrity of these new doors was discredited when Reginald J. Tull booted one right off its hinges and into the hallway past the nose of the supervisor! After a couple of other failures, the decision was made to replace all doors with steel ones.

Bronson Detention Centre was "do more with less" epitomized – the ceilings were low and the décor was art-deco (inadvertently – the furniture was simply *that* old), but some really incredible things happened there – things that would make a person want to keep working with kids, no matter how challenging things were. The staff team was committed and genuinely cared about the clients. Sure, there were some that brought a "correctional worker" mentality to the job; but this was tempered by the willingness to engage in conversations, have some laughs, poke some fun and make the best of the time spent together.

The kids that came to Bronson Detention Centre were usually from Eastern Ontario: Ottawa, Kingston, Cornwall, Pembroke, Brockville and surrounding counties. There were kids from all walks of life: rich, poor, black, white, native – a real quilt of culture. There was also the issue of language; Bronson was the only facility in the province mandated to service clients in English and French, so the staff team was comprised of a 50/50 split of Anglophones and bilingual workers. This was particularly interesting when kids came from the Toronto area or from Southwestern Ontario; French is not as recognized there, and there were times when it was spoken quite frequently at Bronson.

After a short time, the Bronson site was "developed," meaning that the detention centre was demolished and gave way to condominiums.[1]

The Bronson Detention Centre as I knew it was not a bad place. Take away the locked doors and twenty-foot wooden fence outside in the yard that kept us away from our freedom, and Bronson would have been more like a youth drop-in centre than a youth detention centre. We spent most of our time playing soccer or basketball in the small gym located in the centre of the facility, which separated the administration area and kitchen from the TV room, the games room, and the north and south wing units. If we weren't playing sports in the gym, we were playing ping-pong in the games room, watching television or playing monopoly or cards in the TV room.

For most of us, the food at Bronson was better than the food at home: three meals a day along with dessert and an evening snack. The two chefs rotated shifts. I remember Pete's cheesecake – it was out of this world, everyone's favourite.

The rules at Bronson were simple: no whispering, no swearing, no fighting, and no talking back to the detention centre staff. In other words, just shut up and do what you're told and you will be fine. It sounded simple

---

1   Overview summary written by former staff Cameron McCloud.

enough in word, but it was almost impossible in deed. It was an unfamiliar system to me, because all I knew was fighting and speaking out. The staff knew that they were in for a ride with me, and I knew that I was going to take them for one. I challenged every rule they had in the book.

The place ran on a point system. At the beginning of each day, all the kids started off with twenty-five points. If we broke a rule, we would lose a point. The ridiculous thing about the point system was that the staff would never say, "You lost a point," they always said, "You failed to earn a point." I assume this was to take away the negative connotation of losing something and focus more on trying to earn something positive, such as climbing the levels. We all knew that it was bull – we never earned points – we only lost them.

There were three levels: Entry, Standard, and Honour. Everyone started on Entry level when first arriving at the detention centre. There was also Off Program and Special Program. Both programs were used to isolate the individual from the rest of the kids. If you spoke back to the staff, you were put on Off Program; if you got into a fight or had to be restrained for not following a staff order, you were immediately placed on Special Program and locked in the secure isolation room. There was no bed in the secure isolation room, just four walls, a cold floor, and a wooden door to kick for hours.

On both Off Program and Special Program we were able to watch television, play ping-pong or shoot hoops by ourselves. Occasionally one of the staff would come and join us for a game of ping-pong. We were allowed zero contact with the other kids. The kids on the regular program were not permitted to so much as look at the kids who were on one of the isolation programs.

Climbing the levels wasn't difficult for me. Once I made it to Standard, it was a breeze to get to Honour. Staying on Honour by not losing two points in a single day was the big problem. "You failed to earn a point, Reg!" Cameron would say, after I frustratingly uttered "Shit!" for failing to return one of his high-speed ping-pong serves. It was either my tongue or my short temper that got me into trouble. At times I tried to do well and climb the levels, and at other times I just didn't care about their rules and stupid point system.

As much as I hated the place, Bronson became like a third home to me. It was a safe place. The staff made sure that no one felt threatened or taken advantage of. Other than fighting with the staff and the wooden doors, I only remember one fight that I got into with a kid. It started in the laundry room with a tug-of-war argument over a towel. I decked him in the face and it was over. The fight was quickly broken up and I was placed on Special Program.

Between the group homes and short visits to my mom's, Bronson Detention Centre was where I spent most of my time. I was in and out on a regular basis and I got to know the staff fairly well. Marcel and Valerie were the supervisors. They were different in how they dealt with the kids. Marcel was good at being a jerk at times, especially when it came to me. He was a quiet French Canadian who didn't speak much but observed everything. He looked to be in his mid-thirties and carried a small beer belly. Marcel and I never got along, nor did we ever hold a conversation of substance. I avoided him like a plague, but he always found a way to call me out or get me in trouble for something. Bronson was a small place, so there wasn't much room to sneak around or get away with breaking the rules, especially with Marcel's eyes pinned to us at all times.

Valerie, on the other hand, would talk to us and make us feel as if we were somebody more than just a kid in jail. She was about the same age as Marcel, maybe a few years younger. She had straight blond hair that hung a little past her shoulders and was about fifteen pounds overweight. She seemed to take an honest interest in the kids. She spoke to us kindly and respectfully; most of the staff did, but it was evident who really cared and who was there just to collect a paycheque. Valerie didn't come down hard on us. She preferred to give chances rather than cut off our heads. Although Valerie was softer than Marcel, all of the kids respected her. We knew that if Valerie tilted her head forward, raised her eyebrows, and looked directly at us from above her glasses, she meant business, and we would quickly fall in line.

Most of the other staff at Bronson were sticklers, but there were a few that were all right. Cameron was everyone's favourite. He was a clean-shaven good-looking Caucasian guy in his mid-twenties and stood over six feet tall. I admired Cameron because he was easy-going, fair with the kids, and held a black belt in karate – or so he said. Whether this was true or not, it was apparent that he could hold his own if it came down to it. He wasn't massive or anything but he was physically fit, and fast, hence the reason I could never beat him in a game of ping-pong. My attempts to win were always thwarted due to his speed and amazing ability to play the game. Whether I liked or disliked the staff at Bronson, I always despised it there because I wasn't free, and it only catered to the white kids. Although I never experienced racism, it was extremely biased, and other than the Caucasian culture, no one else was able to live out or experience theirs. Instead of altering between Rap City and Power Hour, the staff would get us to vote, knowing damn well that my single vote would be outnumbered every single day. I was never able to watch anything that represented my culture or background. Guns and Roses, Motley Crue, and Metallica blasted from the television speaker, irritating my ears for an hour every day. I found solace in listening to my Walkman in my room. I was able to break away with Run DMC, LL Cool J, Public Enemy, Boogie Down Productions, Ice-T, and N.W.A.

The staff ran Bronson as if it were their own home. The six o'clock news played each day, in which none of the kids had a vote. I found the Gulf War to be interesting to watch. I couldn't understand why Iraq wanted to invade Kuwait, or why George W. Bush wanted to get involved and help the Kuwaitis when the US invaded countries all the time. It didn't make much sense, but it was both entertaining and educational.

During the weekdays, school was mandatory, with the exception of those who were on Off Program or Special Program. The school, which was just a portable classroom, no different from the ones in regular schools, was located only eight feet from the main detention centre building, surrounded by a twenty-foot-high wooden fence similar to the one that that kept us in the yard. I couldn't have cared less about school. It was boring. We had to work out of the correspondence courses they gave us. It took me all class period to answer one or two questions because all I did was daydream; my mind was always on the outside. I just wanted to be free and I couldn't think of anything other than what I would be doing if I were on the other side of that fence. I wanted to break out, but it was impossible to get over the fence – at least that's what I thought, until the day I witnessed a kid do it.

This new kid wasn't scheduled to be released any time soon, but he was determined that he was getting out that day, and on his terms. About ten of us entered the portable classroom and took our seats. The new kid sat at the back of the class to the right of me, close to the portable's rear door. All the schoolwork had been handed out and everyone was settled in. There was only one staff in the class monitoring the kids, and he was distracted by a conversation he was having with the teacher. The new kid took advantage of the opportunity and reached for the door handle. He twisted it and pushed the door open, leaving it ajar less than an inch. When he noticed that I'd seen what he had done, he threw me an impish grin, put his index finger to his lips, and whispered, "Shh." I thought he was just being mischievous by opening the door. I never thought that he was actually planning to escape. He waited a few moments with his eyes locked on the staff and teacher talking at the front, then quietly and slowly pushed the door open and slid out, closing the door softly behind him. I was the only one who saw him go. I sat in my seat astonished, wondering how he was going to climb over the fence. It took the staff until lunchtime to realize that there was a missing kid. We were all lined up when the staff did their head count and realized they were a kid short. He had a good forty-minute lead. It was fun to see the staff scramble around the detention centre in search of this fifteen-year-old fugitive. They couldn't find him anywhere. He was long gone, and if he could have kept himself out of trouble, maybe he would have lasted longer than a week in the free world. I later found out that he never actually climbed the fence. He climbed to the roof of the portable classroom and jumped over the fence, and onto the grass on the other side. That was something I would have never done; if I'd gone with him, I would have been recaptured on the roof for hesitating too long, in fear of breaking a leg or two.

After completing my first two-month bit in Secure Custody behind locked doors and extremely strict rules at Bronson, I was transferred to the Roberts/Smart secure treatment unit, where I met up with Steph, my close friend. I was then sent to a group home called Cramer House to serve a six-month Open Custody sentence. Open Custody was just that. They still had custody over you. Any time you wanted to leave the house without a staff escort, you had to have a pass that had to be signed by your probation officer, the staff supervisor, and your social worker. Passes were only given for the purposes of school, work, family visitations, and some special exceptions. The passes allotted only enough time for you to get to where you needed to be, do what you needed to do, and then get your butt back – or back to Bronson Detention Centre you'd go.

Cramer House was a group home for both Open Custody young offenders and kids living in the custody of the Children's Aid Society (CAS). I happened to be both. There were three other kids in the home but I was the only one on Open Custody. It could have been hard for me to see the kids come in and go out every day, but it wasn't. All the kids in the group home, with the exception of Alisha, were homebodies. Roy and Steve didn't have any friends and stayed home all of the time. I spent most of my time in my room recording mixed hip-hop cassettes or listening to dancehall reggae, which I had just discovered when I found a tape that Orval had given to me a while back. I had never listened to the tape before, and I got so excited about the music that I wanted to share it with someone. I called Terry up to my room. He was the only black staff, and he was from Jamaica. I knew he would be able to relate to my excitement.

"What's up Reg?" He said as he entered my room.

"Listen," I said excitedly, and played the tape.

"Yeah. Reggae," he said nonchalantly.

I wasn't sure where to take the conversation. I was so eager to share this newfound genre of music with someone, and the only person who I thought would love it as much as me seemed as if he didn't care, or that he hadn't even liked dancehall reggae. "It sounds good, eh?" I said, not knowing if he was going to agree or not.

"It's okay. It's reggae." He shrugged his shoulders and left the room.

I felt a little awkward because of the amount of excitement I had expressed, but it was no big deal. I went on and fell in love with the music. Shabba Ranks, Buju Banton, Supercat, and Ninjaman were my favourite – they were the big superstars of dancehall in the early 90s. I had grown up listening to my mom's reggae, Bob Marley and Gregory Isaacs, but to me, nothing was like this cassette. I had the music blasting from my ghetto blaster in my room every day. Other than dancehall reggae, Maestro Fresh Wes, the hip hop king of Toronto got his fair share of play.

The staff at Cramer House were nice people. Cindy was a slim, plain-looking lady in her mid-twenties. She had a few freckles and light red hair. Ken was in his mid-thirties, and he was the spitting image of Rod Stewart. We were able to talk to Ken about anything; he was just that kind of guy. Terry, the only staff of colour, had been in Canada for so long that he didn't speak with a Caribbean accent. When he tried to speak *patois*, I called him a Jafaken for fun because he sounded like a white boy trying to talk black. He'd probably lost his roots throughout the years and maybe that was the reason he wasn't too gung-ho about reggae music. Rick was the size of a sumo wrestler, weighing in at over three hundred pounds and barely able to fit into his little Volkswagen Golf.

There weren't a lot of rules or stress at Cramer House. We made our own schedule and did our own thing. I enjoyed working out at the YMCA with Terry. I watched all of the big guys lifting weights and I fell in love with bodybuilding in the same way I'd fallen in love with reggae music.

Cramer House was the best group home that I had ever been in. I received a weekly allowance and a monthly clothing budget. The staff took us almost anywhere we wanted to go. I did things that I would have never done living with my mother because the money just wasn't there. We went downhill skiing on the fluffy snowy hills of Quebec. Our first camping trip was to North Algonquin Park, and it was awesome. We canoed for several kilometres, portaging through the woods with the canoes over our heads and large backpacks on our backs. I swam three kilometres across one lake with one of the staff canoeing next to me in case I needed a break – I never did. The water was so clean that we could scoop up a cup of water from the canoe and drink it without having to pull over on land to build a fire to boil it. When we ran out of powdered milk, we just used orange Kool-Aid mixed with lake water and poured it on our cereal. On the last night of the camping trip, we stayed at the main campground with people who came from across Canada to get a taste of one of Ontario's largest parks. Around the picnic tables near the lake, there was another group of kids from another group home, mainly black; they were from Toronto. I listened as one of them bragged about going home, "I can't wait. Tomorrow, big city, bright lights." He made sure that our group could hear him loud and clear. I wanted to switch group homes and go with them.

Even though I was happy at Cramer House, I still took fits and went into a rage when I didn't get my way. One time I destroyed my entire bedroom, throwing the bed across the room and tipping over the dresser. It looked as if a tornado had passed through. I had a million opportunities within arm's reach and a ton of support, but it wasn't enough. The desire to do whatever I wanted, legal or illegal, always outweighed anything else. I knew nothing about delayed gratification or the fact that I couldn't just take whatever I wanted just because I wanted it. And it was that very attitude that destined me to spend the next seven years, my entire teenage life, in and out of group homes, detention centres, and jails.

CHAPTER EIGHT
THE JOYRIDE

Ken yelled up from the bottom of the stairs. "Hey guys, we're going to have a quick meeting. Can everybody come downstairs to the living room?" He was excited about something, and Ken didn't get excited about a lot of things, or at least he didn't show it. Usually when we had group meetings it was to tell us about next week's plans, upcoming changes that would be implemented, or to give us an opportunity to express our concerns about things and make suggestions, the usual group home stuff. However, his enthusiasm grabbed my attention, and I was the first one downstairs, sitting on the couch in anticipation. Alisha and Steve came down after a few minutes. "Roy come on, we're waiting for you," Ken shouted, eager to get started. Unmotivated and reluctant to come to the meeting, Roy came downstairs and entered the living room in his boxers, a white vest, and a pair of mismatched socks, with his thumb in his mouth.

When we were all settled, Ken began. "Guess what kids, next week we're going camping out near Kingston. We will be staying in tents and cooking our food over a campfire for four days. It will be the real deal, camping out in nature, except of course, there will be bathrooms. We will have two tents, one for Alisha and Cindy, and one for the guys. We'll be driving up in the two group home cars in order to have enough space for the coolers and our bags. It'll be nice to get out of the house for a bit and spend some time in the outdoors.

"Steve, I know you will be visiting home next week and you won't be able to come. Sorry, I tried changing the date to accommodate everyone, but unfortunately I wasn't able to."

Steve seemed as if he didn't care either way.

Roy and Alisha weren't too excited. Roy sat silent with his legs crossed and his thumb still in his mouth. Roy didn't want to be taken away from his daily routine of sitting around the house all day doing nothing, and

Alisha would be missing her kleptomaniac boyfriend, Dennis. I was okay with anything. I liked going on long trips.

"Is anybody else as excited as me?" Ken asked.

"Do we have to go?" Alisha asked.

"Of course you have to go, Alisha," Ken said. "Where else are you going to go? There's not going to be any staff here while we're away. Don't worry, I think as time goes on and you guys start packing for the trip, the excitement will kick in. Now look, here's a list of the things you will need." He handed us a sheet of paper. "It has all of the things that you should bring and also the stuff you shouldn't bring. You guys should start packing in advance so that you're not left in a last-minute haste. Take this list of the campsite rules as well. Please read them thoroughly so that there are no surprises. Any questions?"

We all got up and left the living room.

The following week we headed out as planned for the two-hour drive to Kingston. The ride was smooth from beginning to end. The windows were down, and the fresh air blew throughout the inside of the car as the B-52s' famous song *Love Shack* played on the radio. I liked the feeling of the powerful wind against my arm as it hung outside the window. Roy was in the back fooling around with his leg out the window. "Roy, put your leg back in and stop acting like a clown," Ken told him. But Roy was having too much fun and refused to listen. Next thing you know, his shoe went flying off, and the joke was on him. Ken refused to stop and go back, and Roy was left with only one shoe.

We arrived at the campground a couple of hours before sunset. We pitched two tents and Ken made a campfire to cook dinner. Hotdogs, beans, potato chips, and Kool-Aid made up the meal. After we ate, we walked around the campsite. There were about six or seven other tents within a twenty-yard radius. The restrooms on the campsite were similar to the ones you'd see at the parks in the city. The campgrounds were fairly plain and simple. Other than hiking it didn't appear that there was much else to do, especially for teenagers. Neither Ken nor Cindy told us what the plan was for the following day, if they even had one. None of us bothered to ask.

Night time came and it was lights out, or rather sun down. There were no lights on the campgrounds and it was pitch dark. The only way to get around was by using a flashlight. Roy, Alisha and I were hanging out in one of the vehicles talking and joking around. Alisha sat in the driver's seat, playing with the steering wheel, pretending to drive. I sat in the passenger's seat and Roy was in the back. It was about two o'clock in the morning when Aisha joked about stealing the car.

"Do you guys want to steal the car? Let's do it," I said, generating an energy of excitement.

We were all down with it. We came up with a plan on how we were going to get the keys. It didn't take me long to think of one. Roy and I would go into our tent on our hands and knees screaming and yelling as if we were playing a prank to scare Ken, meanwhile we would search around the dark tent for the keys.

Ken was not impressed at all. We had just woken him out of a deep sleep and he was mad.

"What the hell are you guys doing?" Ken screamed. "Get out of here if you are going to act like animals and let me sleep!" We ran out of the tent and back to the car where Alisha sat laughing her head off.

"Did you get the keys?" she asked.

"I didn't," I answered. We both looked back at Roy, who sat quietly for a moment until he couldn't hold it in any longer. With a guilty smile, he opened his hand and passed the keys to Alisha. We waited a few minutes for Ken to fall back asleep before Alisha put the key in the ignition and turned it half way to check the gas level. It was on empty.

"That sucks," Alisha said. "That's not going to get us anywhere."

As we sat there concocting another plan to get the keys for the other car, Cindy came out from the girls' tent with her flashlight and went to the bathroom. As soon as she went inside Alisha bolted to her tent. She wasn't in there for more than ten seconds before running back to the vehicle with the keys. We waited for Cindy to get back to her tent and fall asleep, and then we got into the other car. I got into the driver's seat this time; Alisha was in the passenger seat and Roy in the back. We hit the jackpot with this one; the gas tank was full. I started the ignition and put it into Drive. I started to drive forward but couldn't see a thing. "Turn on the lights! Turn on the lights!" Alisha said. After a few seconds of searching for the light switch, I found it in the nick of time as we rolled forward in sheer darkness. The lights saved us from crashing into the tent directly in front of us. I made a left turn on the dirt path that led out of the campgrounds and to the main road. I followed the signs that read "Highway 401." It took only a few minutes to get to the highway. There were two entrances: one that read "West to Toronto" and the other "East to Ottawa."

"Let's go to Toronto," I said. The thought of showing up in my old hood in a brand-new car would have been the coolest thing.

"No, let's go to Ottawa," Alisha said.

"Yeah, let's go to Ottawa. I don't want to go to Toronto," Roy agreed with Alisha.

"We should go to Toronto. I can show you around the city and there's a lot to do." I tried once more to convince them.

"No, I'm not going to Toronto," Roy said adamantly. Alisha was dead set against the idea as well.

I got onto the east ramp and headed to Ottawa. I had never driven on the highway before. The cars and trucks seemed as if they were driving at the speed of a bullet as they zoomed by. It took me a while to adjust to the high speed but I eventually did, sooner than I thought. Alisha came up with an idea to put her watch around the rearview mirror to make sure that we all got equal driving time. We switched drivers every twenty minutes until we got to Ottawa. Whenever my turn was over and it was time for me to pull over, I would take an extra two minutes doing tricks on a dirt road, skidding the tires until the air was full of dust, or reverse donuts on an open grass field.

We arrived in Ottawa just after six in the morning. Our first stop was to pick up Alisha's boyfriend. I knew Dennis from the Bronson Detention Centre. This kid was wild, the craziest juvenile delinquent I had ever met. His favourite music was heavy metal. Whenever it played, I thought he was going to bang his head on something or break his neck because of the way he moved it up and down like a maniac. He definitely loved adventure and lived his life for the next thrill. He was our age and had been in and out of detention centres since he was thirteen. His sentences were usually longer than mine because of his extensive rap sheet for breaking and entering and car theft. Back then, anything over six months was considered a long sentence. He was also a chronic shoplifter. When Dennis entered a store, he would steal anything he could get his hands on. He once told me that every time he walked into a store, even if he didn't plan to steal anything, he felt that they were watching him like a thief. "It's probably because you are," We both laughed.

Dennis lived with his mother in a low-income area of the city on the notorious Blake Boulevard, which was located behind the first school I attended when I first moved to Ottawa, Robert E. Wilson. Blake Boulevard was known in Ottawa as the baddest area in the city. The area had a lot of small three-storey buildings near to one another, and the houses were tiny and in need of renovations. To me it didn't seem like that bad a neighbourhood; its reputation exceeded the reality.

When Dennis joined the party, the entire vibe in the car changed. The adrenalin that we experienced when we first stole the car came back. After being awake all night and driving for so long, we were not tired, but in a relaxed calm mode – until Dennis got in the car.

I parked the car outside of Dennis's place and Alisha went to knock on his door. Dennis was more than excited when he saw us with a hot set of wheels. It wasn't really a hot set of wheels, it was only a Ford Escort, but for a bunch of fifteen-year-olds, it was hot. Dennis ran to his room, jumped out of his pyjamas and into a pair of jeans and a T-shirt, threw on his running shoes, and hopped in the passenger seat in the blink of an eye. "Do you want to drive, Dennis?" I asked.

"Damn right I want to drive." He got out and ran around the front of the car to the driver's side. I opened the door, gave him the keys and walked over to the passenger seat. He had the vehicle started before I could get inside. I sat down and put on my seat belt. *This guy's a little too excited,* I thought. *I hope he knows what he's doing.*

"All right, let's go!" Dennis said, as he rubbed the palms of his hands together. He threw the car into drive and took off with the front wheels skidding on the pavement. He drove even more recklessly than I had imagined. I was fearing for our lives while he drove a hundred and forty kilometres per hour on the back streets without stopping for stop signs. After ten minutes of his dangerous driving, I had to put this to an end. Roy was shivering in fear in the back seat begging him to drive civilized. Alisha was enjoying the ride, as if everything Dennis did turned her on. "Okay man, let me drive. It's my turn," I said. I couldn't take anymore. I thought we were going to die in that car that day, at the hands of that lunatic of a driver.

"Come on man, just give me five more minutes," Dennis pleaded.

"No man, it's my turn. Pull over right there," I said, in no uncertain terms. Dennis was a cool guy, but I wasn't about to lose my life for his enjoyment.

I took the wheel and drove off with Dennis in the front. I wanted to give him a little taste of his own medicine. I was confident with my driving and felt much safer with my stunts than I did with his. I started off at the speed limit until I got to the first stop sign, then ripped right around the corner, shaking everybody up. I got a little wilder on my corner turns and Roy began complaining again. When I arrived on Blake Boulevard I felt more comfortable driving at a higher speed because Blake was a broader and longer street than the other back roads. I hit the gas and floored it, trying to exceed Dennis's speed of a hundred and forty. I achieved it for a few seconds until we got nearer to the end of the Boulevard. I also succeeded in scaring Dennis, who had both feet pressed against the dashboard to cushion the impact in case we crashed, saying with clenched teeth, "Oh god, oh god." Roy would not stop yelling from the back. I calmed down and drove normally. "That was awesome, man. I didn't know you could drive like that," Dennis said, with his hand on his chest feeling his heart.

I drove downtown as we talked about how much fun we just had. "You are crazy, man!" Dennis said to me.

"No bro, you're crazy. I thought you were going to kill us all. You were driving over a hundred on the back streets, zooming past all the cars and going through stop signs. Honestly, man, you were scaring me. That's why I took the car back. You're psycho."

"I was in control," Dennis said. "I've been driving for a long time. You were swinging us around those corners, throwing us all over the car. What was that?"

"I had to get you back for almost making me shit my pants," I said, and we all laughed, except Roy.

"Take me back to the group home," Roy said.

"I'm not driving all the way back to Nepean, especially so early. Plus we still have a lot of gas left to drive around," I replied.

"Then let me out right here. I'll take the bus."

"OK." I pulled over and Roy got out.

"Why does he only have one shoe?" Dennis asked, as we watched him walk up Montreal Road toward the bus stop.

"Because he's a jackass," I said. We all laughed. "The guy sticks his foot out of the car window while Ken is driving on the highway and the wind blows off his shoe."

It was now morning rush hour in downtown Ottawa. We were joyriding, going up and down whatever street looked interesting enough to drive on, but I didn't like the traffic. Downtown was getting congested and I wanted to cruise. I made a turn on a street that wasn't busy. When we got to the first stop sign there was a lineup of at least ten cars, stopping and going as they approached the T intersection, most of them turning left. Beyond the stop sign straight ahead, was a free-flowing road, with trees and grass on either side. I didn't have the patience to wait behind the cars. I made a bold move and drove up onto the curb and onto the grass and sidewalk, void of pedestrians, passing all the vehicles from the right side. As I passed the stop sign, I spotted an RCMP cruiser stationed at the other end of the field. I hopped back onto the road hoping that he hadn't seen the stunt I had just pulled. We all saw him. "Oh shit," Dennis said. I continued driving. We watched the cruiser sit a hundred yards from us. It began creeping toward us. I didn't wait for it to get close. As soon as I saw the cruiser move, I put the pedal to the metal. The cop pursued. There was what appeared to be a military base directly in front of us. I turned left. It was not my intention to get into a high-speed chase with the police. I tried to get as far away from the cruiser for us to get out and run on foot. We reached the Aviation Parkway underpass in less than a minute. I slammed on the brakes and pulled up the emergency brake simultaneously. Dennis and I jumped out of the car while it was still in motion. The momentum almost caused me to tumble to the ground, but I managed to stay on my feet and I took off in the opposite direction from Dennis. He ran up the hill toward the bridge and I ran through a suburban community. Alisha stayed in the back seat.

I made my way along the back streets until I eventually ended up back on Montreal Road. I knew I had nowhere to go. No one I knew was going to provide refuge to a wanted teen who'd run away and stolen a car. I could hear police sirens from all over. I walked east toward the Rideau Centre, expecting a police car to pull up beside me at any time. It didn't take long to come to fruition. A cruiser soon stopped next to me. I also stopped walking. We both knew what we were doing there. I was arrested and taken back to the Bronson Detention Centre.

I was sentenced to two months secure custody and six months open custody which were to run concurrently. My time at Bronson went smoothly and the staff were impressed with my behaviour. I spent most of my time on Honour Level. I did a lot of drawing and reading for the two months that I was there. Cramer House agreed to take me back, which I was surprised to hear considering I had stolen their car.

After two months I walked into the group home again, all smiles. I was excited to see Roy and Alisha and talk about our adventure. The feeling wasn't mutual. Roy was standing in the kitchen and Alisha was sitting at the dining room table when I entered. I went to greet them both, but was welcomed with silence. Alisha ignored me, and Roy walked away and went to his room. *Whatever*, I thought. *They were in on it just as much as me. I don't know what their problem is.* And I didn't care. I went about my regular routine. Eventually we were all speaking again, as if nothing had happened – no one ever talked about the stolen group home car.

There were a few changes. Dennis and Alisha had broken up. Shortly after, Roy lost his virginity in a bathtub, to Alisha, while they were both drunk at a house party. It seemed like a lot had changed since I had left, yet everyone was still the same.

CHAPTER NINE
INNES DETENTION CENTRE

It wasn't long before I ended up back in the Bronson Detention Centre. After a few temper tantrums, destroying everything in my room, and cursing at the staff, I decided I'd had enough of the group home and open custody life, so I ran away. I was never abused or wrongfully treated at Cramer House, I was just fatigued with the open custody rules and group home regulations, and I wanted to be free. I preferred to be around people who were more like me, who listened to my music, wore similar clothes, and spoke the same lingo.

The first place I stayed when I fled Cramer House was to Steph's group home downtown. He snuck me in, and I slept underneath a bunch of blankets on the floor before sneaking out early the next morning and spending my day at the Rideau Centre. This went on for a couple of nights until he too ran away. During the nights we'd stay at different friends' places, and on the weekend when we went to the clubs in Quebec, we slept on the floor of an abandoned house along the Hull strip; in the mornings we showered at a nearby hotel where some friends stayed every weekend. The days were spent downtown at the Rideau Centre with the main crew: Orval, Layton, Troy, Randy, Koby, Lamar, Tyrone (when he wasn't in jail). Our crew also included a group we referred to as, the Haitian Creation: Eddie, Max, Ron and his brother JC. Of course, there was also Trevor, the only whiteboy. Everyone had their own story, their own history.

We had done a lot of junk together. I was involved in more serious criminal activity than when I was in Regent Park. It was nothing to snatch a purse or stab someone in a fight. The debit card and bank machine were only recently introduced into the world. In need of money, Steph, Trevor, and I went on the hunt. After snatching a lady's purse and taking out the cash, we found a card inside with a pin number taped to the back of it. We went to the nearest ATM and pulled out five hundred dollars, splitting it three ways.

Richard was about two years older than me. He was a whiteboy who tried to fit in with our crew but was never fully accepted. I hung out with him a few times. He was physically strong, more so than me in a one-on-one, but he couldn't control his tongue, or back up his talk at times, so he never got the respect. He definitely lost a notch after my sister beat him up in an elevator. He and I also got into a dispute up by the Major Mackenzie Bridge outside of the Rideau Centre. Words were exchanged, and he called me on while I was with Steph and a few other guys on our way into the mall. I pulled out the hunting knife that I had tucked away in the sleeve between my hip and my jeans – the same one I cut my thumb with after smashing the skinhead. I hid the blade behind my wrist as I approached, swinging the bottom of the handle at the side of his head. He ducked and grabbed me with both arms around my waist, but he let go immediately after feeling the point of the blade penetrate deep beyond the skin tissue of his back. My homies and I casually walked into the Rideau Centre, leaving him to scream in pain as the rush-hour bystanders waiting for the bus hurried to his aid.

The following afternoon I entered the downtown McDonald's with Steph, Orval, Layton, Troy, and a couple others. Richard was by himself at the back of the restaurant eating fries. We all walked up to his table and sat down around him. There was no bitterness in the conversation.

"What's up, man? How you feel?" I asked, sitting on the chair next to his table.

"Man, the doctor said that if the knife went half an inch more to the right, it would have punctured a lung and I would have died."

He pulled up his shirt and showed me where I had stabbed him. He then requested to see the knife that I had used. I placed it in his hand. He looked at it almost in admiration, turning it from side to side, feeling the sharpness of the blade, and touching the tip. I was cautious that he had my knife, being only two feet away from me the very next day after the stabbing, but I wasn't worried. He could barely move with his arm in the sling, and I was backed by six other guys, of whom at least two also had knives. He gave back the knife, and we all left him there with his fries. That would be the last time I'd see Richard.

I was on the run for a few more weeks until I was spotted on the OC Transpo by a teacher from Ottawa Technical High School, where I'd attended before I fled the group home. He was one of the only black teachers at the school, and he was a very big guy.

During my short time of freedom, I experienced a great deal. I was constantly jumping around from friend's place to friend's place, a few nights at Eddie's, a few at Tyrone's, and the occasional night at Orval and Layton's house after hitting the night clubs in Hull. I didn't enjoy sleeping at their house as much though. Their mother was a nice, but strict Jamaican lady. She didn't allow a lot of kids to sleep over, so Orval and Layton usually had to sneak me in and have me sleep under Orval's bed in the basement. The floor was carpeted, but not extremely comfortable. There was one Saturday night when she did allow me to sleep over, but I had to go to church with them on Sunday morning. The next day I was regretting my decision. Bored, underdressed in my T-shirt and jeans, and feeling uncomfortable because I didn't know anybody, I was thinking that I should have roughed it out on the rug underneath the bed and then left in the morning. I wasn't accustomed to the church environment because I hadn't grown up in it. Even the occasional times when we visited our grandparents in New Liskeard for Christmas and went to mass at the Catholic Church I felt out of place. I never knew what to do. Do we kneel? Do we sit, or do we stand? I had to look at everyone else and follow their lead. I couldn't wait for the service to end. "How much longer are we going to be here?" I whispered to Layton.

"About four more hours."

"Four more hours? Are you serious?" It was almost one o'clock in the afternoon. *That's going to take up the whole day*, I thought. *By the time we get to the mall it's going to be closed.*

Church ended a few minutes later. "I got you, mon. You thought you were gonna be trapped here all day," Layton laughed.

Orval and Layton's mom stopped to chat for a little while with a few of the members before we left to their house. The brothers changed out of their suits and ties, and we headed to the Rideau Centre to hang out.

The first time I tried marijuana was with Tyrone, Eddie, Steph, Orval, and Layton. We met up with Gary and a few others at a house on our way to go club hopping in Hull, Quebec. Gary pulled out a bag of weed and some hash and rolled up a joint. I wasn't planning on smoking any, but it didn't take much convincing once the joint was being passed around the room. When the spliff got to me, I said no thanks. It was a weak no, more like a thought – should I or shouldn't I? "Yo take a hit off of that, Junior, don't be soft." Gary convinced me. I esteemed him highly among the older guys around the way, as I did Jackson and Richard, Orval and Layton's older brothers. Gary was a pimp as well, but more discreet about it than the others. To me he was more like a player than a pimp. He was a few years older than my sister and was dark, tall, and muscular. He was regularly in and out of jail, which gave him ample time to work out and bulk up. He also had swag and carried himself in a manner that demanded respect. His girlfriend was the shortest girl in Ottawa but had the biggest breasts in the city. These were the kind of guys I felt proud to be associated with. I took the joint and had my first puff. It continued around the circle until it was too small to hold, but Tyrone found a way; he sucked on the joint until it almost burnt his lips, then put the roach in his pocket to roll with the rest of his collection for later. We left the house and spent the night going to different clubs, from Club 747 all the way down the strip to Park Avenue. I was as high as a kite.

My first time smoking dope was nothing like my first time getting drunk. My uncle Leo held a party at his house and all the adults were drinking and socializing. No one noticed the number of times I went into the kitchen and guzzled down a glass of red wine. I was downing one at least every fifteen minutes. When the party was over, everyone had left. My mother and I were staying over for the night. She was already sleeping but was awakened to the sound of me vomiting everywhere. She led me to the bathroom to throw up in the toilet bowl. It felt as if I were puking my guts out all night long with her yelling at me, making my head ring even more than it was.

I continued doing drugs with my friends. It was fun. Everyone was doing them, even the girls. Manon, Eddie's girlfriend, and her roommate Chantel were my two favourite people to get high with. We smoked hash by heating up two butter knives on the stove and then squeezing a piece of hashish between them. As the smoke went up, we sucked it in and filled our lungs. After we got high, we'd go down to the convenient store and steal some snacks because we had the munchies. After smoking, all we did was joke and laugh. We laughed at things that were not even funny had we not been stoned. Tyrone was the biggest pothead in Ottawa. Everybody knew it, and he didn't hide it. Tyrone's apartment was where you went when you wanted to smoke or drink. He would even let you use his bed if you had a chick that you wanted to tap. Tyrone's place was the hot spot for fun and entertainment – until the drugs and alcohol ran out. He then became miserable and rude, at times even aggressive. Eddie and his Haitian crew were the worst to do drugs with. They always wanted to play stupid voodoo games after everyone was high. You constantly had to have your guard up or else they would pull a prank on you, always at your expense, while they got the laugh. I didn't like that, and I didn't trust them. I didn't even trust Orval and Layton when they were with the Haitians, because they were always in on it too. It was usually pick-on-Junior day when we got high together. Maybe it was because I was the youngest. I don't know. When I got high, I just wanted to relax, laugh, or have sex. Manon and Chantel's place was the best for that. Their apartment was the cleanest, and they took care of me like a little brother and kept me out of trouble. They never peer-pressured me into anything or played tricks. They even gave me my own room when I slept over, and they didn't care if I invited a girl. In fact, Manon was always eager to meet the girls I had in my life. Manon was my best friend. I always felt safe with her, and I loved her like a sister whom I could confide in about anything. However, regardless of whose place I hung out at and did drugs, I felt as if we were a community, and it was us against the world.

While I was on the run from the group home, I spent most of my time hanging out downtown at the Rideau Centre or St Laurent Mall. If we weren't break dancing up by the doors at the Mackenzie King Bridge, we were congregating down by the food court, or fighting against the skinheads or Rideau security guards. The food court was where you could find anybody, and if the police were actively looking for me, that was where I could have been found.

It was a bummer getting caught by the teacher while I was on the bus. The bus was full, and I was at the back, about to get off at the Rideau Centre. When I looked out of the window, I saw him across the street. Our eyes locked and he ran over to catch me. I pushed through the crowd and ran to the back doors, but when I got there he was blocking the exit. I tried pushing my way past him, but the six-foot three-inch giant, with the form of a bodybuilder, wasn't going to let that happen. He grabbed my arm and told the bus driver to call the police. The cops came, and I was thrown back into the Bronson Detention Centre.

I spent the rest of my open custody sentence, plus an additional thirty days for being AWOL, in Bronson. I was released and placed in a different group home somewhere in the east of the city. It only took a couple of months for me to get rearrested for robbery. I had hit the big leagues with this charge and was sentenced to six months in secure custody, and I served one month dead time waiting for court. I tried to stay as productive as possible. My behaviour was the best it had ever been. They sent me to another detention centre to serve a portion of my time. It was a bigger facility for youths serving longer sentences, called Rotherglen Youth Detention Centre, just on the outskirts of Toronto. I played football and worked out during my time there. I even learned how to knock myself out by intentionally hyperventilating for thirty-seconds and then pressing the palms of my hands against my throat to cut off the air circulation. I learned it from one of the kids. He was a drug addict, and this was his way of getting high without any access to drugs. He did it all day, every day. I tried it a few times, and that was enough for me. After a few months in Rotherglen, and only being placed in segregation once, I returned to Bronson to apply for an early release. I was granted the release for good behaviour and got out a month early. I spent a total of six months in detention. I was placed in another group home. Though I was on probation, I was free to do what I wanted. My only conditions were to report to my probation officer and Keep the Peace and Be of Good Behaviour.

I was arrested eleven days after my release for assault and spent another four months in secure custody awaiting trial. I was not a happy camper, and my behaviour reflected just that. Steph was in Bronson at the same time, and he was equally as angry. We both added fuel to each other's fire by encouraging one another's bad behaviour. Steph and I were constantly into some sort of trouble on the outside, and it was worse now being on the inside.

I was bitter that I was back in jail after being out for only eleven days. The staff at Bronson never liked referring to it as jail, but it was. We were locked up behind a wooden door every night and we couldn't walk out of the front door at will. If that was not jail, I didn't know what it was; all I knew was that I hated the place more than I ever had. I rebelled, refused orders from the staff, and at times became violent toward them and the other kids on a whim. I was even making unnecessary enemies at other detention centres.

One day I had a court appearance and I thought it would be fun to provoke another inmate from the Ottawa-Carleton Detention Centre, more popularly known as Innes Detention Centre. The maximum-security facility was infamously known for its violence, barbwires, and not-so-nice correctional officers. It held inmates aged sixteen to seventeen, and adult males and females. Since I was in phase 1 and he was in phase 2, there was no way that he could get to me, even though he was less than a foot away from me in the adjoining cell. Correctional Services Canada did not allow for young offenders ages twelve to fifteen (phase 1), ages sixteen and seventeen (phase 2), or eighteen and older (adults) to come into direct physical contact. We could at times see each other through the bars and spit at one another, or talk through the cells at the courthouse, but we couldn't be out of our cells at the same time. If it were inevitable for two phases to be out at the same time, for example in the corridor, going to or coming from the courtroom, the court officer escorting the higher phase handcuffed inmate would stop him and make him face the wall while holding his arm. The younger inmate, also handcuffed, would safely walk by with his escort walking in between them to minimize the risk of an assault on the younger inmate. For this reason, I felt comfortable taunting this guy from Innes, as one would provoke a vicious dog locked up in a cage, knowing that he couldn't get to you no matter how mad he got.

I spent the entire day insulting this guy in the cell next to me.

"Hey, bitch in cell one, what are you in here for?" I asked.

"What did you call me?" He replied, shocked and unsure if he had heard me correctly.

"I said, 'bitch, what are you in here for?' Do you have a hearing problem?"

"Do you know who the f*ck you are talking to?"

"Yeah, I'm talking to you, pussy." I continued to jeer him to escalate his anger by my carefully selected words. It worked.

"Why don't you say that in my face punk?" He was getting furious quickly.

"What do want me to do, open the bars and come into your cell, idiot? Trust me, if I could do that, I would come over right now and slap you across your ugly face, goof." I was relentless with my words, going as far as calling him a goof. That is the fighting word in jail. If someone calls you a goof and you don't fight, you would be deemed as a coward.

"Oh, you're f*ckin dead dude! I'm going to smash your face."

This guy probably could have kicked my ass. He was a short stocky seventeen-year-old. His body looked too big for his height. He probably got all swole from pumping iron while at Innes Detention Centre and eating all that nutritious jailhouse food. I didn't care how he got so big; I was having fun pushing him to the edge. I even spoke about his mother in the most degrading way. I had him rattling the bars, yelling, "I'm going to kill you! I'm going to f*ckin kill you!"

The same week, Marcel, the supervisor, had threatened to send me to Innes Detention Centre because of a fight I had gotten into in the laundry room. The kid was from a small town called Pembroke, Ontario – he was one of the staffs' favourites, so you can guess whose side they took. I was led to my room and locked up.

The threat of going to Innes Detention Centre was music to my ears. My sister was there at the time. She was seventeen years old and doing time in the young offender's phase 2 section, which housed boys and girls in the same unit. I was hoping that Marcel was serious with his threat. I was looking forward to seeing my sister, but the transfer didn't happen. Maybe because I was only fifteen years old, or because Innes refused to admit me because I had a family member there. Instead, I spent five days on Special Program. I never saw Honour Level once. I spent most of my time on Special Program or locked in the isolation room.

About a month later I had another court appearance. Steph's court date was on the same day. The court officers picked us up at 6:30 in the morning. It was winter, so the Bronson staff gave both of us these army-style coats with hoods for the trip. We rode in the back of the paddy wagon together to the Ottawa Courthouse, located downtown on Elgin Street, but were held in separate holding cells. We were only separated by one cell in between us so we were able to talk all day. The saga began when the court officer brought me and another kid back from the courtroom. The newcomer, who was just picked up from off the street the night before on some petty charges, was asking the officer questions about his bail. The officer was distracted and failed to slide my cell door all the way shut. When the guard left, I took it as an opportunity to run around and check out who was being held in the other cells. One of the officers spotted me in the main corridor and yelled at me to get back in. He ran toward me, and before I knew it, two of them were dragging me by my arms to the cell. An argument ensued, and Steph got involved from his cell.

When it was time for us to be escorted back to Bronson, both Steph and I were handcuffed behind our backs and shackled. For this we shouted obscenities at the guards as they led us out to the paddy wagon. While in the back of the paddy wagon I had an idea. I was going to get the cuffs back in front of me by slipping my hands down below my butt and bringing them under my feet and up to the front. Seeing that I wasn't Houdini, it didn't turn out to be the best idea. I got stuck with my handcuffs below my hamstrings and above my calves. I was locked in the fetal position with my hands bound behind me. It was the most uncomfortable position, and to add injury to insult, the court officer was intentionally driving extra aggressive. He was stomping the brakes at the red lights and making sharp turns, throwing us back and forth inside of the steel paddy wagon. It was a big joke to them when they opened the paddy wagon door and saw me sitting with my head on my knees and my hands behind my legs. I asked them to take the cuffs off and put them on normally so I could walk. They laughed at me and refused my request, even when they saw how challenging it was climbing the six or so steps that led up to the detention centre. It must have taken me ten minutes to get to the top. I slowly and uncomfortably walked into Bronson, crouched down, only able to take steps by the inch. On the way in through the doors the court officers were giving us attitude, and we gave it back in return.

We didn't deserve to be handled this way, even for our misconduct, and Cameron was infused with anger when he saw us come in, especially the way I was hunched. He automatically took our side but still had to make sure that we were compliant and cooperated. When the officers took off my cuffs, I was able to stand erect. They told us to kneel on the chair so they could take off the shackles. We refused to kneel and make their job easy. "You bend down and take them off, asshole!" Steph shot.

At this time Cameron was growing concerned because it was lunchtime, and all the kids could see what was going on through the cafeteria window. Tensions were rising and the kids were getting excited. The staff decided to take us to our bedrooms to remove the cuffs. Cameron took Steph to the North Wing and Marcel brought me to the South Wing. The court officers came along because they had the keys. I was cooling off on my way to the wing, but Steph was still angry and kept chirping insults at the officers. One of the officers finally got fed up with the verbal abuse and stepped on the shackles, causing Steph to fall straight forward, and he couldn't use his hands to break the fall because he was cuffed behind his back. The officer then grabbed the hood on his coat and started pulling him towards the wing; the other officer kicked him hard between the legs from behind. Cameron was disgusted with what he had just witnessed and told them to give him their keys and go wait in the lobby.

All the kids in the cafeteria saw what the court officer did to Steph, and it raised the anxiety of the whole group. I was already amped up, and that was the straw that did it for me. With my ankles shackled and my hands free, I began to swing at Marcel and the other staff escorting me to my room. With the help of the shackles, they managed to get me to the ground quickly and effortlessly. They dragged me to the isolation room and restrained me – facedown.

Cameron had managed to get the cuffs and shackles off Steph. After he was strip-searched in the bathroom, Cameron was escorting him to his room to wait for lunch, but Steph heard me yelling for the staff to get off me. He turned around in the hallway and started heading to the other side of the gym to the South Wing. Cameron caught up to him and touched his shoulder to try to stop him. Steph hit him four good shots in the face, and they ended up in a scuffle. When they were finally able to subdue Steph and lock him in his room, they came over to see me. Once I was calm, Cameron used the court officer's key and took the shackles off. They locked me in the isolation room, leaving me flat on my stomach. I wasn't injured, but my ego was hurt, and I was mad.

I got up and went to kick the door. I kicked it repeatedly, as hard as I could, at times laying on my back, kicking with both feet. I could see that the wood was starting to separate from the hinges, which motivated me to kick harder. I stood up, back towards the door, and with all my power, kicked and kicked and kicked with the heel of my foot. Eventually, the door flew off the hinges and was lying flat on the floor in the middle of the hallway. The staff were braced for a nasty encounter, but it never came. After a few seconds, Cameron peeked into the room and saw me standing calmly. I didn't plan for that to happen, so I didn't have a speech ready. The best I could offer was, "There's your f*ckin door!"

Cameron and I looked at each other for a while; with all the nervous energy of the day's events pent up, all he could do was break out laughing. When I saw him, I did the same. We sat down on the floor against the wall. After a brief silence we spoke for a few minutes. I agreed to cooperate and walk to the room at the end of the hall. They didn't bring me to my original room, but at least this one had a bed with a mattress. They brought me lunch in plastic utensils and a drink in a Styrofoam cup.

After I ate my food and drank my orange juice, I pissed in the Styrofoam cup and waited for them to come and open the door to collect the utensils. I wanted to throw my urine directly in Marcel's face. I didn't particularly hate Marcel; he wasn't all that bad of a guy. I just felt that he always had it in for me, and I wanted to get him back for the times I felt that he deducted points and put me on Off Program or Special Program unfairly.

When they arrived, Marcel noticed that my cup was full, but not with the same colour drink they had served me. "He urinated in the cup," Marcel told Cameron.

"Come on, Reg," Cameron pleaded. "I thought you were going to cooperate."

"Don't worry, Cameron. This is not for you. It's for that asshole."

"OK, have it your way." Marcel clearly had enough of everything. They left from in front of my door.

I could hear Steph on the other wing; he had started banging on his door again. I joined in. I wasn't angry anymore; I only wanted to keep irritating the staff. I even ripped apart the mattress in the room.

Two hours had passed, and I was tired of banging on the door. I was pacing my room, waiting for them to bring me back to my own room so I could at least read a book or draw. I heard a tap on the small plexiglass window in the centre of the door. When I looked out I saw Cameron, Marcel, two police officers, and two correctional officers with patches on their jackets that read, Ottawa-Carleton Detention Centre. *Oh, shit, what the heck is going on?* I thought

"Reg, I want you to pour the cup of urine on the floor in the corner and come and stand at the door." Marcel said in an authoritative tone. I didn't have much of a choice; they weren't leaving me any room to negotiate or debate. I complied and they took me out of the cell. One of the correctional officers handcuffed me and led me to the front. Steph was already there, sitting down handcuffed and ready for the big leagues. My sister had already been released – now it was Bronson's opportunity to get rid of their two main problems. Steph and I were both still fifteen years old, but the jail made an exception to take us because we were considered violent offenders. We were the youngest inmates to have been admitted into the Ottawa-Carleton Detention Centre.

Entering a maximum-security jail for the first time, with the perimeter surrounded by a barbwire fence, was both intriguing and intimidating. It was intriguing because I was always curious as to what was on the inside of this well-guarded fortified building, surrounded by razor wires and camaras pointing in every direction. I had known a lot of people who had passed through it and made it out unscathed. I always wanted to know how it was inside of those walls. It's not that I wanted to be incarcerated;

I just wanted to know how people lived and survived under such conditions. It was intimidating because of all the barbwire, high fences, metal doors, and iron bars. The noise inside the jail added to the intimidation. It echoed from all directions, bouncing off the brick walls and steel doors. You could hear inmates howling from their cells, the steel keys rattling as guards walked down the wing, the heavy doors opening and slamming closed, the voices coming from the correctional officer's radios. And to remind us that we were in a real jail, the guards wore correctional officer uniforms, and the inmates wore prisoner uniforms with blue and white shoes. This culture change was enough to awaken any fifteen-year-old into a reality check.

One of the first things I noticed was that the guards at Innes Detention Centre were much more hardened than the staff at Bronson. Their attitudes reflected the ones of the court officers who escorted us back to Bronson that day. They didn't speak to us as kids, they spoke to us as prisoners. Their purpose was to make it clear who was in charge. It was evident that they would have never tolerated the kind of behaviour that Steph and I demonstrated at Bronson. In fact, these guards would have supported the court officers in the way they dealt with us. I would imagine they would have even taken it a step further and dragged us into a cell and stomped us to a pulp with their black leather boots. That was the impression I got when I first arrived. The officer who admitted us into the jail made it clear that they were not going to tolerate the same behaviour that we were used to getting away with at *Disneyland*. I was convinced of it.

Steph and I had to spend three days in solitary confinement, otherwise known as "segregation," "seg," or "the hole" before entering general population. We were strip-searched and given prison attire: an orange jumpsuit, a T-shirt, boxers that a hundred other inmates had worn, socks, and shoes. They also gave us a towel roll with sheets, a comb, deodorant, and a toothbrush and toothpaste wrapped up inside, and then led us to our separate cells in the segregation unit.

After breakfast the next day, a guard opened my cell door and asked me if I wanted to go out to the yard. Of course I wanted to; I jumped off my bunk and followed him out of the segregation unit and across the range to the yard. Another officer standing at the gate opened it up and let me out. Each day after breakfast, the general population inmates were locked in their cells until lunchtime. Two inmates were allowed out to clean the unit. This was also the time when the inmates in seg were able to take their yard time. Each inmate was allowed out on their own for twenty minutes of fresh air and exercise.

The yard was the size of a basketball court, maybe a little smaller. I stepped out and stood directly outside of the gate looking around at the yard. The perimeter was a tall brick wall that extended even higher up with an iron fence connected to it, and on top of the fence was a roof, to prevent helicopters from flying down and breaking us out. I wasn't out for long when one of the cleaners came to the gate. I recognized him right away. "Open the gate," he told the guard. The officer reached into his pocket, pulled out his key and was about to put it into the keyhole until he heard the guy say, "I'm going to rip his f*ckin head off."

The guard put the key back into his pocket. "I can't let you out there then," he told the kid.

The kid pointed at me. "Today's your lucky day," and went back onto the range to finish cleaning.

It was my buddy from the courthouse; the guy I was taunting in the holding cells a few weeks earlier. Now it dawned on me that I was in the same jail as him, unprotected by the bars or the court officers. I knew I would have to stand my ground. I wasn't afraid though; the whole episode exposed weakness in him. If he really wanted to rip my head off, he wouldn't have told the guard before he opened the door. He would have just let the guard open the gate and come out to do it. It was a display of intimidation.

The intimidation show continued when I was released from segregation into general population. At my first meal I had the honour of sitting directly across from Mr. I'm Going To Rip His F*cking Head Off. I was already seated and began eating when he came and sat down. The rule at Innes Detention Centre was that once you were seated, you were not permitted to stand up for any reason. By standing up at the meal table, it indicated that you were challenging someone to a fight. Before he started to eat, he gave me a few words of caution: "Keep your head up and your eyes open at all times." This guy was appearing less threatening the more he spewed out his empty threats. I didn't say anything back to him. I just kept my head up and my eyes opened, as he said, whenever I walked through the unit. During the time I was there, Mr. I'm Going To Rip His F*cking Head Off never said another word to me, and we never fought. If we had, it would have been a clean one-on-one, because I had backup. Steph was my right-hand man, and Tyrone was also in there with us. We were the only black guys in the phase 2 young offender section of the jail, and we had each other's backs.

I had only been in one fight at Innes. It happened during grub with a guy from the Middle East. He was sitting to the left of me and there was one person in between us. This guy's brother used to run the entire young offender unit when he was there. I had never met him, but apparently, he was a massive seventeen-year-old kid. Rumour had it he took steroids and had an extremely bad temper. He didn't have to fight much because everyone feared his size and his rage. The correctional officers were even afraid of him because he was known for attacking a few of them. It was said that he was the toughest kid that ever passed through Innes's young offender unit, and that he could bench press over 385 pounds.

I guess this cat at my table thought that he could live off the reputation of his brother. He was a big guy too, but more chunky than muscular. We got into a few words and he didn't like the way I spoke back to him. He asked me if I wanted to stand up. I told him to go ahead and stand. He got up, and it was on. Anyone who didn't stand up to fight after a challenge was considered a punk. He put his feet around to the other side of the bench that was connected to the steel picnic table. I quickly stood up on top of the bench. I was usually the first one to strike, and this time was no exception. I jumped down with my fist landing in his face with as much force as I could hit him with. We were both throwing blows, but I don't remember getting hit. I do remember landing a few before the guards stormed in and broke us up. We were both sent to the hole. He was either released or shipped to another jail while I was still in seg. I was glad for that: one less problem for me.

When I got out of segregation I was put into a cell with Carlos. I knew Carlos from the streets. He was a cocky short kid, born in El Salvador but grew up in Canada, adopted by a white family. We reminisced about a vehicle we had stolen on the outside with another kid. We were bored one day, and I suggested that we steal a car and drive it to Quebec. I wanted to see my girlfriend, Brandy. They had agreed, and we went searching for a car. It seemed like back then, people were comfortable leaving their vehicles running while going into the store. It didn't take long to find a van sitting outside of a convenient store on Rideau Street with the engine running. I told them to walk quickly down the side street and I would pick them up. Without hesitation, I went up to the van, got in, and took off to pick up my two amigos. They'd walked about fifty yards up from the store. I pulled up next to them and told them to get in. They looked at each other reluctantly and didn't move. It was like they were surprised that I had actually taken the van. "Get in! Get in! What are you waiting for?" I yelled. They got in the van, and I drove off. "What the heck were you guys waiting for?" They didn't answer – we all suddenly burst out in laughter, them in disbelief, and me because I had a vehicle, and I was excited to see Brandy.

I drove straight to the Alexandra Bridge and crossed over to the Province of Quebec. I pulled over to call Brandy from the payphone to tell her that I was coming with two friends and to confirm the directions. I remembered how to get there because I had been there once before, but I wanted to make sure.

The first time I was at Brandy's house she had a big fight with her mother about our sleeping arrangements. Brandy wanted me to sleep in her room with her because I was allergic to cats, but her mom was uncomfortable with that and preferred that I slept on the couch. Brandy shouted and cursed at her mother, then slammed the door. I ended up sleeping on her bed with her. It was shameful for her mother to allow Brandy to talk to her with such disrespect, and she still gave in to her demands. It was something that I was not accustomed to seeing between a kid and a parent.

The drive along the countryside highway was going smooth, until it started getting too hot in the van. Neither Carlos nor the other kid could figure out how to turn down the heat. It was getting unbearably hot, so I attempted to turn the heater down myself while driving. As I was adjusting the knobs and pressing the buttons, I veered a little to the right, causing the van to slightly touch the gravel on the side of the road. They both screamed in panic as if I was going to smash into a deer or drive off a cliff. The shouting startled me, and I spun the wheel to the left, taking us onto the other side of the highway, again I spun it to the right and lost absolute control. The velocity and speed caused the van to tilt and eventually flip completely onto the driver's side. The van came crashing down on its side with all four wheels facing south, in the direction we came from. The cassette that I had put into the stereo was still playing. The reggae song *Sorry*, by Shelly Thunder was pumping through the speakers as we climbed out of the passenger side window, the way one would climb out of a chimney. We jumped to the pavement and ran through the forest. We were in the middle of nowhere, walking in wet snow: the remains of winter. Our running shoes and the bottoms of our pants were soaked, and our feet were frozen. All we wanted was to get out of that forest and back onto the highway, where the ground was dry.

After an hour of roaming in the forest, we finally found a road. We walked for a few minutes until a white guy in his late twenties stopped and gave us a ride in the back of his pickup truck. When we got to the junction, we thanked him and jumped out. Ironically, we got off just twenty feet from where we tipped the van. We stopped and looked at the remnants of glass from the broken windows and were happy to be alive. We continued to walk north in the direction of Brandy's house. A few minutes into the walk we spotted a police cruiser coming in our direction. We just looked at each other and our expressions said it all. We were too cold and tired to go running through that forest again. We stopped walking and stood there waiting for the cop to arrest us and take us somewhere warm. We were charged with auto theft. We had to sign a document promising to appear in court, and they would release us to an adult who was willing to pick us up and sign us out. I called Brandy, and she asked her mom if she could do it. Brandy and her mother came to the police station, and her mom signed us all out. We ended up spending the night at Brandy's and her mom drove us back to Ottawa the next day.

Carlos and I spent a great deal of time in our cell just talking about life in general. He was a smart kid and always seemed to know what he was talking about. We spent more time locked in our cell than out on the range, there were more than enough things to talk about to keep us distracted. Other than the one time Carlos met Brandy, I never talked about her. She had broken up with me during the summer while I was in Bronson Detention Centre serving my six-month sentence for the robbery. She wrote a letter to me telling me that she couldn't do this anymore and wished me the best in life. To me it was no big deal. There were plenty more fish in my aquarium. Since then, I hadn't thought of her much, until I received an unexpected visit.

The guard opened the cell door. "Tull, you have a visit," he said. I came out of my cell, and he led me across the range, down the corridor, and downstairs toward the visiting room. I didn't have a clue who it was that came to see me. My mother had moved back to Toronto while I was in jail, and Leisa moved back not too long after her release. Usually when someone comes to visit, they tell you that they are coming, and you expect them on a certain day. I was curious on my way to the visiting room to know who was visiting me. To my surprise, I saw Brandy on the other side of the glass, smiling at me with the phone in her hand. She was the last person I expected to see. She looked good, very pretty with her long light brown hair and thin figure, especially given the fact that I hadn't seen a woman in months, except for the female correctional officers, who were suited up in uniform from neck to toe. I sat down and picked up the phone on my end and we started talking. After a few minutes of small talk, she asked me what my plans were when I get out. I didn't really have any plans. She told me that she wanted to get back together, and that she had gotten her own apartment in Ottawa, and I could live with her. It all sounded good to me. This girl came all the way to the jail to tell me that she wanted to get back together with me and provide me with a place to stay when I got out. Wow. This girl either really loved me, or she was just drawn to bad boys. It was a nice visit. I returned to the unit feeling hopeful. The rest of my time in Innes was a breeze. I spent my sixteenth birthday in the jail. I tried LSD for the first time while I was on the unit playing video games with a few of the guys. It made Super Mario Brothers much more exciting. I spoke with Brandy almost every day on the telephone after her visit. When I finally went to trial after four long months, I beat the charges. I was released from the courts, never to see the inside of Bronson Detention Centre or Innes Detention Centre again.

CHAPTER TEN

ONE SHOT OF BRANDY WAS ENOUGH

After ten months of incarceration, with only an eleven-day window of temporary freedom, I was finally out. I had served six months, been released into a Children's Aid group home for eleven days because I was only fifteen, and then been rearrested for assault, for which I spent four months awaiting trial. Now I was sixteen years old, and it was the first time in three years that I was literally free from the judicial system: no lockups, no group homes, no bail conditions, and no probation. The feeling that I could do anything or go anywhere without permission from an authority figure was a huge sense of relief, almost disbelief. I walked out of the courthouse in the centre of the city and watched the people walking around in different directions, peacefully going about their way. It seemed as if everybody had a purpose. I would watch those people from inside of the paddy wagon through the small window on my way to court, or back to the detention centre, and wonder if I would ever have a purpose again.

Brandy was the only basis for me staying in Ottawa. Our relationship from the time she came to visit me in jail was perfect. We spoke on the phone regularly and wrote letters to each other. We were in love. All I thought about was being with her. She was the one for me. She was going to be there for me and support me through thick and thin. We were going to build a foundation and conquer the world. Nothing was going to come between Brandy and me – except Brandy.

The intoxicating feeling I'd had from my relationship with Brandy since the beginning, ended with a hangover and thumping headache. Brandy was not the sweet, soft spoken, lovable girl that I thought she was. She turned out to be more like the Canadian weather: hot, cold, snowy, rainy, and hailing – all in one day. Her mood would change without signs or warnings.

One evening we were cuddled up on the sofa watching a movie. Everything was going well – love was in the air. I held her close. The smell of her hair aroused me as I kissed the back of her head from time to time during the flick. I was more into her than the movie. I enjoyed her company, and I was happy to be with her. As we watched the show, a cute brunette appeared on the screen wearing nothing but a bikini and sunglasses. Brandy noticed that I was a little more attentive to the television than I was to her.

"You think she's pretty?" Brandy asked.

Little did I know, I wasn't supposed to think anyone was pretty except her. "Yeah, she's cute," I answered.

"You're such a jerk! You'd probably sleep with her if you could." She got up and went into the bedroom. I thought it was a joke. I didn't see that coming. *What just happened?* I sat up on the coach and continued watching the television. It was clear that Brandy had some serious insecurity issues.

A few minutes later Brandy came back into the living room and sat next to me. "I'm sorry," she said softly, in an embarrassed tone. She rubbed the back of my head and kissed me. I kissed her back, hoping that it would lead to something further. But before it led to anything else, she stopped, and we continued watching the movie.

It was going on my third night living with Brandy and we still hadn't done it. My teenage hormones were raging. I was sure this was going to be the lucky night. Not that I only wanted her for that, but it would have been a nice addition to our relationship. We were snuggled on the couch when the movie finished. Almost too comfortable to get off the sofa, we ended up making it to the room, and started making out on the bed. We kissed passionately. I caressed her smooth skin, running my hand up from her outer thigh to her small but perfectly formed breasts and back down. It was clear by her response that she loved the way I touched her. She had on a see-through silky nightie. She was wearing and doing everything that turned me on, and the sounds she made aroused every hormone inside me. I was coming along to third base with my hand now moving up her inner thigh. I moved up slowly and brushed my index finger softly against her moistened panties – all of sudden her temperament changed. "Get out! Get the hell out and sleep on the couch! What do you think I am, a slut?"

I was lost. We'd spent twenty minutes fooling around, and when I took a step toward the next obvious move, she freaked out, as if we just met and I went straight for the kill. "What's wrong?"

"Just get out!"

I left and closed the door behind me. I sat on the couch baffled as to how something that felt so right could end in such abruption. *What did I do wrong? I wasn't aggressive, nor did I force myself on her; and it couldn't have been anything I said because I wasn't talking.* I sat in silence and looked around the dark living room, dimly lit from the moon outside.

Fifteen minutes had passed when Brandy opened the bedroom door. She stood in the doorway. "Come back to bed."

"I'm OK out here," I replied. The mood was spoiled. What did she think I was a yo-yo, to be thrown down and pulled up with her little finger? I wasn't going back into that room even if she promised to fulfill all my romantic fantasies.

"So you're not coming back to bed? I'm tired. I want to sleep."

"Then go to sleep. Good night," I replied, knowing that wouldn't be the end of the conversation.

I was beginning to see the type of girl Brandy was. She was a good person, who was in desperate need of love, attention, and companionship. She was afraid of being alone, but too afraid of being close. But I was not in any state to help her. I had just gotten out of jail. I had to work on me. I wasn't going to allow myself to be imprisoned to her emotional instability.

"Come to bed or get out of my apartment. I don't want you sleeping on the couch," she said.

Her last attempt to get me to do what she wanted still didn't work. My pride got the better of me, as it usually did when someone threatened or challenged me. "I'll leave," I said calmly and got up to get my gym bag containing my clothes. She seemed surprised by how easily I agreed to leave. I didn't have anywhere to go, but I figured roaming the streets all night would have been less stressful than dealing with her.

"Where are you going to go?" She was losing control. She knew that once I walked out of that door, I wouldn't need her anymore and her control would be gone. She would go back to her bed – lonely.

I made my way to the door, but when I opened it, Brandy blocked me from leaving. She physically stood in the doorway and refused to let me leave.

"Where are you going to go? You don't have anywhere to go, Junior."

"I'll find a place. Don't worry about me." I tried to pass again.

Tears began to stream down her face. She reached up and hugged me from around my neck. My arms hung down and I didn't reciprocate. I stood still with her sobbing on my chest. "I just want you to come back to bed. Please don't leave."

The hallway outside of her apartment was quiet. The only sound that could be heard was Brandy's crying and pleading for me to come back inside. How embarrassing would that have been if a neighbour opened their door and saw us? It was bad enough everyone on the floor could hear from inside their apartments.

I'm not sure if I went back inside out of sympathy, or because I really didn't have anywhere else to go. We went to bed and never spoke about what happened.

When I woke up in the morning Brandy was on her way out for work. She kissed me on the cheek and left me lying in the bed. It felt good to be alone in the apartment. It was my first time alone since my release. I desperately needed some time to myself. I ate breakfast, took a shower, and watched some TV. I called my mom in Toronto to see how she was doing. All was well, and she suggested that I come down and visit her for the weekend. I was more than happy to head down to my home city for a few days. At that time there was nothing more that I wanted than to get out of Ottawa and be in Toronto.

I didn't tell Brandy right away about my plans to visit Toronto. I knew she would oppose, and I didn't want to hear about it all week, if we made it through the week. I told her two days before I was about to leave, and as predicted, she was not as excited about my trip as me.

She stood up from the couch and put her hands on her hips. "Why didn't you tell me you were planning to go to Toronto?"

"It was just a spontaneous decision after speaking to my mom the other day."

"You're making long distance phone calls from my phone? Who's going to pay for them? You're not working. You already ran up my phone bill with collect calls."

"Is there a need for all that? I'm going to see my mom." I was getting annoyed with her belittling remarks.

"You're not going to see your mother. You're going to see your slut girlfriends. You think I don't know you, Junior."

I had had enough. I stopped talking and ignored her until she went into the bedroom. I needed fresh air and went for a walk around the neighbourhood. When I returned the door was locked. I knocked quietly and there was no answer. I knocked a little harder thinking she might be sleeping and couldn't hear the door. It was after eleven at night and I didn't want to disturb the neighbours by pounding on the door, so I waited a few minutes before knocking again. Brandy opened the door in her pajamas. She was fully awake; it was evident that she was ignoring me while I was knocking. She turned and went into the room, shutting the door behind. I made my way to the couch and lay down. *I had less stress when I was in jail,* I thought. I just wanted to get away from this girl. I didn't change out of my clothes. I wanted to be dressed in case she decided to kick me out again. I fell asleep on the couch.

In the morning Brandy woke me up before getting herself ready for work. "You have to leave with me. I don't want to leave you here when I'm not home."

I didn't object; it was her place. I took a quick shower, put on fresh clothes, and went downtown to the Rideau Centre. I spent the day hanging out with Orval, Layton, Eddie and the Haitian Creation. Steph wasn't there because he was still in jail.

Later in the evening we all ended up at Eddie's apartment, not too far from the mall. There was always something going on at Eddie's place, and it always had to do with drugs and alcohol. That night most of the guys were doing acid and smoking weed and hash. I decided to try it again. The first time I experimented with LCD in Innes, it didn't have much of an effect on me. This time was no different. In fact, the piece that Eddie gave me was too small for me to feel anything at all. Eddie was kind of cheap with his drugs, so it was no surprise that I got such a tiny sheet of acid. Nonetheless, I put it under my tongue and let it dissolve. Everybody thought I was high because they knew I wasn't a big acid user. Apparently the drug was supposed to cause you to hallucinate. They had stories of people doing crazy things like jumping from a ten-storey building due to hallucinating. I believed them, and I was content with my little piece, even though it did nothing to me.

Eddie thought it would be fun to play a voodoo game and initiate me as the subject. Initially I said no, but before I could stand on my word, I was being peer-pressured by everyone – the joys of being the youngest one in the room. Manon was there, along with a couple of other girls. Manon tried to tell them to leave me alone because it was obvious that I didn't want to play. They ignored her and continued pressing me until I finally gave in.

129

It was supposedly a Haitian voodoo ritual, but I knew that it was just another one of their stupid games. It involved the subject stripping down to his underwear and kneeling, chanting something in Creole with his hands up. After a few minutes someone snuck up behind the subject and threw warm water at his back. Apparently if the person was *high* enough on LSD, they were supposed to hallucinate and think their back had busted open. Maybe it would have worked on me if Eddie wasn't so cheap with his drugs.

I stayed a few hours before leaving with Orval and Layton just before one o'clock in the morning. We caught the last bus heading up Rideau Street. They got off before me and I continued to Brandy's.

I dreaded showing up at her place at this time of the night. I could only imagine the conflict that was going to take place. I walked from the bus stop to the apartment building, bracing myself for anything. The important thing was that I maintain my composure. I had one more night after this one before catching the Greyhound to Toronto. I was even mentally preparing myself to spend both nights roaming the downtown streets of Ottawa until it was time to board the bus.

When I arrived at the door, I heard the television. Maybe she'd fallen asleep with it on. I wouldn't have expected her to be up at this time watching TV on a work night. I knocked on the door, and she answered as if she had been waiting for me. I noticed her eyes were red and puffy from crying all night. As soon as she saw me, she wrapped her arms around me. "I was worried about you." She sniffled between words with her head pressed against my chest.

It was the opposite reaction than I expected, like the time when I ran away from home when I was ten years old after getting suspended for jumping on the roof of a car during lunch recess. The last thing I expected to hear from my mom when I returned home was "I was worried about you." But it was genuine, a heartfelt feeling of unconditional love. Coming from my mom, those words meant: I value your safety and protection; I am happy that you are back in the sanctuary of my love and care; you are welcome home anytime. And mom didn't expect anything in return.

Brandy's reaction was genuine as well, but emotionally self-serving: *I was worried about you because I was lonely; I was worried you were going to leave me; I was worried I wouldn't have anyone to hold me and make me feel safe; I was worried that if you were not here I would sink into depression and* not be able to get out of bed in the morning. I was worried that if you didn't come back, I'd have no one to control.*

I put my arms around her and assured her that she didn't have to worry about me. We went to bed, cuddled together until the sun came up.

In the morning I woke up and found that Brandy had already left for work. I lingered in bed until about ten o'clock before getting up to eat some cereal. I spent the entire day in my pajamas watching my favourite shows and thinking about my trip the next day.

When Brandy returned from work she looked tired. She took off her shoes and came and plopped down on the couch next to me. I didn't even know what Brandy did or where she worked. I'm sure she told me at some point, and I just forgot. I would have never asked her again though, that was for sure; she would've stormed off in tears, saying that I don't care about her enough to listen, and then kick my ass out of her apartment.

"How was your day?" she asked.

"It was good."

"Did you miss me?"

"Of course," I lied.

"What did you do, sleep most of the day?"

"No, I packed for Toronto."

"Oh yeah, you're going to Toronto tomorrow. Well, I hope when you get back you're going to look for a job. You can't live off me forever. Anyway, I'm going to take a shower, then I'll come watch TV with you. I was thinking about you all day."

"Really? What were you thinking about?" I asked curiously, as she walked toward the bathroom.

"I was just thinking about how handsome you are; but you already know that." She closed the door and turned on the shower.

We ended up ordering a pizza and watching a couple of movies before bed. The following morning Brandy and I left the apartment together. She wished me a safe journey and told me not to have too much fun. After sharing a hug and a few kisses in the parking lot, she got into her car and drove to work, and I took the OC Transpo to the Greyhound station.

The weekend ended almost as quickly as it began; I never wanted to leave. It was always nice to reunite with my mom, sister, and brother. I spent some time in Regent Park visiting Tony and a few other friends. Everyone I was closest to lived in Toronto. I'd had a good five years and met a few good friends in Ottawa, but it had never felt like home. The things I had experienced growing up in the system were anything but homelike, and now with Leisa and Mom gone, Ottawa was just a lonely desolate place where I didn't belong.

The day before I was to head back to Ottawa, Mom and I were visiting Denise, who had also moved back to Toronto around the same time. We were sitting in the living room and I was complaining that I didn't want to go back. I told them about the constant uncertainty of staying with Brandy and her unpredictable personality. My mom suggested that I come back to Toronto. Denise thought it was a good idea and added that it would be better for me to be here because I'd have more support. Mom said that she would talk to her new husband Dexter about me living with them. It all sounded great to me. I was in.

On the Greyhound back to Ottawa, all I could think about was living in Toronto again. I decided not to tell Brandy until the actual day I was to leave, which was the next day.

I arrived at Brandy's apartment a little past nine at night. We spoke for a while and watched television. She was happy I was back. I never trusted her happiness though; it had a way of changing without notice. I kept things peaceful by not mentioning my plans that night. I knew I was going to hurt her by springing the news on her the day of, but Brandy really gave me no other option. She had a good heart and I didn't want to break it, but I didn't want to spend the night roaming the streets like a stray dog either. I kept my mouth shut.

In the morning I packed the little bit of clothes that I had, along with the rest of my items while Brandy was in the shower. When she came out of the bathroom, that's when I broke the news to her.

"I'm moving back to Toronto," I told her as I went into the washroom to take a shower.

"What do you mean you're moving to Toronto?" It was like a bomb had hit her.

"Yeah, I'm moving today." I was now in the shower. She came into the bathroom to continue the conversation.

"What are you talking about you're moving to Toronto today? You're just going to leave like that? You didn't even tell me anything." She began weeping like I've never seen her before. "After all I've done for you, this is what you do to me. You're so ungrateful. I can't believe you. You could've at least had the decency to tell me that you were leaving. What kind of guy are you? Don't ever talk to me again. I never want to see you again."

She left the bathroom, and I could hear her sobbing from the kitchen.

I felt horrible because of how bad Brandy felt. As good as I was at it, I hated hurting girls' feelings. But this relationship was over, and now we both had to come to grips with it and move on. I finished my shower, dried off, and got dressed. We didn't speak about it anymore when we left the apartment, but we did hug, and said our final goodbyes.

CHAPTER ELEVEN
GOOD GIRLS LOVE BAD BOYS

It was the summer of 1991, two years before I would be arrested for murder. I moved in with my mother and her husband, Dexter, until he couldn't tolerate me any longer. Although I didn't feel much love from Dexter, the change in my environment was rejuvenating. It had been years since I had felt appreciated just for being present, without having to prove anything or achieve anything. It was only my mother who gave me that feeling of unconditional acceptance.

I shared a room with my seven-year-old brother, Andrew. The family lived in a small but cozy two-bedroom house on a quiet one-way street in the west end of Toronto, the Oakwood-Vaughan area. Although the street we stayed on was calm, just a few minutes' walk up Oakwood toward Eglinton Avenue West was where you could find crack and marijuana as easy as a Kit Kat. The neighbourhood was predominantly Portuguese and Jamaican. The house was a short walking distance from the school I would be attending in September – Vaughan Road Collegiate – which I ended up hating for several reasons.

I got a temporary summer job through an employment program provided by St. Christopher House, an organization that helped kids find work, along with other programs that supported young people in the community. I was working at Briar Hill Public School, on Dufferin Street near Eglinton Avenue West. The school was closed for the summer, but my job was to clean, organize the desks, move furniture, do minor paint touchups, or help with other tasks that needed to be done to prepare the school for when the students returned. There wasn't much work to do some days, and occasionally my supervisor would send me home early. She always tried to keep me there until the end of the day, but when there was nothing to do, there was just nothing to do. She was an older Christian lady from Jamaica, always serious, but very kind. She would give me sound advice as opposed to lecturing me when I was consistently late or missed days, if she even said anything at all. I didn't think being late or missing a day or two each week was important to the school. After all it was St. Christopher House that was paying me; it still worked out to be free labour for them. Her only concern was that I learn proper work ethics. She wanted me to understand that being late or missing days would not be tolerated at a regular job. I enjoyed working while I was there, when there was actually stuff to do. I felt productive. I also got a steady paycheque every second week, and I was good at making my money last. It also helped that I didn't have to pay for rent or food. I spent most of my money on clothes and going out with my friends, but I always made sure to save a portion of my earnings.

Every day after work I went home, took a shower, put on something crisp, then caught one bus and three trains to get downtown. Yonge Street was the hotspot, with all the skyscrapers that surrounded it, and the multitude of people that filled the sidewalks all the way from Front Street up to Bloor Street and beyond.

After a few years of not seeing each other, I bumped into my old friend James on Yonge Street, and we reunited. James now went by the nickname Baby J. He no longer lived in Regent Park, but he hung out downtown every day. We did a lot of reminiscing. Our first reminiscence was the time when we fought back against DJ, the neighbourhood bully, in front of my building. During the next few weeks, I never took the staircase exit close to DJ's apartment, which was on the ground floor, instead I took the one on the other side, and I also avoided taking the elevator because the lobby was where DJ hung out sometimes and sold weed.

A few years later, after we had left Regent Park, it was said that DJ had lost his mind and became trigger-happy; he went around robbing everyone in the neighbourhood at gunpoint. He shot and killed one of his best friends outside of a night club on Danforth, and later said, "The bully met the bull." He was convicted of first-degree murder and sentenced to life in the penitentiary. It was also rumoured that he'd shot his other friend, who died the following year after he had moved out of the country with the bullet still lodged inside of him.

I also couldn't help but remind Baby J about the time when he threw the rock the size of a grapefruit at the back of my head, and I had to go to the hospital to get stitches. It may have been my fault because I threw it at his leg first, but I never expected him to retaliate with such force. We were friends, and so were our moms. I showed Baby J that I still had the scar. We had a lot to catch up on, and we had all summer to create new memories.

I made many new friends downtown, most of whom were from different parts of Toronto. Our crew started off small. In the beginning there was Tony, also from Regent Park, Sean lived at Pape and Cosburn Avenue in East York, and of course Baby J. Over the course of time we would grow, not into a gang, but into a group of close-knit friends who stuck up for each other and didn't back down from anything.

Yonge Street was a haven for teenage guys and gals to meet and hook up. The environment was inviting, and it only took a few days to feel as if you'd known someone for years. I met my share of fine damsels downtown, at least enough to purify my memory of Brandy. The first girl was Lori, easy going and pleasant to be around. She was a petite white girl with reddish brown hair and a few light freckles spread across her face. My first impression of Lori was that she was loyal, but a bit naive. She laughed at my jokes and was always available for me, whether it was to talk on the phone or connect in person, and she was never late. At the beginning of the summer, we hung out nearly every day, loitering the streets of downtown. As I began meeting more females, I became less interested in spending a great deal of time with any one specific girl. It was obvious Lori wanted more than a friendship, so I gave her more – I added benefits to our relationship. I liked her, but she wasn't the bomb, so "friends with benefits" was as far as I was willing to go with her. I visited Lori's place a few times where she lived near Dufferin Street with two other girls, a mulatto and a white girl in her mid-twenties who was the one that rented the basement apartment. I had a taste of them both as well – on different days, of course.

One Friday after work, I met Lori at the Bloor-Yonge subway station. I wanted to walk along Yonge Street to the Eaton Centre instead of taking the third train. It was only a twenty-minute walk. We were nearing the Eaton Centre when I observed a young lady, nicely dressed, clean, and well put together. She was walking in our direction with an average-looking Asian girl. They didn't look like they were from Toronto. It wasn't difficult to spot people from out of town. They were always in awe of the skyscrapers and the two enormous records brightly hanging above the entrance of Sam the Record Man. I kept my eye on this girl as she drew nearer – glued to her facial features and Coca Cola bottle shape. From a distance she appeared to be the most beautiful woman I had ever seen outside of TV or magazines. I was fixated on her. I wanted to see if her flawlessness would fade the closer we got. It didn't. I marvelled as her soft honey balayage hair blew lightly from the wind. She moved with a shy confidence, as if she knew how attractive she was, but didn't like being the centre of attention.

Suddenly my focus was blocked by two dudes who stepped in between my viewpoint. They were local downtown sharks, out fishing for phone numbers. The taller guy stopped the girl that I was watching. He pulled her to the side in front of the shoe store to talk. The Asian girl and the guy's friend stood off to the side and waited for him to get the digits. Lori and I passed by while he was asking for her number. I noticed his demeanour was pretty aggressive and his approach raw, as if he were talking to a hood rat chick from the projects. He was definitely more demanding than suave, putting her on the spot and making it impossible, or at least uncomfortable to say no. But who was I to judge? His style worked. She handed him a number, and he continued up the road with his buddy. *Wow, that was easy, and he didn't even have game.* Now it was my turn, but I couldn't just go back and ask for her number without making Lori feel uncomfortable. But I had to have her number – I had to have her. It was the perfect opportunity. Who knew if I would ever see this girl again? It was now or never.

"I bet you I can get that girl's number too, after she just gave it to that guy. You think so?" I said to Lori before crossing the street.

"I don't know," Lori answered, seeming somewhat surprised by the question.

"I bet I can. Just for fun, I'm gonna test my game and get her number, then throw it in the garbage." I reached out my hand, and she reluctantly took it. The bet was on. I turned around, put my player limp on, and did my thing.

I subtly approached the ladies as they walked up Yonge Street talking and looking through the store windows. The girl I liked looked just as good from the back as she did from the front.

"Excuse me," I politely said. Both girls turned around, pleasantly surprised by the interruption. I knew they recognized me because we all made eye contact the first time I passed them with Lori. "I was wondering where you girls are from."

"We're from Toronto," the Asian girl answered.

"Ha, ha, no you're not." I couldn't help but to let out a little chuckle. I knew she was pulling my leg.

"Why do you say we're not from Toronto?" she asked.

"You don't look like you're from Toronto. Do you know where the SkyDome is?" I waited a few seconds with a smile on my face.

"I'm just joking, we're from London," she said, and the two girls giggled.

I was already feeling a good vibe from both girls. They were funny and down to earth. "So you girls are down here all the way from England ... Wow." I turned my attention towards the girl that I was interested in, to engage her in the conversation.

"No, we're from London, Ontario," the cute one replied.

"There's a London in Ontario?" We all laughed at my lack of knowledge of provincial geography.

"Yeah, it's only about two hours away from here." She smiled. "I don't believe you've never heard of it; it's boring, but it's not that small."

I noticed she had a distinct accent; one I've never heard before. I wanted to stay and keep talking, but as much as I was captivated by her smile, accent, and brown eyes, I had to cut the conversation short because Lori was waiting for me. It was time to wrap it up and get the digits.

"So what is your name?" I asked. "And by the way, where are you from originally? I hear an accent."

"My name is Bobbie, and I was born in Hungary. This is my best friend, Jackie."

"I'm Junior." I shook both of their hands and asked Jackie where she was from. She told me that her parents were Chinese, but she was born in Canada.

"And where were you born, Junior?" Bobbie asked.

"I was born in Jamaica, but I moved here when I was two," I lied. I just thought Jamaica seemed like a cooler place to be born than Canada. "You know what, next time you ladies are in Toronto we should hang out. I'll introduce Jackie to a friend, and we can all go out to a club."

"That sounds good, we're coming back next weekend," Bobbie said.

"Cool. Do you want to give me your number and I'll call you during the week?"

I pulled out my ready pen, ripped a piece of paper from my Trident gum packet, and she told me her number. I wrote her name and number down twice on the same piece of paper and tore it in two, placing one in my pocket.

"Why did you write it twice?" she asked, somewhat puzzled.

"I just want to make sure I don't lose it." We smiled at each other as I wished them a fabulous weekend, and we parted ways.

I caught up with Lori. "So did you get it?" she asked.

"Of course. I'm the Don." I showed her the copy I had in my hand, crumpled it up, and threw it in the garbage bin on the corner of the street.

"You're too much," she said. "But you got game. I'll give you that. It's the natural player in you."

We continued walking to the Eaton Centre. Nothing more was said about the phone number, the two girls, or the significant role Bobbie would play in my teenage life.

I called Bobbie almost every day that week and we spoke for hours. It turned out that the weekend she and Jackie were coming to Toronto, my mom and Dexter were taking Andrew and going out of town. Before leaving, mom gave me specific instructions that I was not to have anybody over at the house, nor was I to touch Dexter's stereo system, or his jewelry. To me she sounded like a messenger delivering the commandments of Dexter himself. He was meticulous about his things: his car, his track suits, his turntable, and his jewelry. They meant the world to him. He even spent his entire eight-hundred-dollar paycheque on a set of rims for his Trans Am when my mom was pregnant with my second brother. A more accurate word to describe Dexter would be vain; nothing mattered more to him than his greasy Jheri Curls and material possessions.

I couldn't wait to have the house to myself. It was going to be one hell of a weekend. I had already made plans for Donna to spend Friday and Saturday night over, but now that I had met Bobbie, the plan would have to be altered.

Donna was a girl I'd met at the Reggae Sunsplash Music Festival at Ontario Place a couple of weekends earlier. She went to the concert with some girlfriends but lost them amidst the crowd; I went with Lenny and Denise (Lenny's girlfriend at that time), but I lost them intentionally when I met Donna. Our energy connected instantly. We had a magnetic physical attraction to each other from the moment we said hello. We yelled at each other over the deafening bass of the nearby speakers for a full ten minutes as we danced and grinded our bodies to the live reggae music, then decided to find a quieter spot to talk. We left the crowded outdoor Jamaican event in exchange for a secluded area on the grass, close to the water. It was difficult for us to talk, not because the music was loud – the music sounded nicer from a distance – but because we couldn't keep our damn tongues out of each other's mouth. We hadn't known each other for more than twenty minutes and already we were at it. When we did get a chance to breathe, she pointed out the full moon and told me that it was a sign. The stars and the moon and the chemistry between us were eccentric. Everything was prepared by Cupid for a night of lust at first sight.

When the festival was coming to an end, with Maxi Priest performing the last songs of the night, I went to find Denise and Lenny. I introduced them to Donna and asked Lenny if he could drive her home after the show. He agreed, handed me the keys, and told me they would meet us at the car soon; his way of sending us off so he and Denise could drink a couple more beers and smoke one more spliff. It worked for us. Donna and I spent the last half hour making out in the back seat of Lenny's car.

I saw Donna the following day for the next episode, but I didn't know that it was going to go as far as it did. We walked along Bay Street, near City Hall. The heat between us once again began to rise, and the power to contain ourselves dissipated. We finally gave in fully to our lustful desire and found ourselves having sex under the bushes next to Trinity Tower. It lasted for less than two minutes until she said that we should stop. We got up and fixed our clothes.

"Is this what you want?" She asked, pointing at the bush we just came up from under. "Because if this is what you want, we can go back under there and f*ck." She wasn't yelling and she wasn't upset, but I felt that she was testing me. If I said yes, I knew she wasn't going to go back under the bush, she was going home and would probably never speak to me again. Girls could be tricky to read. It was a good thing I had already released and the tension was over or maybe I would have given her the wrong answer.

"No, that's not all I want. I like you a lot." It was the answer she wanted to hear. We walked through Trinity Square hand in hand.

Friday morning came and Mom and Dexter left with Andrew. I watched in covert excitement as they walked through the door and to the car with their bags for the weekend. I skipped work and Sean came over. Bobbie and Jackie were in town. They were staying at Bobbie's sister's place in Mississauga. Sean was looking forward to meeting Jackie, and of course I was overanxious about seeing Bobbie again. After all the hours I'd spent on the phone with her during the week, I felt as if I knew her well. She had a full-time job and earned her own money, as did Jackie. She lived with her parents and older brother. Her parents did not approve of her friendship with Jackie because they thought Jackie was a bad influence. Bobbie and

I had a lot in common; she liked all the same music as me and enjoyed going out to night clubs. She was fascinated with the big city, and there was no better tour guide than yours truly. I was in love with my city, and I knew every part of downtown.

We were meeting them that afternoon at Islington Subway Station. We arrived fifteen minutes early, just five minutes before their bus pulled up to the platform. When both girls exited the bus and we saw each other, it was all smiles. I hugged Bobbie first, then Jackie, and introduced everybody. There was no physical attraction between Sean and Jackie, but they hit it off well. We all stood up on the train and chatted on our way downtown. Bobbie looked better than the day I met her. I think she got all dolled up because she was coming to see me. I had to catch her a couple times when the subway jerked upon acceleration or stopped suddenly. She wasn't accustomed to riding the train.

When we reached Spadina station, two guys entered our car. I recognized them off the bat. It was the same guy from downtown the previous Friday with his sidekick, the guy Bobbie gave a number to. They entered the train, looking up and down at everyone and walking with a limp, trying to be thug. He noticed Bobbie with me and came over to her. He wasn't too happy to see us together, but no one would have expected him to grab her by the wrist and pull her toward him. He'd only met her a week ago and they hadn't spoken since.

"Yo what are you doing with him? You gave me your number last week and this week you're with him. How you gonna dis me like that?" he said as he held onto to her arm as if she was his property.

Bobbie was clearly confused. "I don't even know you," she uttered nervously, not knowing what to do in this awkward situation.

"Yo bredren." I stepped in. "Why you holding onto the girl like that? Let her go."

He showed contempt toward me by kissing his teeth and telling me to get the f*ck out of his face, as he pulled Bobbie even closer.

Being the person I was, protective over my people, my feelings, and my reputation, he passed the point of no return by violating both the former and latter. I didn't know this asshole, so he had no power to hurt my feelings, but to violate the girl I was with, and disrespect me personally, there were going to be repercussions. I smashed him across his face with my fist. He fell back onto the seat behind him. The second punch was a left to the right side of his face. By then Sean was holding onto the subway railing above, stomping him with the bottom of his blue Patrick Ewing sneakers. His sidekick did nothing to help him. We beat that bitch until the train reached the next stop.

The doors opened at St. George Subway station. We had to get off the train. This was not the weekend for me to get arrested on some bullshit charges. Sean and I darted to the closest train doors as they were about to close. "Get off!" I yelled at the girls. They hurried to the doors, but it was too late. The sliding subway doors closed, shutting them inside. The train slowly departed from the station as I signalled to Bobbie to take the next train westbound, and we'd wait there.

The stress of waiting for the girls to return on the westbound train had Sean and me on edge. My worst thought was that those cowards were assaulting the now vulnerable girls, and my other concern was that security or police would arrive while we waited for them. The subway on the westbound platform arrived. We were relieved to see Bobbie and Jackie unscathed, and with smiles stretching from ear to ear.

"Holy shit, what happened?" I asked.

"Nothing," Bobbie answered. "They just sat there in their seats and stayed on the train."

"They didn't say anything?"

"Nope. Nothing."

We took a different route to the Eaton Centre and laughed about what just happened while we travelled southbound on the University subway line. For Sean and me it was pure jokes, another day in the life of our world. For Bobbie and Jackie, they loved the excitement, the fearlessness, and the power we exhibited to inflict enough fear in those jerks to keep them quiet, even in our absence – a story of *good girls* falling for *bad boys*. I'd never fought to impress a girl before, but I could see that I had won Bobbie over, and I wasn't going to turn down the prize. I'd earned her heart and her confidence.

I never saw those guys downtown again.

The train stopped at Yonge and Dundas, and we got off at the Eaton Centre exit. Across the street was World's Biggest Jean Store, that was our first stop. Leroy was outside on the corner, as usual, handing out flyers and talking to everyone who passed by. He was the most energetic employee at the store, in fact he was the most energetic employee I had ever seen at any store. His short stature and heavy Jamaican accent didn't hinder him from being noticed. Everyone who hung out downtown knew Leroy.

He was always determined to get people into the store. If you missed the baton (flyer) that he tried to hand you, he'd cross the street and make sure you got one.

We chatted outside the store for a while before entering. Leroy was delighted to meet Bobbie and Jackie. Although he was in his mid-thirties, he got along better with kids our age. We viewed him as a peer; we never saw him as a man more than twice our age. He fit in with us teenagers. We hung out with Leroy regularly. If we needed liquor from the LCBO, Leroy was the man we went to. Bobbie and Jackie thought Leroy was cool, but they were more impressed with the size of the store. On the outside along the wall hung over a hundred mannequins dressed in different styles of clothing, not to mention the inside: it was an adventure. There were more clothes than one could imagine in a single store, and the second floor was even more ridiculous, with over a ton of jeans stacked everywhere. The place was huge, and it was always packed with customers, browsers, tourists, locals, and thieves.

After our visit to World's Biggest Jean Store, we walked up Yonge Street and grabbed a slice of pizza at The Big Slice. My neighbour worked there so I got my slice for free and treated Bobbie, Jackie, and Sean. I thought it would be a good idea to invite the girls over to the house so Sean and I could DJ for them on Dexter's turntable. He had two record players for mixing, speakers that would blow the roof off the house, and millions of records. They agreed, and we headed to the train station.

I gave the girls an expired transfer and showed them how to walk past the ticket booth without the collector noticing. Sean already had his transfer ready. We waited for a large group of people to enter the station's platform that were coming from the arriving streetcar outside College Station. The trick was to walk in with the group of passengers, flash the expired transfer quickly, covering the issue time with your hand. It worked all the time, and if a ticket collector did call you back to see your transfer, you would just act as if you didn't hear and keep walking to the end of the platform. They would never leave their booth because there were too many passengers entering.

After a few hours of DJing and mixing and scratching records, Sean and I took Bobbie and Jackie back to Islington Subway Station. We waited around with them until their bus came. Once they were gone, I called Donna from the payphone.

"I thought you were never going to call," she said.

"Why?"

"Well, you invited me to spend the weekend and it's already after six. I thought you were going to cancel."

"No. No. Of course not. What time did you want to come?"

"I'll go in the shower now and then leave."

"Why do you have to say that?" I chuckled, "Now you got me thinking thoughts."

"Cool yourself, boy. I'll be there soon. Give me the directions."

"Do you have a pen?"

"Give me a sec, sweetie." I got tingles when she called me sweetie. Her feminine voice brought me back to Ontario Place, to the night when I was caressing her legs and biting her neck. She was the most sensual woman I had ever known, passionate and comfortable to explore. I loved this woman with the strongest sense of lust, the kind I had never felt before.

"Ok, go ahead, I'm ready."

"The address is 364 Winona Drive. You have to go to St. Clair West Station and take the Vaughan bus. Get off at Winona, just before Vaughan Road Collegiate and walk south."

"Got it. I should be there by eight or eight thirty."

"Okay, see you soon."

"Bye."

Sean and I arrived back at my place by seven o'clock. I had time to freshen up myself before Donna got there.

The phone rang. It was Baby J. "What's up, Junior?"

"I'm cool, just chillin' here with Sean. We're about to spin some records. I got this cute coolie thing coming over in a bit."

"That's what's up. So your mom and them left already."

"Yeah, they left in the morning. Remember that girl, Bobbie, I told you I met last week? Her and her Chinese friend were here today."

"Seriously! Did you tap that bro?"

"Nah man, we were just here for a little while playing music. I actually just got back from dropping them at Islington."

"Yo I'm coming over right now." Baby J could never go without missing out on the action.

"Okay I'll see you when you reach."

Sean was on the turntable when Donna arrived. I opened the door, kissed her on the cheek and gave her a welcoming bearhug. Sean was changing records when I introduced him to her and scratched the record trying to turn around to shake her hand, with his usual ear to ear smile whenever he met a pretty girl. She shook his hand, took off her shoes and walked across the living room to grab a seat on the sofa.

"After this song it's my turn on the table," I told Sean, as he reapplied the needle to play *Mr. Lover Man* by Shabba Ranks.

I asked Donna what song she wanted to hear. She told me to surprise her. I played the reggae version of *You Sexy Thing*, walked over to her, took her by the hand, and we danced slowly and closely to the sweet tune of Johnny Osbourne.

Baby J arrived shortly after the song was over and Ninja Man was pumping out of the speakers. We spent the good part of the night enjoying music and chatting. I turned down the volume to an appropriate level because it was after eleven, and I left Sean and Baby J playing on the turn tables. The little house was full with only the four of us. I told the guys that one could sleep in my brother's room and the other on the couch. Donna and I slept on my mom and Dexter's bed.

I finally had Donna in a private and comfortable setting. We were now able to take our time and explore one another. The night was nice, but in the morning, I found Donna to be too aggressive for my liking. It wasn't that she wanted it hard and rough, but she liked to bite and scratch. I was fine with love bites and light scratches, but this girl was trying to draw blood from my lip and tear the flesh off my back. I had to tell her to calm down more than once. It was as if she were not present, but in her own zone. Everything about being with her sexually was great, except I couldn't relax for fear of my bottom lip getting ripped off. I was afraid to kiss her.

When it was over, I left her in the bed to sleep. Baby J didn't expect me to open the door immediately after the love session. I caught him standing on the other side of the door with a perverted grin on his face. I closed the bedroom door as I came out. Baby J was more excited than I was about me getting laid.

"Yo, I heard you killin' it bro. Damn you were putting it down on her," he said, snapping his fingers, and putting his other hand on my shoulder as to congratulate me. Baby J had no discretion as to what spewed out of his Scotian mouth, or how loud it came out.

"Shut up, man. You're so loud," I told him, as I pushed him away from me and further from the door, hoping that Donna didn't hear his big mouth.

"Yo, Junior, check this out." He pointed to his eyes.

Because I was too caught up with making sure that Donna didn't hear, I didn't notice at first that his eyes were green. He had taken my mom's prescription contact lenses and put them in his eyes.

"What are you doing? Take those out and go put them back," I told him.

"Come on man, let me wear them, they look fresh."

"Whatever, man." I didn't see a point in making him take them off after he already put them on.

Sean was just getting up from the sofa when I entered the living room. We talked about going to Electric Circuit downtown and then to Centre Island. Electric Circuit was a live dance music television program that aired on MuchMusic, located at the former Citytv building on Queen Street. They were having their live dance show outside in the parking lot that day. The plan was for Donna to sleep over again, but I wanted to hang out with my friends, and see Bobbie later. I told Donna that my mother was coming back this afternoon; she was cool with it. I invited her to Electric Circuit, and she was happy to tag along. I put on the green Pelle tracksuit that Dexter gave me because it didn't fit him; the only thing he ever gave me. In addition, I couldn't resist the temptation to put on his gold rope chain and six gold rings that were sitting on the dresser. The rings didn't fit, they were too big. They slid down my fingers and fell off if I opened my hands completely. The most logical thing to do would have been to put them back, but they matched the gold chain perfectly, and image was everything. I folded small strips of paper and put them in between the rings and the palm of my fingers to tighten the fit. I left the house looking like a member of Run DMC.

Electric Circuit was fun, even though we couldn't get in because we were late and there were only a certain number of guests permitted on the show. We listened to the music from outside of the fence. There were the same number of people on the sidewalk as there were inside. While on the show, the guests were required to be dancing the entire time the music played. So for me, I preferred being on the other side of the fence, in my comfort zone. I wasn't the best dancer, but I sure was able to bump, grind, and wine with a lady to any reggae tune or love song, but when funkadelic played, that's when I needed a break; it was time to converse and grab a drink at the bar. Electric Circuit played a lot of funkadelic, with cameras on you in full view of the lights and the spectators outside watching in and clowning on all the rhythmless souls like me. I was on Electric Circuit once, and it was the most uncomfortable feeling to be dancing to music that I had no idea how to move to.

At the end of the one-hour segment, Donna went home, and Sean, Baby J and I took the ferry to Centre Island, where we spent the rest of the day.

On the ferry ride back from Centre Island Baby J got into a scuffle with another teenager. The ferry was packed, and a white boy bumped him as he passed and failed to say sorry. The guy was big compared to Baby J, but that didn't stop him from starting a confrontation. The problem with Baby J was that he wasn't always able to defend his talk without drawing on us for backup. Words escalated into a shoving match until the kid sucker-punched Baby J in the face; that was the end of the fight. One of my mom's contact lenses fell on the ground. My priority was to protect that contact lens and get it back home in one piece. I picked it up before anyone could step on it. By then Baby J was complaining that his eye was burning, and he could only see out of one. A few adults stepped in and told the kid to just leave it alone. He scoffed at us and walked to the front of the ferry. We went to the bathroom where Baby J rinsed his eye and I cleaned out the dirt from the contact lens and put it in a condom package to keep it lubricated. When the ferry docked, we went straight to the house, and I put the contact lenses back into the case where they belonged. I knew they'd cost a lot of money, and I was relieved to have gotten them back safely – or were they safe? That week my mother ended up getting an eye infection. I told her what happened, not the whole story, just that Baby J had worn them. She wasn't mad. She told me that contact lenses were not to be shared, and now she would have to buy another set.

The following weekend Bobbie and Jackie came to Toronto, as they did every weekend. Sean and I met them at the Eaton Centre. Jackie was all excited about the new credit card she had received from the bank that week. She withdrew her entire $500 limit from the ATM and spent it generously on all of us. We were able to score a bottle of Peach Schnapps from the LCBO and drink it as we walked up and down Yonge Street. The energy of the city was radiant. Souped up Nissan Maximas, Honda Preludes, luxury BMWs, and even busted up Pontiacs drove up and down Yonge Street with their windows down blasting music.

We drank and smoked weed until late at night. All but Sean. When we were around other people Sean pretended to take a few puffs, never inhaling. He even pretended to be drunk after just a few sips of a drink. Sean was never a smoker or a drinker, he was just a kid who liked to play basketball and hang out with his friends. I didn't like playing sports in my teens except when I was in a detention centre. I preferred sitting on the bleachers looking and smelling good while macking the girls. I didn't like sweating if I was going to be in the presence of females. My sport was lifting weights and trying to be the biggest guy in the room.

Leroy joined us after his shift at World's Biggest Jean Store.

The night had escaped us, and the subways were no longer running. Bobbie and Jackie had no way of getting back to Mississauga, but they weren't worried; they knew we would take care of them. We would figure something out, even if it meant spending the entire night on Yonge Street – something Sean, Baby J and I did often, along with several other inner-city teens. Girls from the suburbs (Whitby, Ajax, and Pickering) would come downtown to hang out with us until the sun came up. They thought it was cool hanging in the big city. Although most of the girls were from well-off families, they were happier on the streets with us. The guys from the suburbs, on the other hand, didn't come downtown so late. At two o'clock in the morning they were targets for robbery and extortion. The girls were always protected. Bobbie and Jackie were content and comfortable with whatever we were going to do that night.

Leroy invited us to stay at his place. The five of us took the all-night bus to Leroy's basement apartment in Scarborough and we stayed until the morning. Leroy gave Bobbie and me his bedroom and he slept in the living room with Sean and Jackie. Bobbie and I didn't have sex that night, we made love. It was my first time making love to a girl. I had lost my virginity at thirteen years old, and I had plenty of girls since, but this was the first time I had felt real love.

When Bobbie and Jackie came back to Toronto the following weekend, they stayed at the Bond Place Hotel on Dundas Street instead of in Mississauga with her sister; it was just a stone's throw from the Eaton Centre, and Sean and I stayed with them at the hotel. We clubbed, drank, and smoked marijuana downtown from Friday night to Sunday morning. I usually missed work on Mondays.

That summer Sean and I went to visit Bobbie and Jackie in their hometown. London, Ontario was known as "The Forest City." It was not as multicultural as Toronto, and it was much smaller, with a population of less than four hundred thousand people. However, London was very affluent, and it was a hub for higher education, medical research, manufacturing, and technology. However, regardless of the huge difference in population, diversity, and conservativeness between the two cities, the youths in London loved partying and drinking, just like in every other city.

During our visit to London, I didn't know if we were going to make it back to Toronto alive or be locked up for attempted murder or aggravated assault for stabbing a guy. We rode the Greyhound Bus two hours to London. Jackie had her own apartment, so the plan was that we would stay there. After we dropped off our bags at Jackie's, we took the bus to a shopping mall. We never actually made it inside the mall. We were walking through the parking lot when I notice a car was unlocked. I opened the door and checked the glove compartment for something to steal. The keys for the car were inside the glove compartment, so I stole the car. Bobbie, Jackie, and Sean got in, and off we went for a joyride through London. The ride lasted for half an hour. I drove into a school yard to do reverse donuts, spinning the car as fast as it could go until it was no longer functional. I didn't know what mechanical problem I caused, but it wouldn't go anywhere. The engine was running, and the car would rev, but it wouldn't move. Bobbie, Jackie, and I got out and walked away from the scene of the crime. Sean stayed with the car, pressing on the gas trying to get the vehicle to drive again. I was calling out to Sean to come, but he was determined to get his turn to drive. I knew the police would be coming soon. I yelled at him again, "Sean, let's go!" When he saw that we were leaving the school yard without him, he left the car and caught up to us.

We went to a nightclub that evening. The club was full of teenagers and young adults drinking and having a good time. The music was all right, but I would have preferred to hear more reggae. When the club was closing the lobby was crowded as people made their way out to the parking lot. There was bumping and shoving going on. I hated it when people shoved or bumped into me. I didn't like unwelcome physical contact from strangers, especially men. I didn't mind if a pretty female brushed up on me. I'd usually smell their hair and tell her how good she looked; some would get flattered and stop and talk, others would ignore me and keep on walking. One dude bumped me, and we got into words. The back-and-forth name calling spilled into the parking lot, where he tackled me against a car. The short stocky half-breed guy rushed me, hitting me with his shoulder in my stomach, and grabbing me with his hands around my waist, slamming me into the vehicle behind me. I pulled the steak knife out of my pocket that I had taken from Jackie's house and planted it in his upper back. It didn't take long for him to let me go. He spun around in circles trying to reach for the knife to pull it out – he couldn't reach it.

I thought that was the end of the fight, but apparently, he had more friends than I had anticipated, and I was in for more than I'd bargained for. It seemed like the entire club knew this guy. Everybody in the parking lot rushed toward Sean and me. We ran down the street to escape the mob. There were well over thirty people chasing us. Sean was a faster runner than me, leaving me in the dust as the gang gained on me. I thought it was over. I couldn't run fast enough to get away. The two of us couldn't have taken on that crowd, and with that understanding, I wasn't upset that Sean was taking off on me. I saw my life about to end. The locals were mad – justifiably – I had just stabbed a regular. The question was, what were they going to do with me? *Were they going to beat the life out of me, or hold me for the police?* I ran as fast as I could, but they were closing the gap. Suddenly, and out of nowhere, a black Nissan Maxima with tinted windows drove up next to me. The passenger had his window down. Inside the car I saw two black guys who looked to be in their early to mid-twenties. I didn't see them at the club and had no idea who they were.

"Are you from Toronto?" the passenger shouted out.

"Yeah."

"Get in."

He pulled over. I opened the back door and got in. I had no time to question who these guys were or why they were helping me, but when I got into the car it was obvious; Bobbie and Jackie were in the backseat. They picked up Sean, then made a U-turn, heading back toward the crowd. *Oh shit, this is a set up*, I thought.

"Why are you turning around? Go the other way," I said. I was terrified after stabbing that guy.

"Don't worry, man, this is the way to Jackie's place," the driver said. "By the way, I'm Calvin." He didn't bother to introduce the other guy, and I didn't care to ask who he was.

Calvin sped through the hostile crowd standing on the street, and someone hit his car with their baseball cap. He slammed on the brakes, and both Calvin and his homie ran out of the car and started beating the one who hit the vehicle. We couldn't see out of the window because the tint was too dark, but it was obvious by the commotion that others had jumped into the fight. Sean and I stayed in the car with the girls, wondering what the hell these men were doing. Why would they get out of the vehicle to take on over thirty people? There was no way I was getting out of the car. I didn't even know if the guy still had the knife stuck in his back. I wanted to be as far from the scene as possible. The rumble lasted less than a minute. Calvin and his friend broke away from the crowd and jumped into the car. Calvin sped off.

"Why didn't you two come out and help, man?" Calvin asked. "We were taking on like ten dudes and a few girls."

"I don't know why you would stop. There was no way we could've beaten the entire club," I said.

"Well, I don't give a f*ck about the club, I ain't gonna let some pussy get away with hitting my car. Besides, I got him pretty good until everyone else jumped in. I think I broke his jaw or something. After I punched him, I heard a snap."

We drove the rest of the way listening to music and talking about the wild events of the night. At Jackie's, the girls went to bed in two separate rooms and the guys hung out in the living room chatting.

"Yo, you gonna sit here all night and talk with us, or you gonna go inside and tap that little sexy thing waiting for you?" Calvin asked me.

"Yeah, I'm going in a bit, man. There's no rush, she's not going anywhere."

After a few minutes and a last beer, I went inside the room where Bobbie was. The room was not furnished and there was no bed. She was lying on a carpeted floor with a sheet spread out underneath her and was covered with a thin blanket. I lay down beside her. I wanted to make love to her, but she looked tired, and I didn't want her to think that I only wanted her for sex. I lay next to her, and we slept. In the morning she confessed to me that she'd wanted exactly what was on my mind.

The next day, Sean and I made it back to Toronto; we got a ride with Calvin and his friend. We had survived that memorable weekend in London.

CHAPTER TWELVE
TEENAGE THUG LIFE

The first time I saw crack cocaine was in the winter of 1991. I had spent the end of the summer and most of autumn in the Toronto West Detention Centre – my training ground for a future of crime. The West was located in Rexdale, and was home to over six hundred prisoners: adult males, juveniles, and for a short period they even had a female unit, which was later turned into an overflow range for young offenders.

I had spent the good part of the summer working during the weekdays and hanging out downtown on the weekends. Bobbie became my bona fide girlfriend. I saw her every weekend while she still lived in London. She and Jackie spent all their time with me and my homeboys; wherever we went, they came. We drank, smoked ganja, partied, and just got downright silly at times. The worst part of my summer came at the end, when the St. Christopher House program ended and I was no longer employed. The days were idle, and the cash flow was halted. With more time on my hands, I found myself downtown every day, and I began getting into trouble with the law.

The first incident occurred with me snatching a tourist's purse on Yonge Street. I didn't plan it; it was a stupid split-second decision. The lady and two men were visiting Toronto from England. When my friends and I heard them talking, we were amused by their accent, and began heckling them. The jesting went overboard, into borderline harassment. The woman became extremely irate with our immaturity and began yelling at Sean and the others, turning her back to me. While she was distracted and going into a frenzy, I noticed her purse dangling loosely from her shoulder. I knew she had money because she was a tourist. I snatched it and ran. I got a few blocks up, but it didn't take long for the police to be notified. There were sirens everywhere. I made it to College Street, where I was confronted by a cop running out of his car with his gun drawn, screaming at me to stop. I dropped the purse in the middle of College Street and fled south on a side street just east of Yonge. I hopped over a six-foot fence, and hid, crouched down in the back of a Yonge Street restaurant doorway. Police sirens in all directions. Cops on foot. I had nowhere to run. My only choice was to stay put and hope they wouldn't find me. It was a matter of minutes until I was handcuffed and placed in a police car. It was difficult to digest that this foolish impulse decision cost me almost the rest of the summer in the Toronto West Detention Centre's young offender unit.

The pig who brought me to the station and led me up the stairs of 52 Division was a miserable abusive son-of-a-bitch. He spoke to me as if I was less than human, and when I gave him a piece of my mouth in return, he let loose on me, pounding my back from behind as hard as he could with a clenched fist. He did this the entire way up the stairs while I was handcuffed behind my back.

The first range I was put on was for geeky white boys. There were no protective custody units in young offenders, but this range was considered one; kids who were afraid to go to the *tough* ranges, went to 1A, directly across from the segregation units and A and D. All the ranges in the West Detention Centre were tough – *all* of them. Juveniles always had something to prove. The weak didn't eat well. Their protein and dessert were taken from them at every meal, leaving them with only vegetables and rice or pasta. They barely got to use the phone, unless they knew someone who had three-way calling, then the other kids took advantage of the opportunity to make free calls. I met Busthead on 1A. He had just arrived, a day or two after me. He was a bad boy Jamaican drug dealer from the streets of Rexdale, and nothing changed with his incarceration. I was impressed with the way he stood up to the range heavy, a Latino cat from El Salvador. Busthead didn't care that this guy was a hundred and ninety pounds of solid muscle, almost twice his size; he stood his ground and gained the respect of everyone on the range. Later, Busthead and the Latino ended up becoming friends. After a week, Busthead was transferred to another range because the guards deemed him to be too aggressive and intimidating. They wanted to reserve at least one range in the West as a safe place for vulnerable young offenders. I too was transferred to a *normal* range.

I was released on bail near the end of the summer. The lawyer who was supposed to represent me ended up being a sellout. After seeing him outside of the courtroom, talking and laughing with the woman and two guys and the Crown Attorney, he came over to me and told me that I should just go and apologize. I thought it was odd since I still had not pled to the charge, but I walked over and said sorry anyway. My apology was not welcomed. When I returned to my lawyer, he told me that I should plead guilty and accept sixty days secure custody that day. I was not prepared to go to the West for two months. I refused. In front of the judge, he said that he would not be representing me and walked out of the courtroom. One lawyer in the court saw what had happened and approached me in the hallway. He told me that that guy was a jerk and gave me a card with the name "Michael Lomer" on it. He told me to call, he would help me.

Mr. Lomer was able to plea bargain with the Crown for a sentence of thirty days open custody. It was the beginning of our long journey together as lawyer and client.

I was sent to a group home on Lansdowne near Bloor. My roommate was a cool white kid. He helped me sneak out one night by filling my bed with pillows in the form of a human body my size. He closed the window behind me when I left and opened it when I returned. I almost got caught on my way out. Our room was on the second floor, and I had to climb onto the roof above the front porch and hang drop from the eavestrough. The eavestrough couldn't hold my weight. It broke, and I dropped to the ground. I took the broken piece of metal and ran along the side of the house to the back. The staff working overnight heard the *thud* and came looking around the porch. Without seeing anything, he went back inside. I took the train to see Bobbie for a couple of hours. On my way back to the group home I bought a quarter ounce of weed and buried it in the backyard.

Sanchez, who I knew from the West Detention Centre, was also in the group home. We were friends in the West, but I didn't like him at the group home. He would steal my clothes from my room; in return I stole his. When my weed came up missing, I knew it was him who took it because he was the only one who knew where it was after we smoked a joint together.

I decided that I didn't want to stay at the group home anymore and ran away.

It was another Friday night on Yonge Street. I was with Bobbie and Jackie just like every other weekend. One of my downtown homies, Russell, was with us. We saw some ruckus going on in front of the Eaton Centre involving two young black girls and two grown men. One of the men was holding both girls firmly by the wrist, as they both screamed for him to let go. The other man was standing by to make sure no one interfered.

Something didn't seem right. They kept looking up and down the street as if expecting someone to drive by and pick them up, at least that's what I read from their behaviour. The first thing that crossed my mind was that these guys were pimps and the girls wanted to go home. Both men were dressed in normal attire – name brand clothes – and both guys were black. I had always been an advocate for peace and justice, and from my perspective, from the outside looking in, these girls needed help. I took it upon myself to tell the man who was holding the girls to let them go. He ignored me, but his friend told me to mind my business.

"This is my business," I said. "Let go of the girls."

The two girls got louder and cried for the guys to leave them alone. Russell was getting agitated as the situation escalated, and joined in. Bobbie and Jackie stood off to the side, along with the public spectators, as the aggression intensified. It became a grabbing and shoving match, until Russell threw the first punch. After that, it was an all-out brawl between the four of us. I wasn't sure how Russell was holding up, but I had my guy up against the Eaton Centre window slamming him with punch after punch until I was grabbed by a few uniformed police officers who happened to be nearby. Russell was already on the ground in handcuffs. That was when the men pulled out their badges and identified themselves. It sucked for Russell and me – as for the girls, they were long gone, along with the items they had stolen from the Eaton Centre.

Russell and I were charged with two counts of assault police and obstruct justice. Russell went to an adult jail because he was eighteen, and I was hauled back to the Toronto West Detention Centre. I was only out for a few weeks, and already back in jail. Trouble had a way of following me.

Again, they put me on the kiddie PC range when I arrived at the West. I would have preferred to be on any other range. The Latino cat had been released and a thick white boy called Mad Dog was running the wimps. It only took a few days for us to get at it. Words exchanged, and he cupped me. In the West, each inmate got their own cup, a solid plastic cup that wouldn't crack if it was smashed against the wall. They were used for juice, hot tea, and weapons, and could bust one's head wide open. He hit me with it on the back of my head. He didn't connect well, but it still hurt. The guard ran over and broke it up before I was able to retaliate. He should have been put in the hole, but because the guards favoured this punk, they turned a blind eye; but I hadn't forgotten. Later that evening in the gym, he was bench-pressing, while I was plotting. I took up the rake from the pool table and walked over to him.

"You want to cup me again, Pussy?"

He put the bar on the bench hinges, and before he made it to his feet, I swung the wooden object across his forehead. I was expecting to beat him with it over and over until the guards arrived. The stick broke in half across his head from the first blow, and within a second, he was on top of me, feeding me his fist. This friggin' guy was way stronger that I'd thought. There was no way I could have taken him. The guards rushed in and saved me. The COs put me in the hole, but he returned to the range and continued serving the evening peanut butter and jam sandwiches that we got every evening in our cells at lockup. He received eight stitches to the forehead and two black eyes from the blood that poured down from the wound. The *rat* pressed charges against me; it's no wonder he was on the pussy range.

The guards must have had it out for me too because they let Mad Dog and his partner serve me the peanut butter and jelly sandwiches that they had made. I took it but obviously knew better. I opened the sandwich to see how much they loved me. Green hork stretched from one slice of bread to the other without splitting apart. I flushed the spit-filled sandwich down the toilette, not surprised with the gift in the middle.

It was time for court. Russell had already pled guilty and was sentenced to six months in jail. I pled not guilty, and against the advice of Mr. Lomer, I chose to testify at my trial. He said that if I testified, it would hurt my case, because the Crown Attorney would bring up my Young Offender record and try to prove my guilt by showing that I was a violent offender. But it just so happened that at the end of the trial, the judge said that I was the only person he understood. With all the conflicting testimony, I was the only one who made sense out of the whole story. All four witnesses had to wait outside of the courtroom while each one gave their version of events. The Crown witnesses were the two undercover officers, and the defense witnesses were Bobbie and Jackie.

The cop who was holding the girls testified that he reached into his pocket and showed Russell and me his badge. It's funny that the girl didn't run away after he let go of her wrist. The other officer said that he was the only one able to pull out his badge because his partner was detaining the shoplifters, while he was trying to control the crowd, contradicting the other officer.

I'd advised Bobbie and Jackie before the trial to tell the truth, regardless of how bad it sounded. They didn't. They blundered when they were asked how they met the defendant. Bobbie said downtown on Yonge Street. Jackie said at a club. But they both said they met me on the same day. When it was my turn to testify, I had to do some minor damage control for the judge to see both girls as credible witnesses. I told him that I met Bobbie during the day on Yonge Street and I met Jackie later at the club. The little white lie was good enough for me since it didn't have any relevance to what had transpired on the night in question.

I was acquitted of the charge.

After spending a few more months in the Toronto West Detention Centre, I was becoming accustomed to the system, both on the inside, and on the streets. You can say I learned a thing or two in the West – things I would eventually use on the outside.

In the West almost everyone claimed to be a drug dealer. We all wore orange jumpsuits and blue and white shoes. If you held any status in the jail, your jumpsuit and shoes were always fresh and new, and you had plenty of extra boxers and socks. It was evident who was on top of the food chain, but when we went to court, that revealed what class one was in on the street, and how much shit one talked in the tank. Because when we went to court, almost every inmate changed into their street clothes. The real drug dealers wore the brand spanking new Air Jordan sneakers, Canada Goose coats, and Fubu jeans. The wannabes wore clothes from Stitches and World's Biggest Jean Store. And the ones who smoked the crack, they were dressed in what looked to be hand-me-down old shoes, dirty jeans, and a coat that usually had a tear somewhere on it. I appreciated the hustle, and I was determined to move up from my Stitches gear and single pair of red Champion sneakers that Sean had given me, to wearing whatever I wanted without a budget – and Courtney, AKA Cash, made that all possible for me.

Cash was my cell partner. He was a known drug dealer in Toronto, but he didn't hustle on the street, he supplied the dealers on the corner with 8-balls and half balls. During the time we shared a cell together I asked Cash a lot of questions about the game, and he schooled me. He chopped up a bar of white soap into little pieces resembling crack cocaine and showed me how much each piece was worth: from a twenty piece up to an ounce. I was eager to get out and get started. Every day Cash and I talked about selling drugs. I never got bored listening to his stories; it was street life – and I loved the streets.

I was released from the Toronto West Detention Centre before Cash. It didn't take long before I forgot about him and the stories he told me. We never stayed in touch, and I never expected to see him again, except maybe back in jail.

By the time I got out, a few things had changed. Sean moved out of his mom's house and got his own place. He rented a room upstairs in a rooming house near Greenwood and Danforth Avenue. I wasn't able to go back and live with my mother because Dexter viewed me as a criminal and didn't want me in his house. It wouldn't be hard to blame him for what he thought of me. The first time we'd met was at their wedding. At the time I was doing a six-month sentence at Rotherglen Detention Centre for the robbery but I was able to obtain a day pass to attend the wedding. Escorted by a detention centre staff, I walked into the church, late. The staffer who was escorting me was not familiar with Toronto and depended on my directions. I led him down Yonge Street, knowing full well that it was out of the way, but I couldn't resist the urge to take a trip down my hangout spot. In addition, when we got to the West End we took a few wrong turns trying to find the church located on Ossington Avenue, an area I wasn't familiar with at the time. When we first met, I got the notion that Dexter was a good guy but learned that same day that he was a good pretender. The wedding reception was being held at their house on Winona Drive, where my eyes were opened to the true Dexter. Two of my uncles had written "Just Married" with shaving cream on his burgundy Firebird. When he came outside, he laughed about it with them, but when my uncles went back into the house, his smile vanished as he kissed his teeth and uttered to Lenny in his Trini accent, "I just washed dis f*cking car, man." He showed me that just one statement could reveal a person's true character.

I ended up going to stay with Sean, who was more than happy to take me in – he was my homie. The average-size room was pre-furnished with a bed, a dresser, and a desk next to the closet. I had no problem sleeping on a carpeted floor; it was much better than a jail cell bunk. There were two other rooms on the floor, the one to the left was vacant, and the one to the right, closer to the bathroom and the top of the stairs was occupied by a white man in his twenties who was rarely there. Both rooms downstairs were occupied. There was a "no guest" rule in the house, but the landlord didn't live there, so that rule didn't apply to us – neither did the other rules.

Living with Sean was an adventure. We had almost no limits. One night we were on the subway heading home from downtown. We sat in the first car where the operator drove the train. It was a regular weekday night, a little after ten o'clock with a hand full of passengers in our car. The train was approaching Greenwood Station when I noticed a man at the very front relaxing, his eyes closed and feet up on the seat in front of him. He looked like he was on his way home to drink a few beers after a hard day of work. He had a twelve-pack of Molson Canadian on the floor and a ghetto blaster on the seat next to his feet. I suddenly got thirsty. I told Sean that I was going to grab the guy's beer when the doors opened. He just grinned and followed me to the front of the car. I thought he was coming with me for *moral* support, or to have my back, as he always did. It ended up Sean had his own agenda.

We stood in front of the doors located closest to where the man was sitting. The train slowed down and he opened his eyes to see which station he was at. I waited for the doors to slide open, then snatched the case of beer from the ground. Immediately after I grabbed the beer, he lunged forward to take them back but got distracted when Sean snatched the ghetto blaster from the seat in front of him so fast that one of the detachable speakers fell off. We both fled with the man in pursuit, shouting at us to come back with his stuff. We sprinted down the subway corridor, up the stairs, and out the closest exit where we went north to Strathmore Blvd and then turned right. We hid behind a car in the first driveway we saw. Seconds later the fellow came walking by, confused, looking up and down the dark street wondering where we had disappeared. Once he got far enough up the street, we left the beer and the stereo hidden behind the car and ran to Sean's place. We stayed low-key for twenty or so minutes before returning for the stuff. That night I quenched my thirst while Sean played music on his new one-speaker ghetto blaster.

Another significant change since my incarceration and release was Bobbie moving to Mississauga to live with her older sister, Szofia, and her husband, so that she could be closer to me. We were able to see each other almost whenever we wanted. She took the bus to Toronto regularly, and I even visited her a few times at Szofia's condo. I was fond of her sister. She was pretty, pleasant, and hospitable, always asking if I wanted something to eat or drink. She came across as a genuine person. Her husband on the other hand acted polite and was friendly, but he didn't strike me as sincere. It could have been because of what Bobbie had already told me about him, and his choice of words when referring to other races while in their absence. She also told me that she was awakened one night while sleeping on the couch to find his hand down her top. I wanted to punch him out, but that wouldn't have solved anything. I had no interest in speaking to him; he was boring, and there was no substance to our discussions. The only thing we had in common was that we were two straight males, and we both liked Bobbie's tits. When we did talk, it was a dull conversation about nothing; my mind only ran on Bobbie, and how much I wanted to get out of there and be alone with her.

Bobbie was free to come and go as she pleased while she was staying at her sister's, but when her parents were visiting from London, it was a different story. She had rules. She wasn't allowed to stay out overnight, and of course, I wasn't welcome to visit. I was fine with it. Bobbie had already told me everything about her family and their views on interracial relationships. It didn't bother me, and it didn't bother her to be with me. Bobbie gave me everything: her time, her heart, her body, and even her money if I needed it. Her time with her parents was her time, and if for whatever reason they didn't want to accept me, it was no skin off my back; she loved me whether they liked it or not.

The relationship between Bobbie and me grew fast and strong. If we weren't together in person, we were on the phone. We often fell asleep with the receivers against our ears and woke up with it lying next to our head. Bobbie became a part of my family. I've always been reserved when it came to bringing girls home. I felt like they wouldn't like me anymore because I was from the lower-class spectrum. Girls I usually went out with were from middle- class homes. To me, that meant rich. Bobbie didn't care. To her, I was Junior, the guy who swept her off her feet with his charm and punched out a guy on the train for messing with her. After months of dating, I couldn't see myself without Bobbie. As much as I couldn't sing a note if my life depended on it, there was a song I sang to her all the time by Ritchie Valens called, *Donna*. I changed the lyrics and said Bobbie in place of Donna: "I had a girl, Bobbie was her name. Since she left me, I've never been the same, cause I love my girl. Bobbie, where could you be?" It was silly, but she loved it and it made her happy every time I serenaded her with it. My mom loved Bobbie, and surprisingly, my sister liked her too – and Leisa never liked anyone. We were only sixteen years old, but we were going to grow old together.

As much as I loved and cherished my relationship with Bobbie, I had a problem with monogamy. It was impossible for me to be with only one girl. I had to have several. I had grown into a sex addict over the few years since I'd had my first kiss at camp. Or maybe I wasn't addicted to sex; maybe I just craved the affection and attention of a woman. I wasn't into pornography or extreme erotic fantasies. I was drawn to the emotional intimacy of love making. I desired women for their femininity. I was more attracted to the pretty-but-plain morning weather reporter than the bombshell porn star who would be willing to satisfy a man's every desire. It could have been the reason why good girls were drawn to me in turn – and Bobbie was a good girl. Not everything she did was good, but her heart was always in the right place, even when she gave me a hundred dollars to buy my first half-ball of crack cocaine to sell.

I had met Bobbie at Islington Subway Station that day. Her parents were visiting, and therefore she wasn't allowed to sleep out. Jackie was to meet us at the Greyhound station downtown and stay over at Shawn's with us for the weekend. As Bobbie and I were about to walk down the stairs to the train's platform, I bumped into my ex-cell partner, Cash.

We shot the breeze for a few minutes before he asked me if I wanted something. Thinking it was weed he was referring to but unsure, I asked, "What do you got?"

"I got shit, man."

"Come on, man, I don't smoke crack," I replied, surprised by his offer.

He came a step closer and leaned in, speaking from the side of his mouth: "Not to smoke, to sell."

I was immediately sold on the idea. "Wait here."

I went over to where Bobbie was waiting for me and enthusiastically asked her to borrow a hundred dollars for my new business venture. She gave it to me like a proud woman, happy to see her man making progressive moves in life. *Aww, look at my baby, always thinking like an entrepreneur.*

Cash and I went into the bathroom to make the deal. I gave him the hundred-dollar bill and he gave me a small bag with one solid piece and a few small pieces of crack. Although a half-ball went for a hundred and twenty dollars, I still asked him to throw in two more of the smaller pieces. As he handed them to me, I asked him how much they were worth.

"Those are twenty pieces," he told me. I knew I was going to make a good amount of money off what he sold me.

That night I cut up the solid piece into the same size as the loose pieces, wrapped them up in plastic, and went out to Sherbourne and Dundas to hustle with Jackie. The first sale I made was to Congo, from Regent Park. When Tony, Jerome and I were kids we would provoke him by singing a song that went: "My name is Congo, I live in the jungle, I get five dollars a day, I give it to Lucy, she gives me her pussy, and that's what I do all day." We made sure to sing it from a distance, because he would chase us, and whenever he caught us he roughed us up with body blows until he decided we'd had enough. At first I thought Congo was going to rob me. Maybe he still viewed me as the little kid that ran around Regent Park fighting and causing trouble. He was happy to see me after five years but even happier that I had what he was looking for. I gave him two pieces and he handed me two twenty-dollar bills and continued across the street.

I made over five hundred dollars that night in only two hours. I think Sean was getting a hard-on as he lay on his bed and watched Jackie and me counting the money on the floor. Needless to say, Sean got into the game not long after. At lights out, Jackie and I shared the floor, with a sheet under us, and a blanket over us. Sean kicked us out of his room and told us to go to the vacant room down the hall when he heard us making out. We went, and Bobbie's best friend and boyfriend had their fill of lasciviousness.

Sean started hustling on the block with me. We walked along Dundas Street from Parliament to Jarvis; that was our strip. I never entered Regent Park to sell, that would have been infringing on other dealers' turf and wouldn't have been embraced with a very warm welcome. When our strip got too hot with police, we moved on to Parkdale, a free-for-all turf, as were the Dundas and Jarvis and Sherbourne blocks.

My first attempt at drug dealing didn't last long. I was busted in the late fall and spent the holidays and my seventeenth birthday in the West Detention Centre. I wasn't actually selling drugs when I was arrested. I was arrested in an alley off Jarvis, just south of Dundas, but the story goes back to Roxy's, a club at Danforth and Greenwood. Roxy's was a popular spot in Toronto. The owner sold weed downstairs while dancehall reggae made its way through the speakers upstairs – interspersed occasionally with the sound of a gunshot.

Being the diversified individual that I was, I bought a quarter ounce of weed to sell on the street along with my crack. Sean and Tony and I lingered in the club, listening to the music, chilling on the movie theatre seats that faced the stage in front. Roxy's had once been a cinema before being converted into a night club, and it still had the chairs and aisles leading down where the big screen once played movies.

There was a cat named Drift, an acquaintance who I knew from the places I frequented. He happened to be at Roxy's that night and asked me if I could spot him some weed until he sold it and made up the money to pay me back. A few weeks had passed when I saw Drift at Dundas and Jarvis. There was a restaurant and donut shop next door to each other; they shared the same public washrooms. He was chopping a custie (making a drug deal) in the foyer of the restrooms. I waited for him to close the deal and collect the cash, and then I confronted him for the money he owed me. Judging by his attitude, I could see that he had no intention of paying me back. I didn't have time to continue pressuring him for my money. I saw four police officers enter the donut shop. I walked past them trying not to look suspicious, which was difficult to do, as I had a chopped up 8-ball in one pocket and seven grams of marijuana in small packets in another. I avoided eye contact with the officers and walked straight out the door. I turned and walked south on Jarvis, hoping that they wouldn't stop and search me. Stop and search was a common practice in that area, but only if you were a black youth dressed in new clothes with a little bit of gold and a pager. I made it maybe thirty feet down the street when I heard one officer yell out for me to stop. I saw two cops walking quickly, gaining on me from behind. I took off running down Jarvis Street and made a right, somewhere before Shuter Street. I ended up in an alley with a police cruiser tailing me. A cop jumped out and tackled me to the ground. I had four pigs on me: one sitting on my back with my arm behind me, one on each of my ankles to prevent me from kicking (although I was completely compliant), and the fourth pig was standing over me with his boot pressed down on my neck. I never found out what came of that piece of shit, Drift.

Sean had stopped selling drugs during the three months that I was in the West Detention Centre. When I got out, he started again. It didn't take me more than twenty-four hours after my release for me to hit the streets with an 8-ball of crack. The first place I went was to the welfare office to grab an emergency cheque for almost six hundred dollars. Once I cashed it, my next stop was to Richie's place up at Caledonia and St. Clair to purchase the drugs from his neighbour, who I started buying from before I was busted because I'd lost touch with Cash. I had met Richie earlier that year at the Eaton Centre. He was coming up the escalator talking on one of those big old Motorola cellular telephones. I thought it was cool that he had a cell phone. The only people I knew who had cell phones were the thriving pimps I idolized in Ottawa. We bonded immediately and the rest was history. I called him crazy Richie. He was the only one in our crew who pushed the limits and did more insane things than me. When he told me how he got his cell phone I couldn't stop laughing. There was a Chinese man strolling along Yonge Street having a conversation on his Motorola, when Richie suddenly ran by and snatched it from his ear. He then ran around the corner into the welfare building, went to the bathroom, and stood on the toilet to look through the window. He could see the man in a police car searching the area looking for him.

After my brief visit to Richie's, I met Tony downtown. I didn't have time to chop up the 8-ball and package it into individual twenty pieces; I chopped up a few pieces on the streetcar. Tony and I were walking east on Dundas Street when a crackhead approached me and asked if he could get two for thirty. I agreed and we turned up Mutual Street, away from the main street. Tory continued along Dundas, holding the majority of the 8-ball for me, as I had just gotten out of jail that day and it was too risky to be carrying an entire 8-ball and selling at the same time. I just had fifty dollars' worth in my pocket for a few quick sales on the way to his house. Normally we packaged the twenty pieces in plastic and kept them in our mouths so that when the cops stopped and searched us, we could easily swallow it.

I had the crack in my hand and was about to hand it off to the crackhead when an unmarked police cruiser pulled up to us and two uniformed officers rushed out of their car. I dropped the piece of crack on the sidewalk and tried to walk as far away from it as I could. I made it only five feet before the cops were up in our faces questioning us. It was obvious that this guy and I had nothing in common: he was an older white man in his forties and looked like he had been smoking crack for a few years. I was a clean cut and well-dressed brown sixteen-year-old – I perfectly fit the image of a drug dealer, based on their stereotypical judgement. One of the officers told us to empty our pockets while the other searched the sidewalk. I still had about four hundred dollars after buying the 8-ball. The cop asked how come I had so much money. I told him the truth. I stood there and watched the other cop standing directly over the piece beside his boot. I waited for him to spot it and was prepared to snatch my money from the officer in front of me and flee. The cop must have been blind. My ID and cash were given back to me, and the crackhead and I walked off together in the same direction that Tony had gone. The crackhead asked me if he could have the piece on the ground for the thirty dollars. I told him yes, and he went to hand me the money.

"Keep it down," I told him, through clenched teeth. "Just keep walking."

When I looked back and saw that the cops had left, I took the two bills, and he ran back to retrieve the rock.

The most humiliating thing about returning to jail, was returning on the same day you were released. I was shaken up by the incident and threw the rest of the 8-ball in the garbage.

Sean had moved out of the rooming house and into an open-concept basement apartment. I went to stay with him. Our friend Markie, the white dread with hair down his back, would visit often. Three weeks after my release from the West, I had run out of cash. Markie was over when I came up with the idea to go down to the spot and sell Vic (the street slang for fake crack). All of us were broke, so it was a perfect idea. We wrapped up twenty pieces, half-balls, and 8-balls into clear plastic, sealing them with the hot metal part of a lighter. Then we put Anbesol on the outside to numb the lips and tongue as the client tore the packaging with their teeth to verify that it was real.

We got to Jarvis and Dundas and found two guys from India who wanted a half-ball. I handed it over to one with the hundred and twenty dollars in his hand. He didn't give me the cash right away. It was a lot of money and he wanted to make sure that he was getting the real deal. I told him to hurry up and give me the money as he was taking his time to open the package. I walked along the two men; Sean and Markie followed from a foot behind.

"Yo, just give it back, man. You're being a heat score," I told him.

Sean tapped me on the arm. "Let him open it and try it," he said.

I didn't trust that. These guys wanted to thoroughly check what it was they were getting. "Yo, give me my shit back. I don't want to deal with you guys. You're going to get us busted."

I needed to put pressure on him. It worked; he hesitantly handed me the money. Without counting it, all three of us darted across the street and got lost in the dark. The next day, we bought a half-ball, split it up into three, and made enough money to buy our own half-ball, then 8-ball. We hustled on the streets every day. At times I got greedy. Once a car pulled up travelling north on Sherbourne Street. It was clearly Markie's deal; he was ahead of Sean and me, already making his way to the vehicle. I ran in front of him. The guy in the passenger seat asked for three for fifty. He had a ten-dollar bill wrapped around two green bills. I handed him the three twenty-pieces at the same time I took the money. The car sped up the road, leaving me with a Canadian ten-dollar bill, and two Canadian Tire five cent bills.

"That's what you get for being greedy, you f*cker you!" Markie said.

They both laughed at me the rest of the way up the street.

The streets were dangerous at times. Everyone had to have a way to protect themselves, especially at night. If you didn't have a gun, a knife, or a bredren nearby, you were vulnerable. One older crackhead was a skinny, fragile lady. She carried a needle filled with her AIDS infected blood. Everyone knew about her weapon for survival, and no one bothered her.

I bought a lot of clothes, gold, and shoes with the money I earned selling crack. My fingers were decked out in rings, my wrists with a nice sized link, matching the chain around my neck. I had an Uzi earing and a gold cap with the letter *J* on my left fang. I took girls on dates to the movies, and if felt good to pull out a wad of fifties and twenties as I paid for the tickets. *What do you do?* was a typical question when they saw me with so much cash. *I'm into pharmaceutical sales. I have my own business*, was my answer.

Bobbie and I had lived at a few places. She was no longer happy in the relationship because I was never there. We didn't spend time together anymore. I was out selling drugs, hanging with the homies, or cheating on her with another girl. We rented a rooming house in the St. Clair West and Old Weston Road area. I only saw Bobbie late at night when I returned from hustling, and I left when I woke up. The laundromat was a ten-minute walk. She stopped doing my laundry, and I never had time to. I bought a new set of clothes every day from the Eaton Centre to wear on the following day as my dirty clothes piled up in the closet. She left me and moved back in with her sister after I was arrested the second time for selling drugs.

Again, I wasn't selling crack when I was picked up, but I wasn't innocent either. On my way to Tony's house, a crackhead asked me to trade a twenty piece for the bike he had. Why not, it was worth it. I gave him the rock, jumped on the bike, and rode to Regent Park. After spending some time at Tony's, I rode the bike along Dundas, passing Sherbourne, where I saw the same guy, but on a new, nicer bicycle. I told him that I would give him another twenty piece and this bike back in exchange for his new one. When I was casually riding along my way, testing the gears and looking down at my new bike, a car cut across the street to my side. Driving in the wrong direction, I knew they were cops. They slammed the brakes on in front of me and I couldn't turn the bike around quick enough. I jumped off and ran up a side street. I was going to swallow the packages I had in my mouth, but the gold cap that I wore on my fang popped off and would have cut the inside of my throat. I spit the packages out one by one, hoping that cops in pursuit wouldn't notice. I was talked to the ground. One of the cops had his hands around my throat, screaming at me to spit them out. The crackhead came to court willing to testify that I had sold him the crack for twenty dollars. His charges in return were dropped. I never fought the case. Mr. Lomer got me a sixty-day sentence with a month and a half dead time for a total of a little over three months, just enough time to bulk up and get out for the last part of the summer.

Blackman and his sidekick ran all the ranges they went on – no one could remember his first name, as everyone was called by their last name when in the system. Both were Jamaican. Blackman was muscular and intimidating. Sidekick was light-skinned, thinner, wore a small afro, and acted crazy; his eyes opened widely as he looked at his victims while taking whatever he wanted from their plate. Both were from Jane and Finch. They bullied everyone who was not a part of their crew. The first time I saw Blackman was in the gym. He was on the range across from mine and we all went to the gym at the same time. He was lying on the inclined bench press, not working out, surrounded by five or six guys, probably from Jane and Finch as well. I walked past to use the flat bench on the other side. "What's up, fatboy?" he said. Sidekick grinning, watching my reaction. I wasn't fat. I knew his comment was to get a reaction. I said nothing and just did my sets until gym time was up.

I ran into Sidekick a few weeks later on the court range. I was lying on my bunk reading a magazine when the CO opened the door and let him in. He dropped his things on the desk and told me to go on the top bunk. When I refused, he pulled out the pencil he had in between his ear and his afro, pressed it against my neck, eyes wide open in an attempt to convince me that he was psycho. I wasn't allowing it. He was nothing without Blackman.

"Go ahead and do it. Stab me in the neck and kill me, because I'm not moving."

"What, you don't believe I'll stick this through your neck?"

"I don't really give a shit. If you want to kill me, go ahead." I stared back at him, never breaking eye contact.

"You're f*cking crazy dude. I have a pencil up against your neck, and you're about to die over a bunk. You're crazy." He left me alone and went on the top bunk. We never spoke.

A month later, I was using the phone on another unit that I was running. The returnees and new guys were entering the range. I spotted Sidekick's limp and tough facade walking along the wall, pillowcase, and belongings over his shoulder as he made his way to his cell at the end. Without hesitation or delay, I approached him. When I got five feet in front of him, he recognized me and smiled, saying what's up, as if we were old friends. I pelted his face with my fist nonstop, as he ran to the gate he just came in through, screaming out to the guards to let him out. His back was toward me. I punched his face on both sides from behind until the guards finally opened the door and rescued this poor victim. It was the most rewarding three days I had ever spent in the hole.

My encounter with Blackman didn't end with such action. Near the end of my sentence, I was put on the female range that they had converted into a young offender unit. On his second day he was already trying to make a name for himself. The night before, he was successful at intimidating the white boy in the cell next to him into sending across his last cigarette, with the threat of bashing his face in the next day if he didn't. I avoided Blackman, but during dinner he sat next to me. He pulled my tray toward him. I held on to it as he told me he was going to take my food. I didn't let it go. He was underestimating me. He had no clue that if he had let go of my tray a few seconds later, his head was going to be split in two from my cup sitting in front of me.

When I got out of the West, I quit selling drugs and went to live with Lenny and his new girlfriend, Sharon, at Kingston and Woodbine. This time I stopped for good. But I was still hanging out with the same crowd, and we were still taxing white boys for their hats, and whatever else we wanted to take. Richie started a war with the Italians at St. Clair and Caledonia after he snatched a hat from one of them outside of their poolhall.

The Italian kid didn't accept the taxation and ran inside the poolhall. He and five others exited with pool sticks and rakes. They chased Richie, Tony, Danier, Garfield, and me across the street to the baseball diamond where there was a kids' league game going on. I ran straight to the bag of bats and started throwing them to all my boys. The chase had reversed, with us in pursuit of them. All but one had got away untouched. The unlucky Italian slipped on the gravel as Garfield swung the aluminum bat at the back of his head, missing by just a few inches. Garfield fed him a few body-blows with the bat as the kid limped off running.

Our next encounter with the Italians took place in the same parking lot outside the poolhall. I had a starter's pistol that I carried with me just to scare people. It didn't work on the Italian after I rammed it in his face twice, leaving two round marks from the barrel. Richie, Tony, Danier, Garfield, Locksley, Winston, and I continued along St. Clair to Dufferin, where we waited for the bus to go to our favourite night club, Max. It was the only night club in Toronto that had three floors and played three different genres of music on each floor: reggae upstairs, house on the main floor, and hip hop below. The bus stop was around the corner on Dufferin. It must have been a voice telling me in my ear to look down St. Clair. I walked backwards away from my homies to take a glance around the corner where we had just come from. Twenty feet from me was approaching a gang of at least ten Italians carrying baseball bats and other weapons. I bolted up Dufferin, running along the yellow line through the traffic; if something was going to happen to me, I at least wanted witnesses around to maybe help me. Richie darted through the dark parking lot and along the back streets, thinking I ran because I spotted the police coming. For some unknown reason, Locksley and Winston didn't move, while everyone else took off in their own direction.

When we all met at Max later on, Locksley told us that one of the Italians pushed a 9 mm handgun in his face, and told him to give the guy with the little pistol, and the dark-skinned guy a message: *When we catch them, they're dead.*

The following day, we retaliated yet again. We gathered up a large crew from Yonge and Dundas, all the homies and then some. We went to Richie's place on Caledonia where he lived with Garfield. We collected weapons and planned our attack. We filled our pockets with wooden bed legs to throw, some took knives, others brought bats. All twelve or so of us had a weapon or two. We hid behind the bushes across the street from the poolhall, where they were cornered in the parking lot hanging out. We counted to three before taking off toward them, but our plan was thwarted by a police car coming down the street. We threw our weapons on the grass near the bush and walked in the opposite direction, unnoticed. Ten minutes later, we returned, regrouped, rearmed, and stuck to the original plan. We got them good. We ran them out of their own turf, beating them with baseball bats and all the other things we brought to the battlefield. The wooden bed legs even came in handy for me when a few guys jumped in a minivan and fled the parking lot. I whipped the bed leg through the back window, shattering it as they drove away. That was the final conflict with the Italians.

We also made enemies with the Latinos. That didn't work out too good for us. I was the one who started this feud. Richie, Garfield, Tony, Danier, and I were passing their main spot, a club just next to the graveyard on St. Clair West at the top of Lansdowne. I made a near deadly mistake by taking the Latinos and putting them in the same category as punk white boys. They were anything but punks. I hollered at one of the girls standing outside with two guys smoking a cigarette. She ignored my flirtatious remark, and when I didn't give up, one of the guys stepped up and told me to keep walking; I did, but not till after I slapped him in the back of the head, sending all three of them running into the club and up the stairs. My homies and I continued along St. Clair, without giving them a second thought, until what appeared to be the entire club come running up from behind. I ran along the sidewalk where there were large black garbage bags waiting to be picked up in the morning. In an attempt to slow the angry Latinos down, I grabbed a couple and threw them behind me. It wasn't effective; I headed for the middle of the street where they caught me, surrounded me, and beat me. They walked back to the club, and I took the alleyway behind where my friends had taken off through. My back was killing me as if I had been beaten several times with a sledgehammer. I had trouble climbing over the fence into the cemetery due to the excruciating pain. My silk shirt was stuck to my back from the top to the bottom. *Why was I sweating so much?* Richie pointed out that my shirt had two holes in it. It wasn't sweat that drenched my shirt. I had been stabbed in my upper and lower back. We made it back to Richie's place making our way through the side streets in the dark. The two girls we had left at Richie's were still there. I stripped down to my underwear and they helped me in the shower, rinsing and drying my wounds. By the time I got my pants on, the police and ambulance had arrived. Richie had notified my mother, and she'd called 911. Two officers and two paramedics entered Richie's room and questioned me about what happened. I told them that I was wrestling with my friend, and I had rolled into broken glass. They didn't buy it and insisted that I go with them to the hospital. I refused and they made me sign a waiver before they left.

Bobbie stayed with me most of the time. She came by the night I was stabbed, and the next day I tried having sex with her, but my entire back seized up on me and I couldn't move. The worst pain I had ever experienced. I didn't argue with her about going to the hospital; it was no longer an option.

CHAPTER THIRTEEN
VICTIM OF MY ENVIRONMENT

I was eighteen years old, and six months was the longest I had stayed out of jail since I was thirteen. My desire now was to progress in life, and do it the right way. I was determined to never return to crime. I was still living with Lenny since my release, in a decent area near the Beaches. The townhouse had three floors. On the bottom was the living room and kitchen. The second and third floors each had two bedrooms and a bathroom. Bobbie later moved most of her things in; she still had a room at her sister's place, but she stayed with me almost every night, and half the closet had her clothes in it. The only time she slept at her sister's was when her parents visited, or if we were quarrelling. She even had a key, but never used it unless I was at the house or meeting her there. She only came downstairs and interacted with Lenny and Sharon when I was with her. Both were Jamaican, and their accents a little hard to understand at times. Bobbie was a shy girl and didn't like coming out of her comfort zone.

It had been almost two years since Bobbie and I had begun dating. We were at the zenith of our relationship. We had been tried and tested, and we'd made it through the fire. It took Bobbie lots of patience and love to deal with me. I was a tough rigid hothead with a ghetto attitude, but she helped soften me, not completely, but enough to motivate me to choose better in life. She always had goals and was confident and excited about striving to achieve them. I was also ambitious, and the energy that she radiated caused me to strive harder.

Bobbie and I both had full time jobs, which we obtained through the St. Christopher House, where we also shared the same placement counsellor, Bob. He was extremely helpful in getting us to where we wanted to be. Although I opposed homosexuality, and almost everything they stood for or taught about morality, I respected Bob. He was the only gay man that I knew personally. At the time I was more judgmental and opposed to faggots in all ways shapes and forms, not realizing that my fornicating habits were just as sinful as theirs. I valued Bob's opinion and took heed to his advice. The only other interaction I had with a homosexual was when I had to meet a man at the Barn, a gay night club on Church Street, to deliver a half ball of crack. It was an uncomfortable experience for me to put mildly. The way they gawked at me made me feel like a piece of meat on a grill, surrounded by ravenous men – the same way I looked at women. I just wanted to get in – and the heck out. Bob never made me feel uncomfortable. He was always professional, and treated Bobbie and me fair. He also didn't hide the fact that he had AIDS and may not be around to see us through to the end of the program. He died the following year. Bobbie and I talked about going to his funeral, but we never did.

The program Bobbie and I were placed in was a temporary three-month summer program to provide us with work experience, with hopes of staying with the company permanently. She worked for Meals on Wheels, and I worked at Toys 'R' Us. Bobbie loved working with Meals on Wheels. Every day she had an exciting story to tell me about the elderly people that she served. She enjoyed making a difference and seeing the smiles on the faces of people she was helping. I liked my job too, but there was nothing morally rewarding about stocking shelves with remote control cars and teddy bears.

Although I was working five days a week and had a somewhat live-in girlfriend, I still found time to hang out with the boys and maintain relations with other girls. As much as I loved Bobbie and was attracted to every form of her beauty, I was unable to overcome my weakness and desire for other women. I was addicted to females the way a crackhead was addicted to the pipe. I always had to have more, even my love for Bobbie couldn't put a halt to my compulsive womanizing behaviour. When I saw I girl I wanted, I went out of my way to get her. On the subway, on the street, in the mall, in the library, or in jail – yes, I got girls even when I was locked up. In the West, there was a white boy who would let his girlfriend make three-way calls for other inmates. When my phone call was over, and the other party hung up, I spent time seducing her with feel-good lyrics. Unfortunately for the kid giving away the three-way calls, I got out before him. I realized that I had a power that few men possessed – the ability to attract and draw almost any female into my world. I intrigued them. My dad once told me the only men who got more women than him were celebrities and sports figures; the same held true for me.

Michelle was one of the girls I had met along the way. She was a few years older than me, a twenty-one-year-old virgin, and just as tough as me on the exterior. I thought Michelle was cool. She was light skinned and had a banging body and bigger than average breasts. The chase for her virginity was what turned me on the most, but she never let me slide past second base. She was a generous girl but was not willing to share her body. She didn't hesitate to spend money on me. She bought me a gold chain with a cross and told me to never take it off. Michelle's mother was a big white woman who spoke loud and often. Her father was a black Nova Scotian, but he wasn't in the picture. Her father figure was her mother's boyfriend, who Michelle referred to as her stepfather. He was in the Toronto Don Jail on drug-related charges. Michelle was all right to hang with, but she took our relationship too far, too quick. I hadn't known her for three weeks and she was already introducing me to her family as her boyfriend. I visited her a few times at her house in the Christie Pits area, and we went out on one date to the movies, where she almost punched out a girl for making a flirtatious comment. Her jealous nature was too much for me. She never ceased to turn me off with her unladylike ways. We were exiting the College Park subway station when a girl and her friend were walking down. Both girls looked at me as they passed, but one committed the unpardonable sin of making the sound, "mmm… mmm… mmm." Michelle stopped in her tracks, about to turn around and slap the black off her beautiful face. "*What?!*" I gave her a light push from behind. "Just go," I said, mildly irritated with her pettiness. Although nothing came of our friendship, meeting Michelle was a blessing in disguise.

Other than hanging out with females, my favourite past time was bike riding with the homies. When we got together on our bicycles, we rode deep. There were usually ten to twelve of us. If one didn't have a bike, someone double rode him, either sitting on the seat behind the rider, or on the cross bars in front, until the passenger spotted a bike sitting outside of a convenience store, conveniently waiting to get stolen. We did this until everyone had their own bike, then we rode through the city like a motorcycle gang.

While I was trying to stay clear of the law, I was still hanging around a group of thugs that had no regard for it. Richie was still selling crack, although he was laying low because his girl was about to have a baby. Locksley, his brother Winston, and their Eglinton West posse were still looting and robbing businesses and individuals in large numbers. Tony,

Danier, and Sean were not actively breaking the law. Tony and Danier for the most part were law-abiding individuals. Although they usually went along with whatever the group was doing, they were never ringleaders, and they normally took a back seat, only stepping up when needed, such as participating in a scrap.

The days had gotten routine. During the week, Bobbie and I worked from nine to five, and during the weekend we either hung out together or went our separate ways.

One weekend we were babysitting my little brother, Jamal, while my mom went out to party with Dexter. They had separated and lived in different locations because he had gotten his secret Portuguese girlfriend pregnant. Jamal was sleeping, and Bobbie and I were arguing in the living room about something petty. Our attention was diverted out the window to the car parked in front of the building. There was loud arguing and thumping coming from the vehicle. When we looked out the living room window, I noticed that it was Dexter's car. My mom was in the passenger seat, and he had her in the headlock, punching her in the face. The car rocked back and forth with her struggling to break free from his grip. I had never seen anyone beat up on my mother like that before. I snapped, as any son would. My mind went into defence-and-attack mode – defend my mom and attack the aggressor. I ran to the kitchen and pulled out a butcher knife from the drawer. Bobbie got scared and blocked the apartment door to prevent me from leaving and doing something I may regret, possibly for the rest of my life. I managed to make it down half a flight of stairs, but the closer I got to the bottom, the more physical and adamant Bobbie became, crying and demanding that I give her the knife. Driven by rage and emotion, I continued pushing through her to get to my mom and save her from this monster. When Bobbie realized that she didn't have the strength to hold me back, she jumped on me, locking both arms around my neck, and her legs around my hips, like a baby chimpanzee locked onto her mother. She begged me to give her the knife. I wasn't going anywhere fast with her hanging from me. After I handed her the knife, she moved out of my way, and I ran out of the building to deal with the matter with my bare hands.

I opened the driver's side door and grabbed Dexter by his Jheri curls, pulled him out of the vehicle, and went to work on him. He was drunk and couldn't stand without wobbling. He tried to explain something to me, but there was no explanation for what I had just saw. I gave him a flying kick to the chest, dropping him to the ground. I continued kicking him several times until my mom ran out of the car and got between us.

Lenny and Dexter were friends, and that week, Lenny told me that Dexter was going to come over and give me a beating. I didn't see Dexter as a revenge seeker, but I was worried that this would escalate. All I wanted was peace with everybody. I no longer had the thug mindset. I didn't expect Dexter to retaliate for me defending my mother, but if he did, I wasn't going to lie down and take it. It never happened. I didn't see Dexter for years after.

I was at a place of peace, being out of the drug game and out of the judiciary system altogether. There was no more cloud hanging over my head. For the first time in my life, I was making plans, and setting goals. To me, there was nothing I could not do, nothing I could not achieve. I saved up a thousand dollars and put it down towards my first car. The total cost was twenty-five hundred dollars. It was a grey Toyota Corolla SR5, the stick shift sports model. I didn't know how to drive standard, but I knew I would learn once I got the car. Bobbie and I studied the Ministry of Transportation Driver's Handbook together, and we went on the same day to take the written test for the learner's permit; at the time it was called the "365." We both passed the test. I scored perfect, and Bobbie got three questions wrong. I told her it was because I was a better driver. A month later we got our full driver's licences and we were ready to hit the road; all I had to do was pay the remaining fifteen hundred dollars.

Every day when I took the bus to work, I thought of my new car. I was going to drive it all around the city, playing music with my windows down and my arm hanging out. My summer was going to be fabulous.

There was less than a month to go before the official start of the summer season. It was the Victoria Day long weekend, also known as the May Two-Four weekend. That holiday Monday I had plans to go with Bobbie to Szofia's place for dinner. My plans changed after Tony called me and told me that everyone was going to Ontario Place. Little did I know, the choice to follow my friends would change the course of my summer, my year, my life.

CHAPTER FOURTEEN
THE TORONTO DON JAIL

The unmarked police cruiser rolled up to the gate of the Toronto Don Jail with me in the back, handcuffed and shackled. It was a beautiful mid-June afternoon – for most people. For me, it was gloomy and depressing. Once the cops identified themselves, the thick metal door was lifted by the press of a button from the guard inside. I was led through a short corridor with cells on either side where the arresting pigs transferred me over to the Don Jail correctional officers. I was placed in a cell with four other newbies closest to A and D, where men could be seen bending over and opening the crack of their ass for the guards to look up while they did their strip search, all in the presence of female guards and nurses, who would sneak a peek at the exposed penises every now and then. When it was my turn for processing, I was asked a slew of questions, most of which the officer already knew because he had my file in front of him on the desk. After I was registered in the system, strip-searched, and in my new jail house attire (an orange jumpsuit, orange T-shirt, and blue and white shoes), I was put into another cage with eight other men, where we were served a cheese sandwich and tasteless watered-down juice in a Styrofoam cup.

The Don Jail was different from any place I had ever been to. Most of the men were in on gun and drug charges, which downtown hoods like Regent Park, Moss Park, St. Jamestown, and Parkdale were well known for. However, the jail was also home to robbers, sex offenders, and murderers. I knew I wasn't getting out any time soon, so I vowed to make a name for myself. I was going to keep my shoes, and I wasn't backing down from anybody. The new inmates were usually given new shoes upon arrival, and if you allowed anyone to take them from you, it was like giving up your manhood. I would protect myself and my little bit of property at all costs. I observed all the prisoners and guards closely. It wasn't difficult to decipher the alphas from the fakes. The chatterboxes who boasted about their crimes and glamorized the criminal lifestyle were usually the cowards hiding behind their tough talk. The alphas didn't have to talk much at all. The atmosphere was negative and intimidating, a world filled with animosity, violence, and hatred. I was taken to the court range along with all the other inmates that were going to court the following morning. We arrived on the range ten minutes before lockup, and on court range we were not assigned cells, we had to find our own. I found a bottom bunk near the middle of the range. A clean looking quiet Vietnamese guy occupied the top bunk. I didn't get a chance to make a phone call because people were using all three phones. I waited for a few minutes, hoping that someone would hang up. With only three minutes remaining, I decided to head to the back of the range for a shower to wash the stench of the holding cells off my skin. I was successful in soaping and scrubbing every part of my body, but then the water shut off before I was able to completely rinse the suds off. I stood there for a minute thinking about what I was going to do. Maybe I should go to my cell and rinse off by using the sink in there, but then I would make a mess all over the floor and disturb my cell partner. Maybe I should use my towel and wipe the soap off, but then I'd feel uncomfortably sticky all over. As I stood there clothed with only soap suds, the guard who turned off the shower valves emerged from the back. "Hey boss, can you put the shower back on for a minute, please?" I asked.

"You got thirty seconds! Make it quick!" he replied. I was grateful that he was considerate enough to accommodate my request. I rinsed off, dried up, and went straight to my cell feeling fresh and clean, like a bar of Irish Spring.

I didn't speak a word to my cell partner. I spread the two sheets over the thin lumpy piss-stained mattress and slid between them. I had a pillowcase but no pillow; I put my extra pair of socks and boxers in the pillowcase to elevate my head. When I was settled in, I lay on my back, hearing the all too familiar sounds of jail: men speaking between cells with their voices echoing off the bars and steel picnic tables. The television mounted to the bars out on the range, playing nothing I was interested in watching. Angry inmates rattling their bars and yelling profanities from the other range. We were like animals trapped in a cage, only to exit and enter at the master's command. I was cold, lonely, and scared. I lay on my bunk and silently cried myself to sleep.

In the morning I went to court. I was the first one to see the judge. Bobbie and my mom were already in the courtroom waiting as I walked in. The court officers didn't handcuff me as they led me from the holding cells, down the corridor, and into the courtroom from a door that led straight into a prisoner box. I was expecting a bail hearing, but instead, the Crown Attorney stood up and told the judge that they were dropping the charges, and the police would like to apologize for the inconvenience. The judge looked at me and said, "Mr. Tull, the Crown has withdrawn the charge of second-degree murder and you are free to go." I stepped out of the prisoner's box, walked over to my mother and Bobbie, and embraced them with tears of joy. I walked out of the courthouse with my two favourite ladies, and into the beautiful warm spring breeze of freedom. I was free again – until the loud clanking of all eighteen thick steel bars slid open simultaneously, and the bright ceiling light illuminated the cell, waking me up – and once again – stealing my freedom.

I lingered on my bunk for a few minutes, lacking any motivation to get up. When I did make it to the breakfast line my cell partner was already at the table eating his toast with peanut butter, boiled eggs, and Corn Flakes. To complement breakfast, there were two large brown Cambro containers on the first table along with Styrofoam cups. One container was filled with 2.5 gallons of scorching coffee, which on at least on one occasion, I was told, was opened and dumped on another inmate's head and face. The other Cambro contained artificial orange juice made from crystal sugar and tap water.

There were over twenty inmates going to court from the Don Jail. Eight of us from general population were scheduled at Old City Hall, and three from protective custody. The others were going to different courts throughout the city: 1000 Finch, Scarborough Courts, High Court, and even as far as Halton Court in Burlington. We were all handcuffed and shackled together in groups of three or four and sent off in various paddy wagons to face a judge who would determine our fate. I hated being chained to other inmates. Sometimes they smelled so bad you would have to elbow them in the face and tell them to breathe in the other direction just to protect yourself in case they had tuberculosis.

The bullpens at Old City Hall were full to the brim with prisoners from all over Toronto and the surrounding areas: Toronto West Detention Centre, Toronto East Detention Centre, Hamilton-Wentworth Detention Centre, Maplehurst Correctional Complex, Mimico Correctional Centre, and of course the Toronto (Don) Jail. It didn't matter which jail you were being held at for other charges, if you committed a crime in a certain district, you went to court in that district. A fifteen-minute trip in the paddy wagon from the Don Jail was uncomfortable enough. I couldn't imagine a five-hour ride from the Ottawa-Carleton (Innes) Detention Centre if I had been held there instead of with Bob and Sandy, flying in first-class to court five years earlier for the stabbing charge I faced when I was thirteen.

I was held in the bullpen next to the bail court. The first thing that strikes a visitor is the odour – a concoction of sweat, bodily waste, stale breath, and moldy bologna. The cell was smaller than the main bullpen, maybe four hundred square feet, with a concrete bench running along the walls, and a toilet and sink in the back corner. The cell was over crowded with about fifteen men. All the seats were taken; men were lying or sitting on the dirty floor; some were pacing the cell; others stared out of the cell bars staring at the white brick wall in front, depressed with their current situation. There wasn't much talking among the prisoners, but there was noticeable tension that could be felt the minute you stepped in.

One inmate got kicked several times in his face unexpectedly because he sat on the bench. When a medium built thug from the West Detention Centre got up to take a leak, the nerdy white boy with a build of the Toothpick Man, fresh from 52 Division, probably his first time in jail, sat in his spot. His ignorance for thinking that he could take someone's seat when they got up cost him dearly. Without word or warning, the kid was kicked in his face and getting stomped on the ground as he laid in the fetal position with his hands and arms trying to protect his face and head from the vicious blows. His mistake cost him a broken nose, two black eyes, and a swollen cheek. He probably also suffered a concussion or severe headache judging by the number of times his head hit the ground. The kid got up, embarrassed and humiliated, and walked over to stand by the bars. A court officer passing by saw the kid's face and asked him what happened. The kid told the officer that he fell. He was removed from the bullpen, and never returned.

My bail was denied due to the seriousness of the charge and my young offender record. I got back to the Toronto Don Jail shortly after dinner. I was assigned to 2C South, a Jungle Range, which was predominately black, but also housed the Vietnamese gangs. 2C South was one of the most loud and intimidating ranges in the jail – it was a test of faith, courage, and strength.

A range is a big common area cell that all the individual prisoner cells open into. It has several steel picnic tables bolted to the floor where the inmates sit to eat meals, watch television, or play cards or board games. Inmates can also use the phone and take a shower. In the Toronto Don Jail, most ranges had a guard stationed outside at a desk looking in, with a blue button on the wall in case violence erupted. However, in the Don, the regular ranges were separated by north and south wings. On 2C, 3C, and 4C, the guard's desk was stationed on the north side, which left the south side completely unsupervised unless the guard left his desk and walked around. There were no cameras on the ranges, making them even less supervised and more dangerous.

The Toronto Don Jail had six types of ranges: jungle ranges, pen ranges, and protective custody ranges were the regular ones. Then there was a work range, a hospital range, and a psych range. Each regular range had four Quartermen. They were responsible for handing out the food when the meal cart arrived, cleaning the range, handing out the evening jug-up, and running the range. The Quartermen stayed out of their cells during the daytime lockups, which were two and a half hours after lunch and again after dinner. It would take them normally fifteen minutes to clean the cellblock, and the rest of the time was usually spent on the phone. They also stayed out of their cells for an extra half hour at night lockup to clean and hand out the jug-up from cell to cell, which was usually a muffin, a cookie, or an apple. It was always the top Quarterman, also known as the heavy, who handed out jug-up. He kept any extras, and if there weren't any extra muffins or cookies, he would skip cells and pick and choose who gets one. It was usually the new white boys that missed out. The heavy also kept the extra bread and peanut butter to share with his friends to eat during night lockup. The heavies and the Quartermen controlled pretty much everything on the range, from the phones to the food, and to a certain degree, approving or disapproving fights. Not every range had a heavy, some ranges were run by the Quartermen, who shared equal power and were all friends.

The Jungle Range was often loud and chaotic. The prisoners constantly fought over food, the phone, which channel the TV was set to, and who the next Quarterman was once one got released or transferred. The Jamaicans caused the most trouble. They yelled at the top of their lungs while playing dominos or were bullying someone for something. The Scotians were more laid back and easier to get along with. The Vietnamese were quiet, respectful, and usually stuck to themselves, but would joke around with you if they knew you. Though they were tiny, no one dared mess with them, because if you f*cked with one, you'd have nine swarming you, stabbing you with pencils or hitting you over the head with a broom or whatever else they could find. I got along well with the Vietnamese; they were the most peaceful group in the jail.

The Pen Range was the complete opposite to the Jungle Range. It was run by huge white pen timers who were soon being transferred to the penitentiary to serve years in prison, or they came from the penitentiary and were in the Don awaiting court for other charges or appeals. The Pen Range was so quiet you could hear a pin drop. The inmates even whispered while talking on the phone as to not disturb anyone. The bread wasn't handed out by the Quartermen like on the Jungle Range; it was placed on the tables and each man took his two slices. In the evening, every prisoner got their jug-up; there was no bullying or punking off. The pen timers rarely used the phone, so one was always available, and there was never any fighting over the phone. Everyone knew who the heavy was on the range and respected, even feared him, in contrast to the Jungle Range, where there was often a struggle for power. The pen range was a peaceful place to do your time, unless you crossed someone the wrong way; but if you preferred action, you'd lose your mind.

It was a privilege to be on the Work Range. Only inmates with non-violent offences and had no misconducts were permitted to work. There were several jobs available but working in the kitchen was the best because you were able to eat as much as you wanted. Inmates nearing the end of their sentence were able to work outside picking up trash on the grounds. They usually had their people on the outside drop drugs on the property the night before, and the inmate would sneak them in by hooping them up their buttocks or ingesting them.

The Hospital Range, also known as Medical Range, was for the sick, for those who had gotten beaten and needed medical attention, and for people coming in off the streets going through drug withdrawal, which was common. However, every incoming inmate had to pass through Medical Range for a physical and tuberculosis test. After a couple of days, the nurse would come down to the ranges to check the results of the TB test. If your arm was normal, you were clean; if your arm was swelled up and bruised, you were removed from the range and treated for tuberculosis in the Hospital Range.

The Psych Range was the most disturbing. Inmates walked back and forth, zoned out and in another world. These men were completely out of their minds – and it was scary. I got a peek into the Psych Range when I was being transported through the jail, and I was in complete shock from what I witnessed. Men hitting themselves in the head, pulling out their hair, screaming in agony, shaking in the corner. It was a disturbing site to see. I wouldn't have lasted a day on that range without going insane myself.

Protective Custody was for the rats, rapists, child molesters, ex-cops and jail guards, or inmates who were afraid to be in General Population. Once an inmate checked in to PC, it was difficult for him to reenter General Pop, because it was noted on their paperwork, and most guards didn't have a problem informing their favourite inmates that the person who just entered the range was a diddler or a snitch. Though it was difficult for a General Pop inmate to physically harm a PC inmate, it was easy to get to them in different ways. Their punishment usually came from the inmates working in the kitchen, who found the nastiest and most vile ways to mess with their food. They ejaculated in their soup, smeared feces in their burgers, horked in their sandwiches, and pissed in their juice – they did whatever the human mind could concoct to get to the protective custody prisoners who they perceived as the scum of the scum.

The Quartermen had already finished cleaning the range, and all the other inmates were still locked in their cages when I entered 2C South with three other inmates. The medium-size white boy with the buzz cut appeared apprehensive, frightened of what was on the other side of the gate. The two Vietnamese lightweights with gang tattoos coming down their arms from out of their orange prison jumpers were confident, as if they were returning home to be with family. I was prepared for whatever.

At the front of the range there was an inmate working out with his shirt off and his jumpsuit rolled down and tide around his waist. He was built like Mike Tyson but stood an inch taller than the champ. His workout was briefly interrupted as the guard in the control booth buzzed the second door opened and all four of us entered the range. I was impressed with his makeshift triceps pushdown machine. He placed a mop handle through the crossbar of the gate, pressed down, and brought it back up in a teeter totter motion, dipping the head of the mop into the bucket of water on the other side of the bars to create resistance. He looked each one of us in the eye as we entered the range. I was the only one he nodded his head to, indicating respect. It was evident by his confidence, size, and demeanour that he ran 2C South.

I was assigned cell eighteen, the last cell at the back of the range. It was the worst cell on all the ranges because it was next to the showers and the shitters, and the TVs couldn't be seen, only heard, which made the sound of them a nuisance when you were locked up in your cell at night.

I walked toward the back of the range trying to look as confident as I could without coming across as arrogant or macho. Some inmates watched as if they were expecting me, and in fact they were, maybe not on their range, but they were expecting my arrival to the Don Jail. It was customary to watch the noon and six o'clock news in all jails, and my picture and name were plastered on the news and in the newspaper. The Toronto Star read:

Store Clerk Charged in Teenager's Slaying

An 18-year-old store clerk was to appear in court today charged with second-degree murder in the fatal stabbing of a teenager during a Victoria Day fireworks display at Ontario Place.

"We got a lot of help on this one," said Detective Sergeant Tom McNamara of the homicide squad, the lead investigator on the Mathew Smith slaying.

McNamara thanked the slain teenager's family for calming Smith's friends, who had vowed revenge for his slaying and had set out looking for the killer.

The family's help bought police time to put the case together and find the suspect, he said. No weapon has been recovered.

According to friends, Smith, 18, of Flemington Rd., North York, was trying to break up a fight in the crowded parking lot of Ontario Place on May 24 when he was stabbed in the chest.

One of Smith's friends accidentally bumped someone in the holiday weekend crowd of 700 that had gathered in the Ontario Place parking lot to watch the annual fireworks display, and an argument ensued, friends said.

Smith, a weightlifter who was almost 6 feet tall and weighed 190 pounds, wasn't carrying any weapon when he was stabbed.

McNamara said the dispute leading up to the fatal stabbing played itself out over several minutes as the two groups involved moved about the crowd and jostled each other.

First-aid workers for Ontario Place desperately tried to help the teenager until an ambulance forced its way through a heavy traffic jam along Lake Shore Blvd. W.

McNamara said yesterday's arrest was the culmination of numerous interviews with witnesses who were at the fireworks display that night.

Reginald Junior Tull, 18, of Kingston Rd. in Toronto was arrested yesterday at the store where he works as a clerk. He is scheduled to appear today in court at old city hall.
Smith was Metro's 25th homicide of the year.

I had read a few of the articles earlier that day from newspapers I found lying in the cells in A and D. I wondered where the police were getting their information. It couldn't have been more contradictory from the truth, and because of the cops' sloppy investigation and hasty decision to throw a black man in prison, there I was – a victim of my circumstance. Although I was innocent, my charge gave me clout in the jail. On my way to the cell, I heard my name called. Usually when someone called you by name, it was your last name they used unless they knew you personally.

"Hey, Junior. Welcome to the Don."

How could anyone have known me by Junior? The news used my first and last name, and Junior was what everyone called me on the outside. I looked to my left where the voice came from and saw a short guy with a small belly walking toward me with his hand out and smile on his face. We shook hands, and he introduced himself.

"I'm Allen, Michelle's stepdad. I spoke to her today; she told me to make sure you were all right. Listen, you don't have to worry about nothing. Me and my boy Courtney over there working out, we run things here. If you need anything: the phone, extra food, cigarettes, just let me know. You can move into my cell, number eleven, it's a TV cell. Take the top bunk. Trust me, you don't want to be in the cell at the end. You're a good man, I got your back, we're fam."

After that welcome, I didn't feel like I had much to worry about on 2C South.

"Thanks, man," I said, and went into the cell to put my things on my new bunk. Courtney came over and Allen introduced me to him as Michelle's boyfriend.

Although I hadn't had sex with Michelle like I wanted, our relationship ended up coming with a different perk. She introduced me to everyone as her *man*, and even told Allen about me. Because of her, I was right up there with the shot callers in one of the most dangerous ranges in the Toronto Don Jail.

CHAPTER FIFTEEN
THE NEW HEAVY ON THE CELL BLOCK

Courtney ran 2C South with an iron fist and a shank that was hidden in Allen's cell, accessible for us to use when needed. Courtney didn't need a shank. Everyone on the range already feared his size and savage temper, but if anyone even batted an eye at him, he would have them up against the bars with the sharp homemade knife pressed against their neck in fear of their life. At times Courtney would go into fits of rage if someone pissed on the toilet seat or didn't flush it or didn't clean the shower after they used it. He banged the steel table with his fist, making an echo throughout the entire range, catching everybody's attention. "YO... WHO THE F*CK PISSED ON THE SEAT?" The range would grow silent. The only ones who continued doing what they were doing without paying any attention to Courtney were the Quartermen and the Vietnamese guys playing cards on the floor outside of their cells. "If I catch any of you nasty motherf*ckers pissing on the seat, I'm going to put your f*ckin face in the toilet!" I always chuckled inside whenever Courtney got mad; he was always so extreme. I'd look around the range, and it humoured me to see the inmates who weren't cool with Courtney tremble with fear.

During the first week of my incarceration, my father paid me a visit. It was the first time I'd seen him since I was thirteen. He'd heard about my arrest through the local Toronto news, as had most of my friends and family. I was overjoyed to see him and grateful for his support during this difficult time in my life. For the duration of his twenty-minute visit, we spoke standing up, through a bulletproof glass. I assured him that I had nothing to do with the murder, and he seemed to believe me. I left the visit feeling encouraged and uplifted because my father was in my life, and in my corner. I called him a few days later. I was eager to speak with him again, but his tone suggested that the feeling wasn't mutual. He began to tell me that he couldn't be a part of this because he was concerned about what his friends might think. The last thing I expected to hear from my father were the words of a coward, who wouldn't stand by his innocent son because he was afraid of what people would think of him. I hung up while he was still talking. I felt hurt, discouraged, and lonely. I got up, grabbed my towel that was hanging from my cell bars, and went into the shower – the only place I could cry without anyone seeing me.

After six months of running 2C South, Courtney was released. I'd been there for only two months, a short time in comparison to the majority of the other men, but I felt the desire to take charge and fill the position of Quarterman. I knew that I would be challenged; it was a bold move on my part, because there were other men ahead of me in line, and it was a coveted position. I didn't care. I was fed up with spending sixteen hours a day in my cell. I wanted to talk on the phone and take a shower while the range was quiet or hang out and play cards with the other Quartermen, anything but stay locked in a cell.

Although prison is ruled by jailhouse politics, there are definitely no elections, nor is there a democracy. When one Quarterman leaves, the next one emerges through force, intimidation, or the support of the other Quartermen. I would use whatever it took – it didn't matter – it was jail.

After lunch, when it was afternoon lockup, I picked up a broom and started sweeping the floor. Terry, one of the Scotians, told me to go to my cell because he was now the new Quarterman. My reply was swift and certain. I told him that he better go to his cell before I beat him down with the broom. An argument ensued that caught the attention of all the inmates. I could have beaten the living snot out of this skinny forty-year-old with my bare hands, but that would have done nothing for my reputation. Plus, I liked Terry. I wanted to put on a show for everyone. The inmates already respected me, but I wanted them to fear me. I wanted to run the range, and I was going to do it like Courtney, through fear. But there was a difference between Courtney and me – I was in for murder – he was in for rape. He had to watch his back for the inmates who were willing to go out of their way just to stab a rapist and make a name for themselves before getting shipped off to the penitentiary.

I threw the broom in Terry's direction, as if to hit him, but missed intentionally. Then I went to my cell to retrieve the shank that was hidden in Allen's mattress. I felt nothing like how I was acting. I exaggerated my rage dramatically and charged in his direction with the shank in my hand, telling him that I was going to kill him for disrespecting me. Terry was liked and respected on the range, and I knew that Allen wasn't going to let me stab him. Terry ran around the range fearing for his life, until Allen and Redman (another Quarterman), along with Derrick, the range "saint," who hated violence, stepped in between us. They held me back and pleaded for me to relax and chill out. I calmed down and handed the shank to Allen, just before two guards came around the corner and yelled, "Lock up!" Everyone, including Terry, went to their cells, while I stayed out with the other Quartermen to clean the range.

After clean-up, I spoke on the phone for a while before engaging in a game of euchre with Allen, Redman, and Kurtis. The guys joked around, laughing and saying that I had quite a temper for a quiet guy.

"I don't want to get on your bad side," Redman said, raising his eyebrows and shaking his head with a smile on his face.

"You're damn right about that. This bwoy don't play. He's almost as crazy as Courtney," Kurtis added.

Allen didn't laugh, he only shook his head during the conversation. I felt good that I had accomplished my goal without anyone getting hurt. Derrick gave me a lecture that evening about how I need to learn to control my temper. Eventually Terry and I began talking again – we knew it wasn't personal – just jailhouse politics.

It was clear after a few more weeks who the new heavy on the cellblock was. I'd run many Young Offender ranges, but in an adult facility, in the most notorious jail in the country's largest city, and on the range with the worst reputation in the institution, there was a greater sense of power. I was used to telling kids my age what to do, but now I was dictating to men twice my age, who were incarcerated for murder, attempted murder, aggravated assault, possession of guns, trafficking drugs, robbery, and the list went on. I was the youngest on the range with the most power and respect. I was locked up but free to do whatever I pleased. I talked on the phone mostly all day, I had extra dessert with my meal, and ate peanut butter and jam sandwiches with my cell partner as we watched a movie from our bunks at night.

Throughout my incarceration I tried my best to stay positive. I spoke to Bobbie every day and to my mom a few times a week. The entire ordeal was extremely difficult for Mom. She didn't just have me to worry about; Leisa had gotten herself into some trouble as well. She was offered a deal with the *devil* that was next to impossible to turn down for a twenty-year-old girl who grew up in the hood, didn't have a job, and wasn't used to having money – ten thousand dollars to smuggle cocaine from Trinidad to Canada. A free trip to the Caribbean, and a whole lot of cash upon return. She accepted the deal, but never received the money; instead, she got a four-year prison sentence. Mom was strong about it; she was accustomed to us being incarcerated at the same time, but now we were in the big leagues. Her two kids, up against years in the penitentiary. I never really thought about how Mom felt. She was always strong, no matter what was going on in our lives, and she was the bravest person I'd ever known. She fought and protected us all throughout our years growing up in Regent Park, and she never backed down from anybody, regardless of how big and bad the assailant was. My mother was my superhero, and she played a major role in keeping me positive while in that place of negativity and despair, but not even she could save me this time; I would have to ride this wave alone.

After three months of incarceration, I'd become accustomed to jail life. A typical day in the Toronto Don Jail was never routine – the schedule for lights out, lights on, meals, and medication were consistent, but the mood consistently changed. When the inmates stepped out of their cells in the morning, there was no telling how the day was going to end.

The cell door bars slid open at 7:00 each morning for breakfast. The meal cart was brought onto the range by the correctional officers, but it was left up to the Quartermen to distribute the trays of food to each inmate as everyone lined up. The tougher inmates walked up to the front of the line and got their meals first, while the others waited patiently in single file. The extra plates went to the Quartermen. If an inmate was new, it was a smart idea to observe where everyone sat before taking a seat, because if he sat in the wrong spot, he could get his meal taken away, slapped across the head, or spoken to disrespectfully. After breakfast each inmate brought his empty meal to put back in the cart. When all the meal trays were counted by the guard, the cart was wheeled out of the range, and the broom, mop, and bucket, along with cleaning supplies were brought in. The cells were cleaned by the men occupying them, and the range was cleaned by the Quartermen: one swept, one mopped, one wiped the tables, and another cleaned the showers and toilets. The heavy chose his chore, and the other three figured the rest out. When morning cleanup was complete, one guard came onto the range to check all the cells while the other stayed in the control room and closed each cell with the touch of a button, as his partner shouted down the range, "18 clear... 17 clear... 16 clear..." all the way down to cell one. The guards usually left the Quartermen's cells on neutral, allowing them to slide open and closed manually throughout the day for us to go in and out at will.

During the day, inmates were able to talk on the phone, watch TV, work out, shower, play cards and other games, read, or take correspondence courses: math and English were provided by the jail. The lunch cart came in at 11:00 a.m. As usual, the inmates lined up, got their food, and ate. Five loaves of bread came with the lunch and dinner cart. The regular inmates got two slices of bread, the heavy took a whole loaf, and the other Quartermen shared the rest, which was put in the cell till later. The Quartermen ate what they could in the night, and the left-over bread was used to make peanut butter and jelly sandwiches, which were sold for cigarettes or other canteen items. After lunch it was lockup until 1:30 p.m., or until the guards decided to crack the cells, which was usually ten to twenty minutes late. All prisoners were expected to be in their cells on time for lockup, but the correctional officers let us out whenever they felt like it. The evening routine was the same: dinner came at 4:00 p.m., and then lockup until 6:30 p.m.

Most conflicts over the phone occurred in the evening, after dinner lockup. That was when the phones were busiest. Inmates arrived from court and needed to call their people: girlfriends, wives, and kids were home from work and school. Lawyers were available to receive phone calls because they weren't in court. With only two hours for forty men to share three phones, the inmates were most volatile.

Some Quartermen took pleasure in watching the inmates fight over the phone. They intentionally stayed on until there was only ten minutes left before lockup, then shouted across the range, "Who needs a phone call?" And walked away, leaving three or four men arguing, at times resulting in a fight. This was a common practice for Courtney; he was relentless at getting inmates against each other. Maybe that was how he held on to power – divide and conquer. But sometimes the men were willing to compromise, agreeing to two minutes each, ending the day in peace.

Once everyone was locked in their cells, the Quartermen gave the range a final cleaning, and the heavy went from cell to cell to hand out the jug-up. Lights out was at 11:00 p.m. Every night we watched the nine o'clock movie that played on City TV. Some inmates were able to see the television from their bunks, others had to stand up at the bars to watch, and yet others were only teased by the sound of the television but couldn't see the screen at all. On the jungle ranges, Friday night was dedicated to 88.1 FM, where we lay on our beds and listened to Reggaemania playing our favourite tunes. My heart grew heavy and my eyes burned with tears at times as I thought of Bobbie while Sanchez sang, *Missing You*. Other songs such as *Batty Rider* and *Love Me Brownin* by Buju Banton put a smile on my face as I thought about my homeboys, and us rolling through the city in Richie's Honda Civic, hollering at girls from out the window on our way to the clubs.

I spent most of my time working out at the back of the range. There were no weights, but there was a chin-up bar and a punching bag, and we made our own weights by using a plastic garbage bag that we filled with water and wrapped up in a sheet. I was getting pretty buff. When I took off my shirt, all eyes were on me, including the female guards', and I loved it. I did at least three hundred push-ups and fifty chin-ups before going for a visit with my sleeves rolled all the way up to my armpits. On the way down to the visiting room the guard usually told me to pull my sleeves down, but once I entered the visiting area, they were back up again.

Receiving visits was the greatest euphoria for an inmate. A visit meant we were loved, and not forgotten by our people on the outside. It meant the world to us that someone would travel such a long distance just to see us through a glass window for twenty minutes. Bobbie visited me twice a week, and she always dressed up sexy, wearing blouses that were easy to button down to give me a quick peep show when no one was looking. After the visit my arms were no longer swollen and bulging from the push-ups and chin-ups, but another muscle was swollen and bulging, which I had to cover with my hands as I walked back up to the range.

Other than visits, the phone was our most valuable possession – it was oil. It got things moving: if you wanted to get out, you needed the phone to call a lawyer; if you wanted money in your canteen, you needed to call family; if no one knew you were in there, and you couldn't get a phone, you were stuck. There were guys who went for days without using the phone because they were too afraid to touch it, and others who used it all day – talking about nothing. If you controlled the phones, you controlled everything. The phone was a stressor, and a stress reliever. The most violence I've witnessed in jail erupted because of it.

Other than working out and talking on the phone, I tried to get off the range as much as possible to pass the time. Yard was almost nonexistent; although it was our *right* to go out to yard an hour a day, the lazy correctional officers only brought us out about two times a week for twenty or thirty minutes. Instead, I went to all the programs: Alcoholics Anonymous, religious services, and the Community Rap Session, which I didn't understand the purpose of, but it was my favourite program to attend. The first time I went, I was expecting us to be rapping and making music, but it ended up being an organization of people who volunteered to come into the jail and talk to the inmates about different topics, mostly what we wanted to talk about. I think these people just volunteered for the program because they'd never been to jail and they were fascinated with us inmates. Courtney and I had girls that came just to see us; when the guards weren't looking they showed us their tits and let us feel them. Courtney's girl snuck weed in for him, which we later smoked on the range and got high. However, after his release she stopped coming to the program, and my girl was too afraid to smuggle weed in for me, so I also stopped attending the program. I spent that time on the phone instead.

Eventually I was transferred to another range. The pig didn't like my attitude, so he told me to pack my things. He even wrote on my card that my Quarterman status had been permanently revoked. He didn't like that all the men on the range supported me because I stood up for myself, whether it was against another inmate or a guard; he also disliked the freedom and respect I had on 2C South, so he put me on 4C North, the Pen Range. I didn't know much about the Pen Range; I just heard that it was run by a bunch of racist white boys sentenced to life in the penitentiary, and if you made any noise, you'd get dummied.

When I entered the Pen Range it felt as if I'd been transferred to another jail altogether. The range was extremely quiet and the vibe was calm and serious. A few men played cards, others worked out at the back of the range, some guys watched the tube with the volume on low, which could still be heard throughout the place due to how silent the place was. Two inmates paced up and down the range talking to each other for hours as if they were going somewhere important. There was only one other black guy on the range. I didn't experience any racism on the Pen Range, just sheer insane boredom. If you minded your own business and didn't cause any trouble, you were all right. In fact, the Pen Range felt safer than the Jungle Range; howbeit, I preferred the action in the jungle.

On my second day there were a few guys working out at the back of the range. They were using more sophisticated water bags than the ones on 2C South. They had small, medium, and heavy bags with loose handles that made them easier to grip. I wanted to use the water bags, so I asked the biggest guy there, who was obviously the range heavy, if I could join in. I didn't know what to expect or how I would be received, but surprisingly his response was quite welcoming. "Yeah, sure of course. Do you want to do your set next?" he asked, and introduced himself as Murdoc. I jumped right in and started working out with the big boys. Murdoc was a pretty intimidating dude, with his body covered in tattoos and his veins bulging out of his biceps and forearms – he was huge. Apparently Murdoc had served ten years in the penitentiary for previous convictions and was now up against first-degree murder. I didn't know why he was so friendly to me, but it triggered my suspicion. He seemed more interested in socializing with me than with his other workout buddies. Though I appreciated him befriending me, I didn't trust anyone on that range. After the workout I thanked Murdoc and went off to hang out by myself. I had no desire to make quick friendships with pen timers.

I was only on the Pen Range for a week before going to court, and I stuck to myself the entire time, except to work out. Upon my return from court, I asked the guard in A and D if he could put me back on 2C South. He told me that it was overpopulated, and assumed that I wanted to live on a Jungle Range, so he assigned me to 3C North. The truth was, I just wanted to go back to my old range where I had friends and people to relate to. I wasn't interested in going to another Jungle Range where I didn't know anyone. I would've preferred to go back to the Pen Range, especially if I had known how much violence I would encounter on 3C North.

CHAPTER SIXTEEN

VIOLENCE IN THE DON

It didn't take long for me to figure out who the heavy was on 3C North. The entire range was sharing two phones, while the third one sat dormant. No one touched it. I needed to make a phone call, and instead of waiting in line half the day for one of the two phones being shared, I decided to check if the other one was working. It might have been broken for all I knew, and that was why nobody was using it. After I picked up the receiver and pressed zero to make my collect call, I heard an effeminate, but firm voice come from one of the tables nearer to the back of the range.

"Yo, who said you can use that phone? Don't you know that's my phone? You got a f*cking problem?" I looked over my shoulder to find a big black dude walking towards me with no shirt on. He had the figure of Terry Crews and was the same size as me, but an inch shorter and more defined. "What's up, man? You think you can use my phone without asking? What do you think this is, the Holiday Inn?"

The man walked and talked like a homosexual. Apart from his size, I couldn't understand how a guy like that could run a range, especially a jungle range. The cellblock was either full of pussies, or this guy had a reputation that I didn't know about. Regardless, everyone feared Willie. I weighed in on the situation and didn't find that it was to my advantage to fight over a phone at this point. I didn't know who on the range would jump me on his behalf. But at the same time, I wasn't going out with my tail between my legs.

"I'll be off in a bit," I said, in a tone of respect. He walked backed to his table and continued with his game of cards, and I spoke to Bobbie for ten minutes before hanging up.

After a month, I fit right in on 3C North. I used the phones at will, worked out with the big dogs, and occasionally got extra dessert and jug-up, but I still didn't feel safe. During yard, I jogged around the small area to build up my stamina as a survival method for the fights I was destined for. My routine was to work out every day and eat as much food as possible: that was my defense.

Willie and I got along alright. We did pushups, chin-ups, and lifted the water bag together. I didn't really like him, and I didn't care if he liked me. The important thing was that we respected each other. The phone was never an issue for us again. Whenever I wanted to use one of the three phones, I left the receiver upside-down, indicating that it was taken.

After supper lockup one evening, one of the new inmates attempted to use the phone I had reserved. He was a mid-size Jamaican cat with a bad attitude and a scar on one side of his face going from his ear down to his chin, hence the nickname Scarry. He was in on drug and firearm charges. He spoke with a heavy Jamaican accent as if he just got off the boat. Our first interaction was negative, and it only got worse as time went on. He was out on the range during lockup because the guards had just brought him up from A and D and was not yet assigned to a cell. Though he fit the image of a criminal by the way he walked, talked, and fit right in with the rest of the inmates, I saw that he lacked understanding of how things were done on the cellblock. He made friends too easy and rubbed shoulders with the range heavies, as if they would protect him in the time of battle. His ignorance and street tough attitude – as he went around intimidating the weaker with his Jamaican talk, and as if he still had a Glock in his waist – would work against him. His demeanour was that of a street thug, not a prisoner. Jail was a completely different world, and he was going to learn that the hard way – from me.

The cell doors slid open almost simultaneously to his collect call being connected. I exited my cell and walked towards him.

"Yo, I got that phone!" *Was this guy stupid, or was he trying to push his luck?* I couldn't tell, because the receiver was clearly upside down, and everybody knew what that meant.

"You want the phone?" he said, in a politely arrogant way. "Ok, that's all you have to say." He told the person on the other end he would call them back and hung up. He looked at me with a piercing glance as he walked away from the phone. I knew we would never be friends.

Three weeks later, Scarry and I got into an argument. How it started remains unclear, but the emotions and hatred that surged through me after he yelled across the range, "Go suck ya mumma, pussy!" would never leave me, until I personally destroyed him. In the Caribbean culture, those were fighting words, akin to calling a white boy on the Pen Range a "Goof."

I went after him, but my hopes of shattering his jaw were crushed when Willie and a few others stepped in between us.

"No fighting on this range while I'm here," Willie said. "I'm not going on lockdown for you two."

"What do you mean no fighting?" I shot back. "You heard what he said to me."

"We just got off lockdown. Next time they'll lock us down for a week with no visits, showers, yard, or phone calls. That's what I mean, no fighting!"

I walked away frustrated, staring Scarry directly in the eyes, and nodding my head, indicating that his day would come. I went to the back of the range to beat up the punching bag until I broke a sweat, then went into the shower. I spent the rest of the evening watching television but thinking about that bitch who told me to go suck my mother.

A month later, Willie was sent back to the penitentiary. I had yet to see an inmate run a cellblock the way he did, with absolute authority, and no apparent friends. He spoke with a soft tone, even when he raised his voice. He was mellow, but everyone was intimidated by him. I was glad to see Willie go. I didn't hate him, nor was I afraid of him; I was just excited about the shifting of government that was about to occur on 3C North now that big boy Willie was gone. I stepped up and took his place as Quarterman. I never became the range heavy; I shared that responsibility with the other Quartermen. Andrew was a light-skinned Indian Jamaican who stood six feet four inches tall, thick but not muscular or fat, just a natural giant, and he had a loyalty that I admired and respected. Andrew was in his early thirties, and was in on drug-related charges. LeRoy was a short slender Jamaican, around the same age as Andrew; he was up against first-degree murder. I became friends with both Andrew and LeRoy. Charles was also a Quarterman, but he didn't help run the range, he was just in the position because of the amount of time he had been there. When Charles got out, Scarry stepped up and declared himself a Quarterman by picking up a broom and sweeping the floor instead of going to his cell, which meant he would be out of his cell each day with me. As far as I was concerned, the beef between Scarry and me was over, but not forgotten. I was willing to leave it in the past, but he was on thin ice.

It was evident that Scarry wanted to be the heavy on the range. He used an aggressive tone, coarse language, and his harsh *patois* to intimidate the other inmates. We never spoke to each other – until the inevitable.

During lockup, the guards would occasionally leave the phone on for the Quartermen to use. On this particular day, I sat on the steel picnic table, my feet on the bench, and talked to Bobbie. The coinless pay phones were bolted to the corridor bars that separated the range's inside from the outside, where the guards walked around to do their rounds. The three-foot-long metal cord connecting the phone and the receiver made it comfortable to sit on the table and talk. I sat with my elbows buried in my knees leaning forward in a relaxed state as I talked to my girl. Through my peripheral vision, I saw Scarry coming toward me pushing the large wooden janitor broom. He stopped short of the phone cord. I knew he was waiting for me to lift up the cord so he could pass and continue sweeping, but I chose not to move, instead I waited for him to use his manners. It appeared that he had left his manners at home and proceeded to pass, ducking under the phone cord, and then spitefully coming up, causing his back to raise up the cord and receiver. I said nothing to him, but told Bobbie what was going on, and if he did it again, I was going to knock him out. Of course she pleaded with me not to, but who could blame her? She had no idea what was going on in here. On the way back, this time he didn't stop. He ducked under the cord and did the same thing.

I flew to my feet, hovering over him at the edge of the bench, he stood four feet in front of me. "You can't say excuse me." I spoke loud enough to draw the attention of Andrew and LeRoy, who were standing outside of Andrew's cell having a conversation.

"Wuh de bloodclot. Wuh me a say excuse me fuh, yuh nuh see me a sweep de bumbaclot floor? Move an gweh, yuh likkle pussyclot." The fool was speaking all his gibberish while unscrewing the bottom of the broom directly in front of my view. A wise prisoner would have said, it's okay, and then continued to sweep the floor until he was out of sight to prepare his weapon, and return, ready to do damage. Scarry wasn't the sharpest tool in the box. His tough *patois* talk worked at scaring the white boys, but it didn't do anything to me, except irritate me. I dropped from the bench, drilling him in the face with my fist. I was finally able to let loose on this guy. I held him in the headlock while feeding him uppercuts, until I felt a sharp pain, a deep penetrating bite on my lower chest, just under my armpit. I let go of him. My overalls were tied around my waist, providing less padding from his bite. I took off my T-shirt, soaked in blood on the left. Blood poured down my side, causing me to become more enraged. Andrew and LeRoy, who were friends with both of us, stepped in to break up the fight. That was not happening. My only desire was to inflict as much pain on this coward before the guard on duty pressed the blue button. The only problem was this big-ass giant in the way.

"Junior, just cool, mon," Andrew said, towering in front of me, as Scarry hid behind him.

"Look at my chest, bleeding from this dog's bite, and you're telling me to *just cool*? You better move out of my way or you and me are going to have a beef." I liked Andrew, but I wasn't going to let him ruin my chance at feeding Scarry what he deserved.

Andrew saw the seriousness in my eyes and the determination in my voice, and without a second thought, he threw up his hands and stepped aside. "All right, go ahead."

Never in my life had revenge tasted so sweet. I didn't waste a second. I rushed him like a tsunami, clobbering him with both fists, swinging as hard and fast as I could move. He tried to escape the blows but found himself up against the bars. I grasped his head with both hands and repeatedly slammed it against the bars next to where the phone was bolted. Bobbie could hear all the commotion from the other end of the receiver. She heard him scream out to Andrew for help.

"Andrew, get him off me… Andrew, get him off me… Andrew… Andrew… Andrew." His calls went unanswered; Andrew knew the rules.

All the inmates on the range were in their cells, cheering and laughing as I beat the living snot out of this big mouth punk. It ended up that his bark and bite were nowhere near his brawling skill set. I continued pouncing on him while blood flowed down from my chest. As expected, the guards came bursting onto the range in large numbers. I stopped the beating before they got close enough to tackle me to the ground, and walked toward them, already knowing where they were going to take me.

Before going to segregation, they brought me to Medical. I was placed in a small cell to wait for the doctor to patch me up and give me a tetanus shot. While I sat on the bench waiting, I saw three guards escorting Scarry, one was pushing him in a wheelchair, head down, too weak to lift it up, body slightly palpitating. The guard in front was getting ready to put his key in the slot to put Scarry in the same cage as me. I got excited. A few more seconds with this guy would have been the icing on the cake, or the nail in the coffin. The CO sitting at the desk monitoring me shouted out for him not to put him in there, that's the guy he was fighting with. They wheeled him passed the cage and directly in to see the doctor. It was clear that his medical condition was more urgent than mine.

I shouted out through the bars and did the next best thing, humiliated him. "What's up now, bitch? You got no more mouth, pussy? Where's your big talk now, bwoy?"

The first thing they did was strip search me when I got to the hole, then left me bare naked in the empty cell for hours before returning my clothes. The cell was about the size of a bathroom. With the exception of two fifteen-minute showers, I was locked up 24 hours a day, without a mattress, from 7:00 a.m. till 8:30 p.m. This was to ensure that I didn't sleep my days away; and books, paper, and writing material were not luxuries I was permitted. The purpose of segregation was to have the prisoner suffer from sheer boredom, loneliness, and depression. I could not image anyone having to spend months, or even years in a place like that. I spent five days in the hole and returned to 3C North. I never saw Scarry again.

Returning to general population was almost like stepping into freedom. It was a breath of fresh air to be out of that nine-by-four-foot box and back on the range, where I could socialize with other human beings, work out, shower, write letters, talk on the phone, and see my Hungarian beauty in the visiting room again. There didn't seem to be much to do in jail until I spent some time in the hole.

It wasn't long before I was involved in another altercation. As usual, it began with an exchange of words, leading up to an argument, and of course resulting in a fight. I had a love/hate relationship with Jamaicans. I grew up with them. I was used to their loud mouths and aggressiveness. Their intimidating demeanour was useful if they were on my team and fought alongside me, but I didn't tolerate them disrespecting or threatening me. I didn't have the energy to argue with them. It always ended in violence, and I was usually the one to strike first, while they were still running off their mouth.

Stretch had nothing to lose. He was in on a slew of drug and gun charges, and once he served his prison time, he would be back on a one-way ticket to the sunny island, where the national motto is "Out of Many One People," eating ackee and saltfish while sipping on a Red Stripe along the beach – compliments of the Government of Canada. With the amount of enemies Stretch made within such a short period of time, I couldn't see him enjoying that type of lifestyle once he got deported. A more accurate depiction of his future would be him sitting in a Jamaican prison on a life sentence or lying in the street dead. Stretch was a violent man.

Stretch and I ended up in a scuffle at the back of the range just after lunch. The old petite Caucasian CO on duty turned a blind eye, pretending to read her newspaper at the desk as if nothing was happening. She didn't care if we fought, if we killed each other, just as long as she collected her paycheque without doing any paperwork. In due honesty, this guard was nice to us inmates, and I didn't know if she let us fight because she got a thrill out of it, or because she didn't want to push the code one button and have us sent to seg. Nonetheless, the fight had to be stopped because it was time for afternoon lockup. She knew that her partner would be coming to assist in the lockup soon, and she made her way along the outer corridor to the back of the range to tell us that it was time to knock it off. None of us wanted to go to the hole; we stopped the fight. Well, I stopped the fight. I had him in a headlock on the ground. After I released my grip, we both got up; he went to his cell, and I helped the other Quartermen with clean up.

Stretch was much taller than me, with a long reach. He wasn't thick with muscles, but he wasn't skin and bones. I believe he was humiliated because I beat him in the fight. I didn't whip his ass like Scarry, but I did come out as the visible winner. For this, he wanted to go another round.

After we cleaned the range, all the Quartermen piled into LeRoy's cell for a brief meeting. LeRoy told me that he wanted us to jump Stretch and beat him down until he cracked (asked the CO to let him leave the range). However, he misinterpreted my response. I should have been clearer in my words, and I may have avoided the near deadly plan of attack that Stretch had up his sleeve for me. If I was a better communicator, I would have told him, "Usually when I get into a fight in jail, I don't expect anybody to jump in, but I do accept and appreciate your offer." I left out the latter, leaving them to think that I wanted a one-on-one with Stretch. What I really meant by the first part of my statement was that I didn't expect that kind of loyalty from other inmates who I didn't know from the streets to help me in a fight. After the meeting we filtered out of the cell and went about to do our own thing.

I sat at the picnic bench reading Proverbs from my little Gideon Bible as I waited for the phone to be turned on. Shortly after all the cell doors slid open, when the female guard's partner left the control booth and went to another cellblock, I heard the familiar voice of Stretch coming from the other side of the picnic table.

"All those push-ups you do every day and that's all you got," he taunted, walking toward the back of the range. I looked over at him. In my naiveté I had thought the fight was over. All I wanted to do was talk to my girlfriend in peace. But this was jail, where peace was promised to no one, but violence was promised to everyone. He nodded his head at me. "Let's finish this."

I got up and walked to the back of the range. A small circle began to form with the first row of spectators. Others stood away and watched from a distance. But all forty-plus men's eyes were focused toward where the action was to take place. Stretch and I faced each other from six feet away. Out of his pocket he pulled out a sock with a hard object inside. *Shit, I should have spoke up at the meeting. I needed the help now.* I had to think quick and come up with a way to attack him without getting clobbered with whatever he had in that sock. It looked heavy and hard, all he needed to do was connect once, and I was out. I noticed that he was holding the top of the sock, and leaving a lot of leeway, with the object dangling at the bottom. It gave for an extended swing but left him with a limited number of times he would be able to hit me if he didn't knock me out with the first blow. Had he rolled the sock completely around his hand, with the object closer to his fist, he would have been able to make contact multiple times. But he knew I was stronger than him and wanted to keep me at bay. I wasn't just strong; I was a thinker; and my thinking was in survival mode.

I faked a lunge at him, and as I drew back to avoid the blow, I heard the *wiz* of the object swing in the air, just inches past my face. His one swing missed. I charged at him, driving my shoulder through his stomach, sending him four feet back, crashing into the cell bars with his back. It made a *thunderous* bang. I gripped the bars as tightly as I could, trapping him between my biceps and forearms, and continually slammed his back against the bars with all my might. My intention was to damage his spine. The little old CO sitting at the desk couldn't ignore the deafening sound of the rattling bars every time his back hit. The noise could even be heard on the other cellblocks. She was forced to press the blue button. The guards swarmed in like bees, and the fight was over. I wasn't sure if he still had the sock at the end, or if he had dropped it, but I didn't get hit once. I spent eight days in the hole for protecting myself.

That wasn't the last time I would be seeing Stretch.

CHAPTER SEVENTEEN
UNITED WE STOOD

Upon my release from the hole, the cops put me back on 2C South. It was no surprise that Courtney had returned. He was a crackhead on the outside and couldn't kick the habit. He was visibly thinner than when he had left the Don not even two months earlier. He had lost a lot of size, but he still had his definition – and nasty attitude. I heard that on the first day Courtney arrived, he started yelling at everyone, as he vigorously cleaned the bathrooms and the range, calling them a bunch of filthy motherf*ckers during the entire time he cleaned. His way of declaring himself Quarterman was through fear. I always wondered how Courtney would have fared had he been put on another Jungle Range, or the Pen Range. Would he still have his bad attitude, or would he be a little humbler?

Raheem walked onto the cellblock a couple of weeks after me. It meant a lot to see a friendly face, one I had known since childhood. Raheem and I became cell partners. It was like sharing a cell with a brother. We were never short of things to talk about, or things to do. We played cards and made-up games. In elementary school we always competed for first place in everything, which caused a lot of fights. We got into several physical altercations growing up because neither one of us knew how to back down. Raheem was in for attempted murder and numerous gun charges. Ever since our teens and into early adulthood, I've always known him to have a gun. He told me the story in detail of how he landed in the Don.

Raheem tried to kill a guy known as Painter, who was also from Regent Park. Painter had a reputation in the hood for robbing other cats for drugs and cash. When Painter approached Raheem and Kris for an ounce of crack, they knew what he was up to.

"I don't have it bro," Kris said.

"What do you have on you then?" asked Painter.

"I ain't got shit, man."

"You sure about that? Let me check," Painter said, stepping closer and becoming more hostile. He grabbed Kris by the collar and slammed him up against the brick wall, clicking open a switch blade.

"Yo, Painter, what the f*ck you doing?" Raheem shouted. "Calm down!"

Kris was trying to resist, shoving back against Painter. Raheem was yelling for him to stop, while looking on the ground for a weapon. The closest thing Raheem could grab was a broken mop lying a few feet away, but before he could reach for it, Painter had already stabbed Kris in the stomach and began twisting the knife inside of him, like a throttle on a motorcycle. Raheem took the mop stick and beat Painter over the head several times, but the blows didn't faze him. He continued savagely twisting the knife as deep as he could in his belly, as Kris screamed for his life in excruciating pain. Realizing that the blows were doing nothing, Raheem pulled Painter away and threw him to the ground. Painter got up and ran away between the low-rise buildings in North Regent, leaving Kris on the ground bleeding. Raheem picked up his cell phone, which fell to the ground because of the scuffle, and called 911. A minute later, Painter returned with the knife in his hand, ready to finish the job. Raheem stood between them with the mop stick, ready to protect his friend at the cost of his own life. It didn't take long for the police and paramedics to arrive. The sirens scared off Painter, who disappeared into the projects. Kris was taken to the hospital. He received twenty-one stitches and was released the next day.

A few days later, Raheem and Kris set out in search for Painter. Raheem strapped with a .32 calibre, Kris with a 9 mm: both fully loaded. They knew they would eventually catch up with him, it was just a matter of time, and a bit of patience. There was nowhere for Painter to go – that was his hood – the only place he knew. They searched every nook and cranny in the projects, from the north to the south, until they found him. It was three o'clock in the morning when they spotted Painter near the high-rise buildings at Oak Street and River. They recognized him in his black hooded windbreaker and baggy blue jeans walking in front of one of the buildings. Both Raheem and Kris pulled out their guns and crept up towards him, ready to put an end to his existence. Painter noticed the two men out of the corner of his eye. They were approaching hastily. He wasted no time and bolted in the opposite direction. Raheem pursued, emptying his entire clip, striking Painter twice in the back. Kris attempted to chase him down as well, but his injury prevented him from doing so. He came to a halt, took aim, and blasted in the direction of Painter, hitting him with one bullet. Painter collapsed to the ground, three bullets in his back. One hit him in the spine, paralyzing him from the waist down – a *life* sentence in a wheelchair for attempting to take *Kris's*. Thinking Painter was dead, both Raheem and Kris took off in different directions.

A resident from the community heard the gunshots and called 911. The police, ambulance, and firetrucks all arrived on the scene almost simultaneously, to find Painter lying on the pavement in a pool of blood. He was rushed to St. Michael's hospital in downtown Toronto. There were no witnesses for the police to question. They had to wait until Painter was conscious and able to talk before getting any leads. The following afternoon, Painter pointed them out from a police photo lineup. Raheem was arrested a week later, booked, then brought to the Toronto Don Jail, directly across the bridge from where the shooting occurred.

There were more conflicts and altercations on 2C South than I was able to keep up with. It was nothing like my first rodeo. Allen was no longer there. Although Courtney was the only permanent Quarterman, while about five of us rotated, the inmates didn't fear him as they once had. There was no leadership. The tough guys fought for power, as the weak sat back hoping that nobody would bother them, and the Vietnamese just minded their business as they usually did. There were arguments and feuds over the phone, food distribution, and who stayed out of their cell during lockup. Although most men on the range were afraid of Courtney, he was unable to gain control. There were too many *alphas* that wanted to do their own thing and would have fought Courtney at the drop of a dime if it came down to it, including me and Raheem.

Raheem and I controlled the middle phone, but sometimes we used two of them if we needed to make calls at the same time. We shared ours generously to whoever needed it, especially to the weaker vessels, who were too afraid to ask for a call. The other phones were reserved by putting the receiver upside down, but not everyone adhered to that. If you had the courage to put a receiver upside down, you'd better have the balls to fight for it if another guy picked it up.

The Jungle Range had become a zoo, filled with untamed prisoners. Inmates were transferring on and off the range because they couldn't handle the constant noise and fighting. It was difficult for new inmates to use the phone, get their jug-up, and sometimes even a dessert at dinner. They were told what to do, where to sit, when to shower. It was a stressful environment for them, and when they returned from a court appearance, they always requested to be placed on a different range. So, in order to populate 2C South with fewer requests for transfers, they began to fill it with only knuckleheads, bad boys, violent offenders, and white inmates who mouthed off to the guards. The COs would throw them on the Jungle Range of Jungle Ranges to see if they were as tough as they talked – they never were. For me, having Raheem there, along with the entertaining chaos, time went by fast. The only things that got to me were the frequent lockdowns for days at a time, and the noise when I was on the phone.

A new nineteen-year-old white boy had entered the range and was assigned to the cell next to Raheem and me. It was his first time in jail. He was small, defenseless, and timid. His cell partner was a shady Portuguese dude named Francisco. On his first night, Raheem and I heard sounds coming out from their cell. Muffled cries and low talking. It sounded like there was bullying going on, but that was a normal thing in those places; we didn't think much of it. During breakfast, Courtney thought it was odd that the new kid was taking a shower instead of eating. He went over to the bathroom to tell him to get his food, when he noticed the boy's hands over his eyes, sobbing like a hurt child. There was mixed blood and water running down his leg from his anus. Courtney asked him what happened. The kid told him that if he told anyone, Francisco would kill him. Courtney assured him that he didn't have to worry, he ran *shit* up on this range. Courtney came to Raheem and me and told us that Francisco had been raping the new boy all night. It didn't take long for us to come up with an idea of what we were going to do to this faggot rapist. After breakfast, during cleanup, we paid Francisco a visit in his cell. Raheem kept six outside of the opened bars while Courtney and I stomped the living shit out of him right in front of the boy. Francisco cracked from 2C South and went straight to PC. The kid got out the next day – scarred for life.

Buddha entered 2C South in a way that caught my attention. He didn't act like a tough guy, but it was clear that he was. I was talking on the phone when he arrived for the first time. Our eyes locked for a few seconds. I knew that he would be a threat to my authority on the range. He had swag, he was physically fit, and he didn't show any sign of fear. He had a boxer's physique and was in his mid-twenties, with a serious demeanour: if he didn't know you, he didn't smile at you. Everything about him said *fighter*. Buddha was a solid dude, a calm soldier, and appeared to be a fierce contender. But I wasn't going to lose the range to him. It didn't come across as if he wanted to run the cellblock, but at the same time, there was no way anyone was going to violate his rights or tell him what to do. Buddha did his own thing, regardless of who ran the range.

The day Buddha arrived, he almost got jumped. I had just finished mopping the floor and was sitting on the table watching a show. Buddha picked up the phone that Raheem had on reserve. He didn't notice the receiver was upside down when he made his call, or maybe he didn't care. There was only ten minutes left before everyone got out from lockup. Raheem said to Buddha through the bars, "I got that phone when I get out, so don't get too comfortable."

"You talking to me?" Buddha replied, irked by Raheem's tone.

"You're the only one on the phone."

"I'll be off soon. If that ain't good enough, you can take it from me."

I kept quiet and observed their interaction. Buddha occasionally looked over at me, catching me size him up. He could tell that Raheem and I were homeboys, but he still looked ready for whatever was about to happen. The cell doors cracked opened. Raheem came out and passed Buddha, walking to the back of the range. Both their eyes locked to each other's. "You got five minutes."

We'd just come out from a lockdown. I didn't want to see these guys fight, but I was backing Raheem regardless. I met Raheem at the back of the range.

"Don't bother with this one. Just go use the middle phone," I suggested. He was cool with that, and that was that. However, if anything kicked off, it wouldn't have been a good day for Buddha.

In less than a week, Raheem, Buddha and I became the best of friends. We were the fearless trio to be reckoned with.

The range was on lockdown when three new inmates entered. The other ranges must have been overpopulated, because our range was already at capacity, with three men in some cells, leaving one to sleep on a thin mattress on the floor with the mice and cockroaches. I stood by the bars, arms halfway out of the cell, resting on the crossbar, waiting to see who was coming into the cellblock. Raheem lay up on his bunk reading a magazine, uninterested in the new arrivals. The first guy came in hugging his pillowcase stuffed with his belongings close to his chest. If there was a portrait of being vulnerable prey, this guy fit the picture. A slender white boy. Young.

It appeared to be his first time in jail. He stared straight down the tier to avoid eye contact with the other inmates watching him as he walked by each cell. Sometimes we joked around if a newbie appeared scared. *"This one's mine,"* an inmate would yell out. *"No, he's mine,"* another would say. *"Hey kid, who you want, him or me?"* The new cat would tremble with fear, not knowing that it was only a prank. When everyone was let out of their cells, the guys joking with the newbie didn't bother him, much less talk to him, the joke was over.

The second inmate was an overweight dark-skinned boy who spoke with a Guyanese accent. He was more relaxed and accepting of his current situation than the white boy walking ahead of him.

I couldn't believe my eyes when I saw the third one. "Yo Raheem, look who's coming on the range."

Raheem jumped off his bunk and rushed over to the bars to see who I was talking about. "Who the f*ck's that? I don't know him."

"That's the pussy that I told you about from 3C North that attacked me with the steel valve in the sock."

Stretch walked past our cell, nodded his head at me, and smiled as if we were friends – the nod I returned indicated the opposite.

Stretch was transferred to 2C South after an altercation with another inmate, where he was sent after the fight we had. I wouldn't be surprised if he was the most hated inmate in the entire Don Jail. I despised his very presence. But I had no plans for jumping him, although I had ample support if I wanted to. It wouldn't have taken much for me to change my plans, however. To beat down a scumbag like Stretch was like a soul cleansing. I didn't know a single person who liked this guy. I've always been the type of person to let disputes go and move forward. I was willing to do the same for Stretch. I didn't trust him, and I didn't mind beating his ass, but it wasn't going to be over a beef from another range. I was ready to go after him for the smallest slight, whether it was directed at me or anyone else on my team.

It only took a week for the volcano to erupt. Raheem and Stretch got into a heated argument over whose turn it was to use the phone. I got involved and told Stretch that he had to leave the range. Stretch refused to crack, and just before we were all about to kick off, the guards came around and shouted lockup. Everyone went to their cells except Courtney and three others who helped with cleanup. During the afternoon lockup Courtney was pretending to play mediator between Stretch and Raheem and me, knowing that we were going to rush him once the cells cracked open and the guards left the control booth. Courtney went back and forth from Stretch's cell to ours, telling everybody that there wasn't going to be any fighting. Raheem told Courtney that Stretch was going to have to leave the range, because there was a possibility that he would attack one of us while the other was at a visit. Courtney refused to support the idea but told us that he wouldn't let that happen. I didn't trust anything that came out of his two-faced mouth. Raheem and I assured him that it was going down, regardless. When we got out of our cells, half the men made their way to the back of the range. Everyone knew what was going to take place. Courtney, acting like the commentator, told Stretch and Raheem, loud enough for everyone to hear, "This is going to be a clean, one-on-one fight. No weapons."

Raheem and Stretch squared off, ready for battle. I was standing directly behind Raheem. Courtney was behind Stretch, holding a broom. Behind Stretch's back, he twisted off the bottom and signaled to me before sliding it on the floor, past the two contenders, and into my hand. Before I even stood to my feet after picking up the weapon, Raheem had already pulled the sock with the bar of soap from out of his pocket and struck Stretch across the left side of his head. He hit him at least twice before they both landed on top of the steel table. Raheem had Stretch in a headlock, feeding him with punches, as the *worm* tried to squirm his way out. I ran around Raheem and began *batting* Stretch's head with the thick piece of wood. He kept twisting and turning, making it difficult to avoid hitting Raheem. I couldn't just go crazy on him like I wanted. I had to take precise and accurate aim each time I swung. I got him good a few times.

The fight lasted for a good three minutes. It would have gone on longer, but the inmates keeping watch at the front of the cellblock shouted, "six up!" When we heard the warning we stopped immediately, but it wasn't soon enough. The guards knew what was up and came around with urgency, busting me red-handed with the detached broom still in my hand and Raheem and Stretched scuffed up, evident that they too were involved. We were all sent to the hole. I spent two weeks, which felt like two years. Raheem was only in the hole for a few days, and I don't know what came of Stretch.

Michael Lomer came to see me while I was in segregation. We met in a small, well-lit room with a large window in the centre of the door, enabling the guards to see through. In the room was a wooden table with four iron legs and two black chairs on either end. Mr. Lomer wanted to go over my version of events one more time before the preliminary hearing, which was scheduled to begin the following week. He brought me the disclosure with all of the evidence against me. A stack of legal sized papers, up to four inches high, and filled with false accusations. Our meeting lasted about an hour. Afterwards I was led back to the hole. The guard told me to leave my paperwork outside of the door. I wasn't permitted to have anything. I took off my shoes, placed my disclosure neatly next to them, and stepped into the box.

When I was released from the hole, my paperwork was gone. Only God knew why one of those pigs would have taken my disclosure.

The preliminary hearing was scheduled for four days, but it stretched out to a span of over three months, continually being adjourned for several weeks at a time. I spent the first four days on the Court Range. I submitted a request for a clothing change, and it was granted. Bobbie had bought me a medium dark green suit, a grey shirt, and a tie. It was the first suit I had ever owned, and I felt pretty damn fly when I put it on for the first time. The only shoes I had to wear with it were a semi-dressy pair of yellow and black leather shoes that I bought on Eglinton Avenue with the money I made selling drugs. I wasn't permitted to wear the tie because it could be used as a weapon – or a rope to commit suicide.

The bullpen at Old City Hall was packed with inmates from all over the city as usual. But the feeling for me was not the same. I wasn't the lonely newcomer, not knowing what to expect, or where my fate lay. I knew people in the bullpen, and I had respect, from both inmates and the court officers. I also felt as if I were at the end of the road with all this; at least I was hoping.

"Tull, you're up for court." My name was one of the first to be called. I was shackled and handcuffed behind my back. Two officers escorted me to the courtroom, one on either side, holding my arms as we walked through the public corridor. Everyone I walked past made sure to get a glimpse of the guy wearing all the iron. I didn't feel humiliated nor embarrassed; I had no reason to be.

I was relieved to see that the judge was a black man. Not that he would show me favouritism, but I felt that he would be fair and impartial in his ruling. I sat in the prisoner box and waited for the first witness to approach the witness box with a mouth full of lies. My lawyer submitted a motion to have all witnesses wait outside of the courtroom until their names were called. This prevented them from hearing each other's fictitious testimonies of the events of May 24, 1993. But the cops were permitted to stay and listen to everything. All the victim's friends were asked the same question after they stated their names for the record. "Do you see the man who stabbed Mathew Smith in this courtroom today?"

All their answers were the same: "Yes, over there," as they pointed their finger at me.

The first witness testified that during the altercation, I walked over to the bushes, approximately fifty feet away, came back with a knife, and stabbed Mathew in the back. The second said that I took a knife out of my sock, walked up to Mathew, and stabbed him in the back. The Crown Attorney and detectives were looking very stupid at this point. The crooked detectives had to do some damage control. As the second witness walked out of the courtroom, one of the pigs left as well, returning a few minutes later with the third witness. The last of the Crown's key witnesses was the most articulate of them all. After being coached by the corrupt detective, the witness was able to piece the blunder together and match the story up. He said that I went to the bushes to retrieve the knife. Then I put it in my sock and walked over to Mathew. When I got closer, I pulled it out of my sock and put it in my pocket to conceal it until I was close enough to stab Mathew in the back. His testimony couldn't have sounded more scripted. It was as if he was reading from a screenplay. I was just hoping that the judge saw the same thing as me.

After the prosecution called their witnesses, Mr. Lomer called up a random witness the cops had failed to include in their investigation. She'd filed a police report the day after the murder. She told the cops that while she was riding the streetcar home that night, a man with his friends came on and boasted about stabbing someone. When she saw the article in the newspaper the following day about a young man getting stabbed to death at Ontario Place, she connected the two and felt compelled to notify the cops. She identified Greg in a police photo lineup as the one bragging about the murder. The court could not take this witness's testimony as facts because it was considered hearsay; it did however take the heat off me.

It wasn't a coincidence that Greg boasted about killing someone on the way to the event, then bragged about stabbing someone afterwards. That night, he was itching to murder someone – and he did. Court was adjourned until December, which meant another two months in jail while they waited to see if they had enough evidence to bring the case to trial. If we went to trial, I'd be in the Don Jail for at least another year and a half, waiting to prove my innocence. How many more fights would there be? How much more violence would I witness? How much more time would I spend in the hole? Wasn't it obvious that it wasn't me who committed this crime?

After the fourth day of the preliminary hearings, I was drained from all the back and forth in the paddy wagon and tired of the bland cheese sandwiches they served us for lunch in the bullpen. I just wanted to get back to 2C South, talk with the guys, and use the phone.

I guess everyone in central Toronto decided to commit their crimes all at the same time because the Don was completely full; in fact most of the ranges were overpopulated. They assigned me to 2A North, a white range with only one other black guy. Diego Serrano, a well-known Italian gangster from the Sicilian Mafia, was the range heavy. He was the leader of Canada's largest cocaine smuggling ring, and he was charged with conspiracy to import and traffic cocaine, as well as money laundering, for which he was sentenced to ten years in prison. Diego wasn't a big guy, but he had power, and he was backed by the Camaro Brothers, career criminals from a Portuguese gang in Toronto's West End who arrived later and also tried to run 2A North. All three men, including a few other pen timers worked together to maintain order on the cellblock. The range was quiet and clean, almost peaceful – as long as everyone followed their rules. At dinner and lunch time, a loaf of bread was placed on each table, and each inmate knew to take only two slices, something that could never be done on the Jungle Ranges. On 2C South, men would fight like wild lions and blood would be shed if the bread wasn't distributed by a Quarterman. During the day, at least one or two of the three phones were available; at times, all three had the receiver on the hook, but the one at the far end of the range was not to be used by anyone except the heavies who ran everything. Nobody argued over dominos or cards. 2A North was the most organized and calm range I had ever been on in any jail – until Raheem and Buddha arrived.

After being separated from my homeboys for a few weeks I sent word, through another inmate who was going to court, to tell Raheem and Buddha that I had been transferred to 2A North. The next day while I was doing pushups at the back, I saw a shorter muscular dude enter the range. It was Buddha. Excited to see him, I shouted across the range. "Buddha! What up, bwoy?" He walked to the back where I was, shook my hand,

and told me that he just got back from court, and Raheem got my message and was trying to transfer. He jumped in and we did a few hundred push-ups and spent some time punching the heavy bag. Working out with Buddha was always physically rewarding. He was a natural street fighter and a trained boxer, and he always pushed me to work out harder. After dinner Buddha moved into my cell and took the top bunk. A couple days later in came Raheem. The guards couldn't honour his request for a transfer because the jail was full, so when he returned from court he lied to the CO and told him that his original range was 2A North. The guard didn't check his sheet, he just brought him up. The same week, Cautious, who I knew from Court Range, and a few other black guys came on the range.

With more blacks on 2A North, the range got racially divided. The whites didn't talk to the blacks and vice versa, unless it was an argument over the phone, extra food, or who stayed out of their cell for cleanup. This was the first time I had experienced such racial tension. It was clear that they didn't want us there, and it was obvious that we didn't care.

The three phones suddenly became more frequently occupied. Raheem, Buddha and I, along with all the other black guys, shared the phone closest to the gate at the front of the range. The other two were controlled by Diego, the Camaro Brothers, and their pen timer buddies. However, they did allow anyone to make a limited call from the middle phone – if they asked. But the last phone nearest to the back, that was absolutely off limits; even if they weren't using it, no one could touch it, especially the blacks, or the white boys on the bottom of the social totem pole.

Tensions over power began mounting between the blacks and the whites. It started with the bread. We didn't like that we were getting overlooked when it came to extra slices. We took a whole loaf for our table and distributed it to our guys accordingly. After a few days the heavies got used to it. They didn't see it worth having a rumble over a loaf of bread. After all, they still had more than their fair share, they just had to be less generous to the other white boys who were not in their direct circle. It was their phone that they were not ready or willing to part with. It came to the point that we were running the first phone and sharing the middle phone with the rest of the range, but with the last phone sitting dormant for hours at a time, it didn't sit right with us. We didn't come from a background where we had to ask white boys to use the phone. Each day when the cell doors cracked open, the tension between the whites and blacks built higher and higher as the hours past. Raheem, Buddha, and I were used to running things on 2C South, and now we were subject to other men's rules and authority – we didn't accept it, only tolerated it – but the day came when the levee burst.

Things finally spilled over one day when Raheem asked me for a phone call. "Hey June, are you going to be long?" He paused for a second, looked at the phone at the back of the range with the receiver on the hook. "Why the f*ck am I asking you for this phone when no one's using that one?" And went directly for it.

Oh shit, I thought, *things are about to kick off.* I watched Raheem pick up the phone and press zero to make his collect call. My heart was beating with adrenaline, anticipating what was about to happen on 2A North right about now. A shout came from the back of the range.

"What the f*ck are you doing n*gger?" It was Joey, the younger of the Camaro Brothers. Reno, Joey's brother, Diego, and another dorky white dude walked up to Raheem. By the looks of it they were expecting him to cower, hang up, and walk away, while we all stood by and watched. But Buddha, Cautious, and I walked up and stood beside Raheem.

"Stay on the phone, Raheem. That's our phone now," I said, in a provoking tone, while looking at the four white boys in front of us, daring any one of them to take it.

The entire cellblock stood in silence. The rest of the black guys came and stood by our side, except the first one who was here when I arrived on the range. He always appeared scared of Diego and the Camaro Brothers. But we weren't. The playing ground was now fair, and we had just as much manpower as them. Out of nine black guys on the range, we were eight strong, and five of us were hardened street and jail soldiers: there would be no backing down. We were prepared to take on all eleven of them to end our oppression and take control of the cellblock. I could sense Joey's fear. He didn't want a full all-out rumble. He took note of our unity as we stood side by side and thought it would be safer to fight Raheem one-on-one instead of getting his head stomped in by all of us. He suggested that he and Raheem duke it out at the back of the range to avoid a lockdown. As much as Buddha and I were itching to fight too, we accepted, and all headed to the back of the range. The whites stood militantly, shoulder to shoulder on one side of the contenders, as we did on the other. Everyone was prepared in case anyone jumped in. Both men danced around, throwing jabs as they circled each other. A few kicks were thrown as well. Raheem connected with a hook to Joey's jaw. He landed on the ground. Raheem kicked him in the face. Blood flew out of his mouth and onto the shoes and pant leg of Menace, standing on the side of the whites. Reno was just a few feet in front of me, his face tempting my fist to start a rumble, but I contained myself. His brother was already getting the shit beat out of him, and there was nothing Reno could do. The brawl didn't last long. After the vicious kick, Joey was out of commission. Raheem sat on his chest and put three more imprints of his fist in his face.

"You want more of this n*gger, bitch?" Raheem said, looking down at his battered face.

"I'm done, man. I'm done," Joey whimpered.

Raheem had settled the battle for us once and for all. Things were much different on 2A North after. We now controlled two phones, everyone else shared one. There were two black Quartermen and two white. We were the ones who decided how much bread each table got, and who got extra dessert. We still gave the Italian mobster and the Portuguese gangsters their due respect, but the balance of power had drastically shifted.

There were other problems in the jail that we inmates had to deal with. There were guards that just didn't think they earned their day's wage unless they made our lives hard. There was one black CO who always walked around with a chip on his shoulder. I was working out by myself one day at the back of the range, doing pushups and chin-ups with my shirt off. I didn't know why he felt the need to make a comment to me.

"Biggin up for the pen, Tull?" he said in a stern tone, assuming that's were my murder charge was going to land me.

"I'm not going to the pen." I replied, looking him dead in the eye on the other side of the bars without a sound of doubt in my voice. My answer caught him off guard.

"Well… I don't want you to go to the pen." He said in a more empathetic intonation.

Another guard thought it would be fun to torture us with scolding hot water for the day. He turned on only the hot pipe for the showers and left it exceedingly hot to the point that it was impossible to stand under the shower without having our skin burned.

I'd had enough of this life; there was no getting used to jail for me.

CHAPTER EIGHTEEN

THE FINAL COURT APPEARANCE

It was now December, and time for me to return for the last scheduled court appearance of my preliminary hearing. The judge was to decide whether the Crown Attorney had enough evidence to bring the case to trial. My lawyer and the Crown made a few more closing remarks in front of the judge. I sat in the prisoner box, and listened in silence. It was nearly four o'clock. There wasn't much time left before court adjourned for the day. I knew nothing was done quickly in court, and they weren't going to rush this through. It was the judge's turn to speak. He spoke for not more than ten minutes before concluding that he would need more time to review all the evidence to make the right decision. I was told by other inmates that at a preliminary hearing, if one person points the finger at you, regardless of how shady their testimony was, the case would go to trial. I had no doubt that I would beat the charge; my worry was spending another year and a half, at risk, in the Toronto Don Jail. I knew of a few men who went into jail on a small charge but picked up serious charges while in, getting over ten-year sentences. I had about forty days to maneuver through the system and get out – unscathed. The judge adjourned the matter to the following year: January 27, 1994.

When the judge exited the courtroom, one of the two court officers told me to stand up and put my hands behind my back. He placed the handcuffs firmly on my wrists and prepared to escort me back to the cage underneath the courthouse. Other than the two court officers, the only people in the courtroom were Mr. Lomer, the Crown Attorney, and the two corrupt detectives who had arrested me at Toys 'R' Us. I was saddened that I would have to spend Christmas and New Year's in jail. What made my pain worse was hearing the cops, the Crown, and my lawyer discussing their plans for the holidays while I stood there handcuffed and shackled. They were all chatting about how they were going to spend Christmas with their families. I didn't like seeing Mr. Lomer talking to them as if they were all buddies. They were the enemy. He wasn't evil like them, but at the end of the day, he was a lawyer, a part of the judicial system. As the court officer opened the box to let me out, I noticed the same detective who had squeezed the back of my neck during my arrest look over at me. His eyes spoke a thousand words. They said he knew I was innocent, but there was no turning back, the damage had already been done. His gaze dropped to the table. He knew he had done the wrong thing. He reorganized his papers and slid them into his leather document bag. He'd have to live with the guilt of his lies and corruption – his sin that would send me back to that cold and lonely place, while he went to celebrate Christmas with his loved ones. How many other innocent men and women were sitting in prison because of him?

On January 27 I arrived at Old City Hall chained up with two other inmates. We arrived early as usual, around eight in the morning. I waited in the musty bullpen with more than twenty inmates for over eight hours. My name was called just after four in the afternoon. We did the typical routine, handcuffed, shackled, and led through the corridor by two guards, like sheep to the slaughter. But in my heart, I knew that there would be no slaughtering taking place. I had the faith that I was being led to freedom. With each step I took, a sense of calm filled my heart. God was not going to permit them to keep me another day in jail for this crime: 226 days was enough.

In the prisoner box with me was a man in his mid-fifties, a slender Rastaman with locks running down his back. He listened attentively as the judge spoke for almost an hour. My focus was not on what the judge was saying. All my attention was on what I was reading from the little Gideon Bible that I was able to smuggle out of the jail. Richie gave me four Psalms to read three times a day. He told me that he went to visit a priest on my behalf, and the priest said that I must read Psalms 20, 26, 35, and 142. He said they would ward off evil people and fight against those that fought against me.

Psalm 20
May the Lord answer you in the day of trouble!
May the name of the God of Jacob set you securely on high!
May He send you help from the sanctuary and support you from Zion!
May He grant you your heart's desire and fulfill all your purpose!

We will sing for joy over your victory. May the Lord fulfill all your petitions.
I know that the Lord saves His anointed.
He will answer him from His holy heaven with the saving strength of His right hand.
Some boast in chariots and some in horses, But we will boast in the name of the Lord, Our God.
They have bowed down and fallen, But we have risen and stood upright.
Save, O Lord; May the King answer us in the day we call.

Psalm 26
Vindicate me, O Lord, For I have walked in my integrity,
And I have trusted in the Lord without wavering.
Do not take my soul away along with sinners, Nor my life with men of bloodshed,
In whose hands is a wicked scheme, and whose right hand is full of bribes.
I shall walk in my integrity; Redeem me and be gracious to me.

Psalm 35
Contend, O Lord, With those who contend with me; Fight against those who fight against me.
Let them be ashamed and dishonoured who seek my life.
Let those be turned back and humiliated who devise evil against me.
Let them be like chaff before the wind, With the angel of the Lord driving them away.
Let their way be dark and slippery, With the angel of the Lord pursuing them.
For without cause they hid their net for me; Without cause they dug a pit for my soul.
Let destruction come upon him unawares, And let the net which he hid catch himself;
Into that very destruction let him fall.
And my soul shall rejoice in the Lord; It shall exult in His salvation.
All my bones will say, "Lord, Who is like You,
Who delivers the afflicted from him who is too strong for him,
And the afflicted and the needy from him who robs him?"
Malicious witnesses rise up; They ask me of things that I do not know.
At my stumbling they rejoiced and gathered themselves together;

The smiters whom I did not know gathered together against me,
They slandered me without ceasing.
Like godless jesters at a feast, They gnashed at me with their teeth.
Lord, how long will You look on?
Rescue my soul from their ravages, My only life from the lions.
I will give You thanks in the great congregation; I will praise You among a mighty throng.
Do not let those who are wrongfully my enemies rejoice over me;
Nor let those who hate me without cause wink maliciously.
For they do not speak peace,
But they devise deceitful words against those who are quiet in the land.
They opened their mouth wide against me;
They said, "Aha, aha, our eyes have seen it!"
You have seen it, O Lord, Do not keep silent; O Lord, Do not be far from me.
Stir up Yourself, And awake to my right and to my cause, My God and my Lord.
Judge me, O Lord my God, According to Your righteousness,
And do not let them rejoice over me.
Do not let them say in their heart, Aha, our desire!
Do not let them say, "We have swallowed him up!"
Let those be ashamed and humiliated altogether who rejoice at my distress;
Let those be clothed with shame and dishonour who magnify themselves over me.
Let them shout for joy and rejoice, Who favour my vindication;
And let them say continually, "The Lord be magnified."

Psalm 142

I cry aloud with my voice to the Lord; I make supplication with my voice to the Lord.
They have hidden a trap for me; Look to the right and see; For there is no one who regards me;
There is no escape for me; No one cares for my soul.
I cry out to you, O Lord; I said, "You are my refuge.
Give heed to my cry, For I am brought very low;
Delivery me from my persecutors, For they are too strong for me.
Bring my soul out of prison, So that I may give thanks to Your name;
The righteous will surround me, For You will deal bountifully with me."

A note was given to the judge from another lawyer who had just entered the courtroom. The judge stopped speaking and politely said that he would continue with my case in twenty minutes because there was a minor matter that he wanted to address before the day was over. The court officer brought me to a small holding cell with a thick metal door and a tiny window; it was the smallest cell I had ever been in. It had a steel toilet with a sink attached to it and a concrete slab bench connected to the brick wall, the size of a loveseat, but there was nothing to love about it. Another test of my faith. I spent the entire time on my knees praying while I was in the cell.

When I re-entered the courtroom, the judge continued where he'd left off, and I continued to read my Bible. The judge summarized the entire case and all the evidence that was given. That was what I gathered from the words I heard every now and again when I gave my eyes a break from reading the tiny font on the pages in front of me. I still didn't look up, I closed my eyes, and opened them again only to read the scriptures that were providing me with any hope for freedom. Everything was out of my hands – out of my power – I had to accept my fate, regardless of what it was.

The last statement the judge said demanded my full attention. "With all the evidence presented, and all the flaws in the witnesses' testimonies, I am left with no other option but to order that the defendant be discharged of the charge of second-degree murder."

The Rastaman jumped to his feet, as did I. He grabbed my hand with both of his and shook it profusely. He wouldn't let go. "Praise Jah! Praise Jah! Praise Jah! Praise Jah!" He shouted. His excitement for me was like one of a father towards a prodigal son, who once was lost but now is found, once was dead but now alive, once a prisoner but now set free. I was never one to express my emotions outwardly, except for anger. That day, the dread expressed everything I was feeling for the entire court to see. The bailiff had to tell him to calm down. When the man finally let go of my hand, I reached over the door of the prisoner box to unlatch the door and let myself out. I fumbled around with the latch but couldn't open it. The bailiff told me to be patient and wait for the judge to leave the court and then he would open it. I had no more patience. It was time for me to go home.

I walked out of the courthouse a free man. Mr. Lomer drove me up to where his office was; my first time in a vehicle in a long time without handcuffs and leg irons. Before letting me off at the corner and giving me ten dollars for a taxi, he explained to me that a discharge was not the same as an acquittal, meaning that if they found new evidence they could rearrest and retry me. The case was still open.

I caught a cab to my mom's place at Dufferin and St. Clair Avenue West. She wasn't expecting me. After I paid the cabbie, I hopped out and jogged across the street to the little brown building where she had been living with my baby brother, Jamal. I walked down the stairs to her apartment, my new home, overwhelmed with joy and excitement as I tapped on the door. Mom opened it as if she had been waiting for me to arrive. She embraced me tightly, as tears streamed down both of our face, uncontrollably. There we began our lives again.

CHAPTER NINETEEN

REDEMPTION DRAWETH NIGH

Life was not a bed of roses when I got out of the Don Jail. I'd survived it, but now I had to deal with my own inner demons: the ingrained, enrooted carnal desires, passions, temptations, emotions. In all my years of incarceration and group homes, the core problem was not addressed or dealt with. How could I deal with my anger, my frustration? Still, I was not resentful. I'd been given another chance. A chance to do good. A chance to make a difference. But like an elastic band – I would have to be pulled back to spring forward.

I had cut off most of my friends. Being incarcerated for a crime that all your friends knew you didn't commit, I thought, would at least draw a little support; maybe twenty dollars in my canteen; a visit; a letter of encouragement. I realized that I didn't have many real friends. I was admired and looked up to, respected and feared, but where was the love? Sean came to visit me once. I was still disappointed that it took him so long, but at least he took the initiative.

The day after I got out, I went to run errands in my new car. Bobbie had paid it off while I was inside. I drove through the city without a single lesson on how to drive a stick shift. I picked up Tony for the company, and he tagged along as I stalled the car at almost every intersection that I stopped at. Driving up the big hill on Dufferin was a horror story as I tried not to roll back into the car behind me once the light turned green. I either screeched away or stalled the car, but I made it through the day.

I had no need for a large circle of friends, so I only kept in touch with Richie, Tony, Sean, Markie, Raheem, and Garry whom I'd met in the West Detention Centre. I picked up another job through St. Christopher House, working at Goodyear, fixing tires and doing oil changes. I worked out with Garry at the YMCA on College near Dufferin. Bobbie also had a membership and came to the gym.

For extra money I babysat Jacklyn's infant daughter. I knew Jacklyn from Ottawa but she now lived less than a ten-minute walk up the street from me. She hustled as a stripper in Brampton, and she paid me well. I made twenty dollars an hour for babysitting, and sometimes she threw me a little extra; occasionally, when she wasn't too tired after work, we even had sex. I never had to do any work because when I arrived, her daughter was already sleeping. I just used the phone to invite girls over. I had a Filipino girl, obsessed with the movie *The Lion King* and dancing. She always asked me how I moved so good in the bed but didn't dance. I had another friend who visited me, she was a Native Canadian who I met through Jacklyn. I liked her, but her psycho boyfriend – who she was trying to leave – I could have done without. Once, we were making out on the couch with the TV on, condom in hand, about to bust the package, when there was a bang on the door. It was him. She ran into the bedroom, where Jacklyn's daughter was sleeping in her crib, and hid in the closet. I opened the door. He rushed in before I could stop him and went straight to the kitchen and grabbed a butcher knife. He came at me, not to attack me, but his body language said that if I got in his way, it wasn't going to end well. I stepped aside with no choice but to let him search the room. He found her crouched down in the closet and relentlessly punched and kicked her in the body and the face, yelling profanities. Whenever I tried to step in, he lifted the knife and moved toward me, reminding me that he was the one in power. I was able to distract him for moment while she made her escape through the door, down the stairs, and out on the street, barefoot. She called me half an hour later on Jacklyn's landline to tell me that she had gotten away, and she was coming back to spend the night. She didn't return, and I never saw or heard from her again.

I should have gotten into the knife industry; it was like there was a knife involved in every corner that I turned. The next time I was with Markie. We didn't have much money, but we wanted to smoke some weed. It was late in the night, so we walked along Danforth and found two black guys on the corner of Greenwood, just next to Roxy's. They said they had weed. We told them that we wanted five dollars' worth. When the one guy opened the palm of his hand to give it to Markie, I thought he was joking. That amount wasn't even enough to roll a pinner. "Are you kidding me?" I said. He wasn't. I slapped his hand, dashing the weed to the ground. It happened so quick. His friend grabbed Markie by his dreads and began punching his face. The guy whose hand I'd knocked pulled out a six-inch Rambo knife with teeth on the other end of the blade and came at me. I took off across Greenwood along Danforth. He wasn't far behind, about five feet when I looked back. He was determined to put that blade through my flesh. Mathew Smith flashed through my mind, still as fresh as the day it happened, and I had only been out for a week. *Was I going to die like him?* Looking back, I slammed into the corner of the beer store, hitting the brick wall with my left shoulder. I landed on the ground in the middle of the sidewalk. My attacker tripped over me with the knife still in his hand. I turned and fled in the opposite direction, crossing Danforth to the northside. The folks who lived in the area had their recycling bins out for pick up in the morning, which probably saved our lives. I grabbed two wine bottles from out of a plastic bin, smashed them on the ground, and went back to chase both men south on Greenwood. Markie and I walked back to his place, him with a few marks on his face and a couple missing dreads, and me with a sore shoulder and a feeling of pride. We ended up scoring a dime of weed from someone else before spinning some records on his turntable in his room.

The next weekend, Markie and I were having a few beers at his crib when he asked me if I wanted to go to a party downtown at Dundas and Spadina. I didn't want to. I wasn't in the mood to be around a crowd, but I said sure, reluctantly. We went to the party, drank a bit more, and after half an hour I told him I was out. As I walked to the train station, minding my own business, a cop car pulled up beside me and two pigs got out. "Excuse me, where are you coming from?" one said.

"Why?"

"Because I asked you where you are coming from. You fit the description of a robbery suspect. Again, where are you coming from?"

"I'm coming from Dundas and Spadina." By now I was frustrated. I hadn't been out of jail for a more than two weeks for a crime that I didn't commit, and now I was being detained by the police for something I didn't do.

"Look." He pointed up at the two signs on the pole in front of me, in the direction that I was walking. One read Dundas, and the other Spadina.

I had no clue which backstreet I was coming from.

"So are you going to tell us where you're coming from, or do we have to take you in?"

"For what? I didn't do anything."

"Let me see some ID."

"Why do you need to see my ID? Because I didn't know exactly where I was? I don't live around here. Why don't you guys go find that robber you were looking for and leave me alone?"

Both pigs grabbed me and slammed me onto the trunk of the cruiser, slapped handcuffs on me from behind, took my wallet out from my back pocket, and threw me in the back seat. After running my name through the CPIC, they let me out of the car, took the cuffs off my wrists, put my wallet in the front pocket of my jeans, and told me to go, adding, "You're lucky we didn't arrest you for public intoxication."

The humiliation and powerlessness I felt from these officer's treatment sent tears streaming down my face as I walked away thinking about all the other times when I was abused by the police. I relived the pain on my back when the cop beat me from behind, the lies that the detectives told in court, and the other abuses of power that were never written. When I got home and opened my wallet, I realized that the pigs had failed to return my license. Now I had to go wait in a government lineup for a replacement.

Downtown in front of the Eaton Centre I bumped into Lloyd, my old acquaintance from that horrible day at Ontario Place, and his crew. He was excited to see me.

"Junior, what's up man.

"I'm good."

"Yo come roll wid us."

Looking at him and listening to him only brought me back to that meeting in the school stairwell after the murder. I declined his offer to hang out with them. The nine thugs went their way, and I went mine.

It was crazy that I was running into all these people who were at Ontario Place that day in May, 1993. I saw the last of the key witnesses, the articulate liar who'd tried to piece all the falsehoods together and get me convicted. He was going up the escalator at the Eaton Centre as I was going down. Our eyes met. When he saw me coming back up the escalator to confront him, the look of fear on his face could be seen from a mile away. I wasn't going to hurt him. I just wanted to know why. Why did he lie against me in court? I never got an answer. He kept silent and continued walking. Afraid I was going to get charged for threatening or harassing the rat, I left him alone. It was enough just to see the terror in him.

Next was Greg, the guy who had stabbed Mathew. I saw him at the Ossington Subway Station. He stood there with his leg in a cast and crutches under both armpits. I walked up to him to punch him in the face. I stopped three feet in front of him. The mood was somber. Instead of hitting him, I asked him why he did it. I knew that striking him would have caused a full-out war, ending in murder. "What are you talking about man?" he answered. That was the extent of our conversation and was the last time I ever saw Greg.

It was summertime, and Ali, my Ethiopian friend and I went to a basement reggae party on Eglinton West. I wasn't there for long before meeting a cute white chick who was down for whatever. I didn't have my car anymore because I had smashed it running a red light while hanging out with Garry on Canada Day, so Ali drove his car. I asked Ali if I could have his car keys so I could deal with my business. He didn't want any hanky-panky going on in his vehicle and refused. I told him I'd be back. On the way out of the party to find a quiet spot to be with the girl, I saw Locksley on his way in. He'd also been part of the Ontario Place posse that long-ago night.

"Hey, Junior! How you doing?" He greeted me, genuinely happy to see me, as Lloyd had been.

When Locksley raised his hand to shake mine, without thinking, I sucker-punched him across the face. He fell back and landed on the ground. I didn't know why I did it; I was just mad at him. He got up and ran into the basement party, and I walked off with the girl around the corner to Eglinton. On the way across the street, I heard Locksley yelling *pussy* at me, coming at me with five other guys. Bold me, or stupid me, turned back to fight them, because I was the tough guy. I didn't look too tough getting beat by six guys with bottles and whatever else they had in their hands. I managed to stay on my feet and only got hit a few times before realizing that I was fighting a losing battle, and took off across Eglinton and through some back streets, leaving the girl behind. The skin above my left eye was busted, my shirt torn, and my gold chain that Michelle had bought me was lying somewhere on the street. I rode the bus back to the east end, full of blood and half covered with a shirt that looked like a ripped-up sheet. That was not the last time I saw Locksley before he was convicted of first-degree murder and sentenced to life in prison.

At times I got desperate. I needed money and turned back to the streets. I got a few twenty pieces from Richie on consignment. After a week, he was asking for his money, but I hadn't sold a thing. It was no longer in me. I thought to dash them in the garbage but that would have made a good friend into an enemy. I gave them back to him and told him that I was out of the game. Shortly after, Richie got into a heated road rage confrontation, popped his trunk, grabbed his machete, and slapped the truck driver across the face with the long blade. Witnesses took note of his license plate, and he was deported from Canada.

After a three-and-a-half-year relationship, Bobbie and I had broken up. One day I wanted to talk to her, so I buzzed up from the lobby of her sister's condo. No one answered. I kept buzzing. A few minutes later a police car rolled up and I was arrested for harassment. I was taken to the West Detention Centre's adult unit because I was now nineteen. I shared a cell with Busthead who was now in on first-degree murder for shooting someone. He'd heard about me beating my murder rap; I had a lot of respect on the range. I also bumped into Gumbo in the holding cells on our way to court. It was cool to see him. Bobbie came to visit me. She felt bad that her sister had called the police. Nothing came out of the charge, and it was dropped later, but not before I had faced other problems as a result of it.

I was released from the West on bail on my own recognizance. The only condition the judge gave me was to report to the bail office downtown once a week. Reporting day was on Fridays. I was instructed that on the first day of reporting I was required to bring my bail papers with me, and every Friday thereafter, all I had to do was show up and sign in. I did what was required of me. I brought my bail papers, the clerk registered me in the system, I signed their form, and I left. The following Friday I returned to the bail office and told the same clerk that I was there to sign in. He asked me for my name, typed it in the system, and apparently couldn't find it. He told me that I had to go home and get my bail papers. I told him that I had registered last Friday with my bail papers, and I wasn't going all the way home and coming back because he failed to do his job properly. Evidently, he didn't appreciate the way I spoke to him and within a minute or two there were two police officers by my side telling me to go with them. Reluctantly, but not unwillingly, I went with them. I had nothing to be concerned about because I had done nothing wrong. I had reported the previous Friday, and I was there that day to report again, as instructed by the judge. They brought me to a small well-lit room with a concrete bench connected to the wall.

"Take off your clothes." The chunky pig with the receding hairline told me.

"What do you mean take off my clothes?" I responded.

"You're under arrest for breach of bail. Take off your clothes. We're conducting a strip search."

"I'm not taking off my clothes. I didn't do anything. I was here last Friday with my bail papers, and I signed in."

"If you don't take off your clothes, we're gonna charge you for assault police on top of the breach of bail." The other pig chirped in.

"F*ck you! I didn't breach my bail. I didn't assault you. And I'm not taking off my clothes."

Both of them grabbed me by the arms and a struggle pursued. They attempted to restrain me in an effort to lock me up in handcuffs. Their attempt was pathetic. I slammed both pigs up against each of the four walls of the tiny room until I realized that I didn't want an actual *real* assault police charge against me, then I gave in and allowed them to cuff me. I even knelt on the bench and let them put the leg irons on my ankles. I was charged with breach of bail and two assault police. I never did take off my clothes for those pigs.

I was taken to the Toronto Don Jail, placed on 2C South, where the inmates embraced me with a warm welcome. I had just beaten a murder rap, now I was in on assault police – I was the don of the Don. In fact, the truth was, I was embarrassed to be back in jail, especially to face the guards that looked up to me and believed that I would do great things once I was released. I felt as if I had let those guards down more than the inmates. The following day when I went to court for my bail hearing, the breach of bail charge was dropped (what a coincidence), but they stuck with the assault police charges, and kept me for three weeks in jail until I was eventually released on bail. I went back to stay with my mother.

I felt betrayed by everyone. While I was incarcerated, my mother figured out my bank card password and cleaned out my entire six hundred dollars because she needed to pay some bills. Back at home, I turned to the Psalms that I had been reading in the Don Jail for comfort. One day I was lying on the top bunk in the room that I shared with Andrew when Leisa entered and asked me a question. I didn't answer; usually when I read my Bible I waited until I was finished before talking to anyone. She grabbed the book and threw it in my face. I jumped off the bunk, chased her out of the room, and struck her once with a closed fist in her face, expecting a fight. I was bigger now and she couldn't beat me up anymore. I wasn't the little Junior that she used to beat up on when she got mad. It was the first time she backed down from me, running out of the apartment to the payphone. I was arrested and taken to the East Detention Centre.

The East was a blessing. I hated the place. I was locked up, alone in my cell. I was granted bail, but my mom was not bailing me out; she took Leisa's side. I had no one. During the day I went to a couple of programs to get off the range. I went to AA; didn't like that. I went to a Christian group meeting; it was OK. I went back to my cell, lay on my bed, looked around at the walls, the locked door, the enclosure that held me trapped. I realized I needed to change or I was going to end up dead or in prison for the rest of my life. I heard the voice of Psalm 27:10 speaking to my soul: *When my mother and my father forsake me, then the Lord will take me up.* I found myself on the floor; on my knees, praying to the God of Shadrach, Meshack, and Abednego, remembering what Derrick had read to me in the Don, and how He saved them from the fiery furnace. Could *He* save me from *myself*? I poured out my heart. Spoke to *Him* with all sincerity. He must have heard my prayer. The next day I got into words with a Jamaican over the phone. Both of us were not letting go of the receiver. I could have flattened this guy like I did the kid in the West, or Scarry in the Don. I let go of the phone and walked away. I spent almost every waking moment reading my Bible and other spiritual books, searching the dictionary for words I didn't know. My mind was opened in a way that it had never been before. There was hope.

I spent a month in the East. The guys on the range must have thought I was cuckoo; I barely said a word to anyone, all I did all day was read, but when the guards called my name to release me, I went around the range and shook every man's hand, wishing them God's blessing.

I went to stay at my mom's for a few weeks until I found my own place. She had moved to Queen Street in Parkdale. I told her that I was a Christian and God had changed my life. That week she had found a tract that someone put on her car windshield. Shortly afterward I started going to the crusade at Perth Seventh-day Adventist Church every night and listened to Evangelist Craig Dossman, who'd come all the way from Oakland, California to preach about the power of God. I was impressed. Pastor Lou, the Chinese Jamaican associate pastor of the church, and Brother Record, an elder from Jamaica, gave me bible studies and supported me in a way that I would never forget. The amount of love that the church members showed made me feel received and welcomed. When I saw the preachers preach from the pulpit in their suits and ties, I wanted to be like them.

My idols were no longer the pimps and drug dealers I grew up watching, they were now the dynamic public speakers and the caring fathers who didn't abandon their kids. These were the men I wanted to be like. By the end of the crusade, I was baptized by Pastor Cassimy.

Shortly after my baptism, I found a rooming house near Dufferin and Dundas. The room was small, and the senior-citizen owners of the house lived below. Their living room was separated by a sheet that hung down from the doorway. The two fought like cats and dogs, every minute of every day. At times I had to intervene when I heard him beating on her. They were constantly drunk and chain-smoked like I had never seen. The entire house, including my room, was always filled with smoke. I could barely breathe at times. To make things worse, the person who had lived in the room before me had owned a cat. I had a severe allergy to cats; it took weeks until I could sleep without wheezing and struggling for air.

The first time I spoke in front of the congregation was to say the benediction. I was nervous and excited to speak in front of over three hundred people, but I was so happy I even invited Bobbie, and she came. But she didn't feel comfortable around my new Christian friends and declined the invitation to come for lunch after church.

I got my first opportunity to speak at the evening youth program, Adventist Youth (AY). I asked the AY leader if I could preach a sermonette the following Sabbath. I was given fifteen minutes to give a testimony. I prepared all week and wrote it out about ten times, memorizing almost every word. After sharing my testimony and preaching my sermonette, I was invited to the churches throughout Toronto to preach for their main services on youth days. I got involved in prison ministry and started a street ministry. Everything I did was different. My team and I called ourselves *All For Christ Street Ministry*. We didn't just go out and hand out tracts, we preached on the corner of Dufferin and Bloor where people waited for the bus. Brother Alexander and my new friend Richard, who joined the church shortly after me, preached with me on the subway while the girls, Kenisha, Michelle, Simone, Eslyn, and my mom (who got baptized and later joined the team) sang. Richard went as far as to purchase a microphone and speaker for the team, which helped us to be heard better on the busier corners like Yonge and Dundas. I'd gone from street *thug* to street *preacher*. Our street ministry team grew, with members joining us from other churches, and before you knew it we were doing big outdoor programs in Regent Park, Jane and Woolner, and other projects throughout the city with professional sound system equipment. Whether I organized an outdoor or indoor church program, I made sure to put the best choirs and singers in Toronto on the roster, with choirs like *Faith Choral*, *In His Name*, and *Divine Word*. I used my favourite singers: Cameron Fray, Everald Bernard, Sharon Riley, Caroline Corbin, and Cheryl Bromfield. The last two girls ended up becoming my girlfriends (although not at the same time).

I noticed that when I spoke in the churches, it was quiet, and people hung on to my every word. To preach and minister was the best feeling, but after preaching my heart out to the congregation, I felt weak in the flesh as I stepped away from the pulpit, vulnerable to the temptations around me. The women in the church were alluring. Every week they dressed in their Sabbath best. I had to pray and stay focused. I had stopped drinking, smoking, and fornicating; the last was the most difficult.

During a weekday, Bobbie came over to my place for lunch. I cooked chicken breast, rice, and veggies. After lunch we talked in my room. I wasn't so strong, and I gave in to her lips. Although she said she had a new boyfriend (maybe she did, maybe she just wanted to make me jealous), we still made out on my bed, but when she got too heated and told me to put it in, I stopped myself and didn't go any further. No clothes were taken off, and no part of her flesh was touched by my hands. It would be the power of my ministry that would give me the strength to be celibate for four years.

It was now time to stand trial for the two assault police charges. I went to court in full force. I had told my entire church about what had happened to me, and those who were able to make it to court came; the rest prayed for me. When I arrived in the courtroom for my trial, I had twenty to thirty of my church family by my side, including my mother. "You have a lot of friends, Junior." Michael Lomer said to me. The trial proceeded, and I beat the fraudulent charges.

Perth chose me to attend the youth conference in St Louis, Missouri. It would be my first time outside of Canada. I was worried that they were not going to let me in the country because there was still a warrant for my arrest in Quebec. I'd missed court for the auto theft charge five years earlier, hoping it would just pass away. I prayed about it before going to the Toronto Police Station to find out about the warrant. There was nothing more I wanted than to attend the conference and represent my church. There were going to be thousands of youths my age from around the world attending. The officer at the desk searched through the system for the warrant. Nothing came up, and he gave me a number to call the station in Quebec where they had arrested me. There was no warrant in their system either.

The trip to St Louis was fantastic. I learned a lot about ministry and met some great people my age who were from the Greater Toronto Area. We all rode the chartered bus over a thousand kilometres to and from the conference.

Pastor Lou and Brother Record encouraged me to go back to school. I had earned two half credits while I was in high school in Ottawa: one for cosmetology, a class I took just so I could be surrounded by girls, and one in math. I attended Adult Day School near Black Creek Drive, along with taking correspondence courses at home, and summer school. It didn't matter what I had to do, I was determined to succeed: when I had no bus fare, I rode my bicycle to school through the rain, the snow, and the slush. I achieved my high school diploma in two years with a grade point average of 3.87.

Soon after, I had the honour of visiting Oakwood College (now Oakwood University) in Huntsville Alabama with a group of kids from the churches in Toronto, including my friend Brian, who I met at Adult Day School. I spoke to him about the Bible every day and he ended up joining the church. I decided that this was where I wanted to continue my education, so I sent in an application.

At the time I was living in a rooming house in The Junction, a part of West Toronto. While I liked the area, I did not like the place I was staying. The room was small, the bed was uncomfortable, but worst of all, the refrigerator made a constant buzzing sound, and it was loud. I had to stop buying food to refrigerate so I could unplug it just to be able to sleep at night. My escape came when I received the acceptance letter in the mail. I was beyond ecstatic that I would be starting Oakwood College that semester, in January 1998.

I got lots of support from my friends, family, and the church members when they learned that I would be studying theology. Kenisha gave me a thousand dollars from her hard-earned savings from working as a waitress, and others also supported with something to help with my first semester.

Oakwood was a historically black school and turned out to be the best experience for me. I sat in the same classes in the Moseley Complex that some of the greatest preachers, evangelists, pastors, and teachers in the world had passed through: E.E. Cleveland, Dr. Shand, James Doggette, Eric Thomas, Andrea Trusty, John Scott, Mason West, Dr. Keith Burton, Dr. Mervyn Warren (my preaching teacher), Dr. Kenneth Mulzac, and of course the "father of preachers," Dr. Calvin Moseley. I too was going to be great.

I spent my first year at Edwards Hall, the dorm for older students. Because I was 22 and older than the average freshman, they didn't put me in Peterson Hall, the freshman dorm. By the time I had waited in a ridiculously long lineup to register for classes and get financially cleared, there were only a few campus jobs left to choose from. My first job was the gym supervisor. It paid very little, but it was worth it. I spent hours studying and working out. Working in the gym helped me to get all A's and make the Dean's List my first year.

Other than talking on the phone until the wee hours of the night with my girlfriend, Cheryl, I was focused on my studies and the ministry. Cheryl ended up attending OC the following year. It was a perfect opportunity for us to spend time together and realize that we were not meant to be. She was a lovely girl, sweet, kind, and caring, but no match.

After I stopped seeing Cheryl, I had my eyes open for someone who was like her in terms of character, spirituality, and intelligence. She would have to be fun to be around, but emotionally stronger and more independent than Cheryl had been. There was a girl that I had a crush on. To me she was the full package. She was the best singer that I had ever heard live – a Whitney Houston on the stage. I fell in love with her every time she touched that mic, and when she played the piano, I got chills. I just didn't understand why Sheléa, who could have gotten any decent guy she wanted, was dating this thug-looking hoodlum who couldn't even sit up properly in the church pew. After Crip walking down the aisle, he'd slump down and lean back with his arm up on the backrest and his legs wide open. I guess I couldn't have had them all.

My first summer job was at a Seventh-day Adventist camp: Camp Frenda. What a summer that was. I was a camp counsellor and mountain biking instructor. I was blessed to work with kids from eight years old up to sixteen. I also worked with the legally blind. The most relaxing session was family camp. The parents took care of their own kids while the staff only taught four classes during the days and went to morning worship and campfire at night.

The following semester I switched jobs. I was a Resident Assistant at Peterson Hall, which paid much more. I wasn't paid in currency, but the job provided room and board, which was an almost four-thousand-dollar expense per semester. I also joined the Literature Evangelist Training Center (LETC) and worked under the leadership of Pastor William Smith and Elder Dsouza. Over the years of Pastor Smith's guidance, I learned a significant amount about working with difficult people, and how to be humble. He wasn't a teacher, but he taught me things that I never learned in the class listening to professors with master's and doctorate degrees. My first lesson came when I led my first LETC team in Warner Robins, Georgia. *There wasn't much to it* – or so I thought. All I had to do was teach a group of students how to sell books door-to-door. But with Anthony on my team, I was in for more than I had anticipated. Anthony was an older student, somewhere in his thirties. He was an ex-cop from Trinidad – I was an ex-con from Canada. We were both in the United States trying to do positive things with our lives. His head was hard, and mine was no softer – we butted them on every conversation. He wasn't accepting my leadership and I wasn't accepting his defiance. I decided to send him back to Alabama. I called Pastor Smith to inform him that I was purchasing a Greyhound ticket and kicking Anthony off the team because he was impossible to work with. Pastor Smith overrode my decision and told me that if I wanted to be successful in life, I had to learn how to work with difficult people, and this was the perfect chance. I did what he said. I had no choice; he was the boss. After the campaign, Anthony and I returned to Oakwood College – best friends.

I began leading LETC teams in different states during the breaks. Thanksgiving and Christmas, we worked in cities down south, usually in Florida. During the summer we went further north to Columbus, Detroit, or Chicago. And during the spring breaks we stayed closer to Huntsville and went to Atlanta, Memphis, and New Orleans. Day, Carl, Aisha, Christine, and Nigel were usually on my team. There was only one team in the LETC camp that sold more books than us and made more money. No matter how hard and long we worked, Delicia's team always beat us.

One summer I recruited a powerhouse LETC team. The publishing director and associate director of the Ontario Conference came to Oakwood to recruit a team to work up in Toronto. They met with me because I was obviously interested in working in my home city. The meeting went well. They told me that every student who signed up to work with the Ontario Conference would receive a three-thousand-dollar base, regardless of how many books they sold, and we would receive one hundred percent of the donations that people gave, if they preferred to help with a donation but didn't want to purchase a book. I used that as the basis for recruiting my team. However, when we got to Toronto, the directors were singing another tune – a song that wasn't too pleasing. In training, they told us that we would be getting only fifty percent of everything we brought in, and everyone was expected to earn three thousand dollars, which meant even the weakest literature evangelist was expected to raise six thousand dollars in sales. I knew that would be impossible, and even unfair for some that gave up their summer jobs to come all the way to Canada expecting a base at the end to pay for their tuition. As the leader, it was my responsibility to fight for the team. They ended up giving us what they promised in the beginning. We worked hard and did well.

In the middle of the campaign, I even took a vacation to Jamaica to visit Richard's family – my first time in the Caribbean. We stayed in Montego Bay for a week before going deep into the countryside for a few days to visit his aunt and uncle. My brother's dad, Keston had moved back to Jamaica, and we went to Rocky Point to visit him. While we were in a restaurant, we heard a commotion outside. There was a man without a shirt running around with a machete in his hand. His chest was slashed at least eight inches from top to bottom from another man's machete. Yet another man emerged from behind a car, also brandishing a machete. I had never seen anything like this. It was a machete war. Men running in different directions. Keston ushered us out to his truck as fast as he could before the guns came out. Four kilometres down the road we passed one police cruiser on its way to the fight.

Later that day, Keston hooked us up with a personal rental car from a guy he knew in his area. We used it to drive to Richard's people's house in the country. Every morning Richard's aunt cooked ackee and saltfish, Jamaica's national dish, with provisions: sweet potato, yam, boiled dumpling, and the works. For dinner it was either jerk chicken, curry chicken, oxtail, or snapper fish with rice and peas. We were spoiled on the Irie Island. On our way back to Montego Bay, we used the car as a taxi to try and make some of our money back for the rental. We didn't know the price for the distance we carried the passengers, we just took whatever they gave us; they were locals, so they knew how much the fare was. I didn't have a Jamaican accent, so I just kept my mouth shut and drove, while Richard shouted out "Taxi! Taxi!" to everyone we passed on the side of the road. Our taxi was always full. The only problem was when the customers would say, "gimme me change." Then Richard would say, "oh sorry, how much ya need?" The trip to Jamaica was worth every minute.

When I returned to Oakwood, I accepted the position of night dean at Edwards Hall, but I ran into a couple of problems during my tenure there. I oversaw the dorm at night, and among other responsibilities I had to have the students sign in if they came in past curfew. One student attempted to slap me across the face because he didn't like my decision. My reflexes were fast enough to turn away, allowing him to only graze my chin. I flew from around the desk and addressed the issue head on – the *street* in me was about to be unleashed. I told him to box me again and see what I would do, this time it would be self-defense. The lobby area was silent. Other students watched on; they knew that this cat was a hothead, and something was about to go down. He walked away, and the next morning apologized to me. I respected him for being a man. The other issue came with a guy I respected. Shane was a built, clean-shaven Jamaican who lived in Florida. I never knew what he did or how he made his money, but he drove nice cars, and for the yearly banquet, he showed up with his date in a brand-spanking-new Ferrari. He always ran around with a crew of young men who followed him and did what he said; some of them were from the hood in their respective cities and some were sent to Oakwood by their parents who had enough money to provide an education. I didn't know what kind of business they were all into, but it was evident that Shane took care of them. We always got along well and engaged in small talk; we were in one class together, social psychology, which he rarely attended. This night I had refused one of the kids in his crew a request because he got back to the dorm way past curfew. He called Shane, who lived off campus, and Shane arrived within minutes. When he got to the locked door, he was heated and demanded that I open it. I opened it, not because he told me, but to have a man-to-man talk. A lot of the students feared Shane; I didn't. We spoke for no more than two minutes. He told me that not everyone was there for school, and he was coming to knock out the person who disrespected his boy; but when he saw me, he realized that it must have been a misunderstanding because he knew that I treated all the students fairly. We still talked and got along after.

Starting a new semester after the summer and meeting new people was exciting for all the students. This particular semester I met someone that, maybe, I should have run in the other direction when I first set eyes on her. She was a mixed-Asian shorty, super fine. We met at one of the churches off campus, where I was introduced to her by a mutual friend. Physically she was a hundred percent my type, but we were on different spiritual paths. One night, we got into talking for a long while on the phone. It was past curfew, but by the way she made me feel, I had to see her. I was a changed man. I had no plans on doing anything naughty with her; if I had, I would have stopped at a gas station along the way to purchase rubbers. When I arrived at her apartment, she answered the door in a tempting sundress, revealing too much leg for a weak Christian young man who had been celibate for four years. We sat on the floor and started watching a movie for no more than ten minutes. We were glued to each other, hands exploring everything. I couldn't go any longer; I was about to explode. I had put myself in such temptation that I had no power of resistance. We drove to the gas station together at my suggestion. My hand stayed inside her panties for the entire trip in a successful attempt to suppress my conscience. We returned to her apartment, and when we were done, saying no to my carnal nature became even more difficult, especially being surrounded by the ravishing young ladies at Oakwood College.

I continued praying and trying to overcome my lustful desires, so much so that a girl I met working at Walmart and attending Alabama A&M University asked me if I was gay because I never made a move on her. She soon found out that I wasn't.

The following summer was a wild one. I brought the LETC team back up to Canada with a few new members on board. There was another falling out between us and the directors. We were supposed to work in Toronto but instead they put us in Hamilton, an hour outside of the city. I called Pastor Smith and he made a few phone calls. The next day Elder Lambert drove up in a big white fifteen-seater van, and everyone headed south to Columbus, Ohio. I drove the little red Acura Integra that I had bought a few days prior, but I didn't have time to register it. When we got to the New York border, Bobby lent me his California license plate from his Jeep. He still had his valid temporary paper handy to place on the windshield. Reuben drove down in his Ford Escort.

Elder Lambert was the absolute best. He set us up in a big yellow duplex house in the middle of the hood. The house was nice and big, but we couldn't sell our books because nobody in the neighbourhood could afford ten dollars to buy them. We had to drive to the higher-end areas. Elder Lambert found us two brand new rental cars. I had a burgundy Ford Taurus, and Jackie, my partner, had a green one. We used our cars both for work and to race on the highway and through the city; sometimes we used all five vehicles, weaving and bobbing in and out of traffic. We had to return a rental for a new one at least two times because we drove them like dune buggies. On one occasion I brought the car up to a high speed, attempting to fly up a five-foot hill and land on the other side of the train tracks without touching. I didn't go fast enough on the first try. I had too many passengers; there were three of us in the front, and three in the back. I tried again. I drove at a speed that caused the Taurus to soar into the air, over the tracks and the hill on the other side, thumping crazily onto the flat road, Day hitting his head on the ceiling. The next morning the car started, but when I pressed the accelerator, it only revved, it didn't move. Underneath the vehicle there was a puddle of red liquid. All the transmission fluid had leaked out.

The Columbus campaign was not a spiritual revival by any means. Nigel was into Kerri-Ann, Bobby was into Janelle, and I was into every girl in the state of Ohio. Jackie was Reuben's girlfriend. Mel was the only white girl on the team. I thought she was cute, and I could tell by the way she looked at me that she liked me to, but she was off limits. I didn't know what anyone else in the house did, but for me, I played it clean with Mel; I was her leader and her friend. Day was a virgin, but that only lasted until we went to the Allegheny West Conference camp meeting. He met a massage therapist a couple years older than him, and on his days off, he was nowhere to be found.

When I got back to Oakwood, I knew I needed to get back on the spiritual path. I felt as if I was falling from grace.

It was at a Wednesday evening prayer meeting where I met a beautiful, brown-skinned young lady from Birmingham, Alabama with the cutest southern accent. She attended the University of Alabama in Huntsville (UAH), studying nursing. One of her class assignments was to attend another religious institution that the students were not familiar with and write an essay on it. She sat directly behind me at the Oakwood College Church with a male classmate, whom I thought was probably her boyfriend. When the pastor told the congregation to break up into groups of twos and threes for prayer, I prayed with the two students from UAH. We joined hands and the guy and I said a short prayer; she was too shy to pray aloud. While holding her hand, I knew I never wanted to let it go. It was not a sexual thing; there was a spiritual connection. She introduced herself and her classmate, and I gave them both my number to keep them posted on upcoming church events. Only Shoshannah called. She was baptized shortly after. Seven months later, I asked her to marry me – she said yes.

Shoshannah and I started doing Christian relationship workshops together. We studied as much as we could about how to develop healthy relationships through communication, abstinence, and putting God first. We did one on Oakwood campus and another at a church in Toronto. I did one on my own on a LETC campaign in Detroit. Shoshannah's father was a pastor but not from the same denomination. Her parents took well to me. They appreciated how I was a positive force in their daughter's life; she built me up as well, and we grew spiritually together.

Anthony and I decided to run for government office in the United Student Movement (USM). I won the seat of Religious Vice President by a landslide; he was not as liked by the students on campus and lost the race for Academic Vice President. My friend Marlon won the presidency. My previous position as Public Relations Director and promoting myself by doing the relationship workshop on campus and preaching played a big role in winning the election for student pastor.

After the elections, all the USM electees flew together to Los Angeles to take part in leadership training seminars before school let out for the summer. We were met by all the other electees from the colleges and universities from across the country. We stayed for four days at La Sierra University.

That summer I had been invited to do a series of street ministry workshops for GC 2000 in Toronto, the official world meeting of the General Conference of the Seventh-day Adventists, which is held every five years in different countries. I was also asked to share my life testimony at the Toronto Congress Centre in front of five thousand people. The event was to last for five days. I also had to get my LETC team prepared and ready to go for the summer. It was a double team. My job was to spend one week in Detroit training Robyn, a new leader, then take my team to work in Chicago. One week turned into two, which turned into three. When we finally made it to Chicago, we spent only a week in the Windy City before heading to Toronto for GC 2000. Robyn had asked to attend the General Conference but was denied. She went anyway. She gathered her LETC team and headed to Toronto, parking the big white church van near the Detroit/Windsor border. They crossed on foot and took a Greyhound three hours to the city. That didn't pan out too well with the publishing director of the Lake Region Conference, who oversaw both the Chicago and Detroit teams. The director had a meeting with us all, and Robyn was demoted. The teams were combined into one, and I was sent back to Detroit to lead thirteen literature evangelists. My commission that summer was the highest it had ever been.

I used a lot of the money I earned to pay off Shoshannah's debts. She had told me once that she grew up believing that black people were meant to be in debt. I refused to believe such rubbish and wanted us to get married debt free.

I returned to Alabama two days before registration. I couldn't check into my dorm early, so I stayed in Shoshannah's dorm at UAH. She had previously told me about her father's temper. He would get into rages and get out of his car to fight, and he would rage and beat her mom. The day before registration, I saw something in Shoshannah that I hadn't seen before. We got into a minor dispute about something, and I told her I was leaving. If my reflexes had been a fraction of a second slower, the cup that she whipped would have smashed in my face instead of the wall behind me. By her expression immediately after, I knew she hadn't meant to hurt me. She sobbed and told me that she'd thought she had overcome her anger. I stayed with her and assured her that everything was okay.

In my fourth year of college, I was excited to serve as Religious Vice President. It was a rewarding experience. I was afforded the chance to take the gospel outside of the church and into the streets, just like the unorthodox way I did it in Toronto. We conducted a Friday night AY program in the projects of Huntsville, Alabama, and the Divine Service main program the following morning. Marlon spoke Friday, and I spoke that Sabbath morning. I organized buses from Laidlaw to transport the students from Oakwood to the hood. Both programs were a success, and after the Sabbath service, lunch was served to the entire community.

I ended up losing my job as night dean. Security was cracking down on students parking in front of Edwards Hall. I had parked there for about twenty minutes; when I came out, I saw one of those annoying orange parking violation stickers covering almost the entire driver's side window. Tearing those things off your car was a pain in the ass. You'd see students driving around campus with the ugly white remnants on their windows for days, everyone knowing they had committed a parking infraction. The security guard hadn't pasted it very well this time, so I slowly peeled it off without tearing it or leaving any residue, walked over to the closest stop sign, and plastered it on. I never took into consideration that my license plate info was on the sticker. After getting fired, I moved off campus into a nice one-bedroom apartment with a big balcony facing the outdoor pool in the back. The rent was only $420 a month, a lot cheaper than remaining on campus and paying my own room and board. Getting fired didn't affect my position as Religious Vice President.

That semester, I was discouraged. It was supposed to be my last year. I hadn't failed any courses – in fact my grades were good – but because I had never visited the guidance counsellor, I ended up having to do another year. Each semester I'd chosen only classes that I wanted, mostly electives that wouldn't count towards my theology degree. Four semesters of Greek were required, and the emphasis was the ancient language. None of the theology majors liked it, but most stuck with it and completed it; I earned one credit, received a C, and shunned the other three semesters, focusing on my psychology minor and taking more electives than required classes. I was majoring in minors.

My eyes began to wander again, and I was doubting if I still wanted to get married. I was stuck in the valley of decision. I thought at twenty-six I needed more time. I brought Shoshannah to one of our favourite restaurants to tell her that we should reverse and just be friends. I chose less direct words, but that was how she took it, and that was how it was. She gave me back the engagement ring and told me when I was ready, then I could give it to her. We didn't stop seeing each other right away.

Elder Dsouza needed to ship some old computers to his homeland of Guyana, and it was much cheaper to ship them from New York City. He needed someone to help him drive the big white van with ten or so computers neatly stored in the back. I'd never been to New York, so of course I volunteered to help him drive. When one of us drove, the other was lying on the mattress in the back sleeping. Elder Dsouza, being three or four times my age, did most of the sleeping; even when I tried to convince him that I was too tired to drive and I was falling asleep at the wheel, I had no choice.

New York changed me. I went searching for my grandmother with the address that my mother had given me. I knocked on the door in Brooklyn and a pretty black lady answered.

"Hi, I'm looking for Enid Tull," I said.

After a moment of looking at me, this woman I had never met grew the biggest smile when she discovered who it was knocking on her door. "Junior!" She embraced me and told me to come inside.

How did she know me? As I entered her home, it was clear how. My picture, along with my sister's was on the living room wall. She introduced herself as Shirley, my aunt. My grandmother wasn't there, but two days later, I met the entire family on my father's side: grandma, uncles, aunts, cousins, everyone who was living in New York was there. It was an overwhelming experience, but never once did I feel out of place. I was welcomed as family with open arms. The following day my uncle Tony came to pick me up and take me around New York. He brought me some gifts: a pair of Nike shorts and a collection of postcards of all the landmarks of New York City. He took me up the Empire State Building and to Junior's Restaurant and Bakery in Brooklyn, famous for their cheesecake. *How did he know I loved cheesecake? Or was it because my name was Junior?* Aunt Shirley and my cousin Merleen showed me around the city as well. She let me drive and was impressed that I could keep up with the New Yorkers on the road. We passed by the Twin Towers. I was in awe of how high they stretched up into the sky. Aunt Shirley gave me my father's number, and I decided to reach out to him when I returned to Alabama.

When one of the pastors heard from Elder Dsouza that a student from Oakwood College was in Brooklyn, he invited me to preach at his church. I spoke at the small church, and after the sermon I was invited to come back and do a youth revival for a week: ten sermons in seven days. I was paid a thousand dollars and all expenses covered. The host church member I was staying with even gave me his Mercedes Benz to drive for the week. I already had an LETC team ready to roll for the spring break campaign. I brought them to Brooklyn with me but couldn't lead the team and be the keynote speaker for the revival at the same time, so my good friend Anthony led the team. After work each evening, they came to the church to hear me preach. We went back to Alabama with joyous hearts and a sense of accomplishment.

It was Tuesday September 11th, 2001. Shoshannah had stayed over at my apartment the night before because it had gotten late and she was too tired to drive back to her dorm. In the morning, when she realized the time, she rushed out the door to make it in time for class. I got up and turned on the television. One of the Twin Towers was down and the other was on fire from planes crashing into them. "Oh my God," was my reaction. I ran to tell Shoshannah, but she was leaving the parking lot in her car and probably had the music on, because she never heard me shouting to her at the top of my lungs. I went back inside to see what the heck was going on in New York. Another plane had crashed into the Pentagon, and yet another went down in a field in Pennsylvania. I was in complete shock, as was the rest of the world. I stayed pinned to the television, only leaving to attend the emergency USM leadership meeting on campus for about an hour. When I got back to my apartment, I didn't leave for days. I don't even remember sleeping; if I did, I woke up on the couch with the TV on as it replayed the planes crashing into the buildings, repeatedly, from different angles.

Shoshannah and I had come to the end of our relationship. I was failing all but one of my classes, in which I ended up with a C because of the teacher's grace. I didn't have enough money to get into college the following semester. The attacks on the US, the breakup with Shoshannah, the failing of all my classes, and not having the money to finish college caused me to sink into a depression. I was fixated with CNN and Fox and what was going to happen next. I didn't go to classes for almost two weeks, and when I started going back I wasn't doing the assignments. I was too far behind, and I couldn't catch up. I continued on as Religious Vice President, but inside I had given up on the ministry. I was showing up to my classes high after smoking weed. I was in the class *Daniel and the Prophets* with Marlon, the USM president, and he would try to talk to me after class about a program that we were having, but I would brush him off by telling him that I was in a hurry, and we would talk later. In the evening I'd buy a six pack of Guinness or Baileys or Peach Schnapps or whatever else I remembered drinking when I was with my friends. The first time I bought a six pack of Guinness, I woke up with a heavy head and hangover, and there were still four and a half beers leftover. I started going to the clubs in Huntsville with my friend Steve, who attended Oakwood and was from the same city as me. When I walked into the club, I was getting stares from all the Oakwoodites. It was the last place they expected to see their Religious Vice President – it was the last place *I* expected to be when I'd entered the ministry. A girl who was in one of my psychology classes approached me and said, "I see you're doing big things." Whatever she meant by that, I said the same thing back to her.

After presenting the relationship workshop at Oakwood with Shoshannah, like a bunch of experts, and then breaking up, like a bunch of failures, it was embarrassing to show my face on campus. I shunned speaking at programs and events because it was hypocritical, but since I was still the Religious VP, I couldn't avoid them all. The ones that I couldn't get out of, I used as a means of getting back on my feet and gaining some spiritual strength. It worked for the first few days while I prayed, read my Bible, and prepared my notes, but once I was done preaching, I had a fresh bottle of Baileys in my fridge and a new girl in my bed.

I had friends who were in the theology program studying to be pastors, and after partying, drinking, and fornicating, they got up the next morning and preached a powerful heartfelt message. I couldn't do it. My sermons felt weak, and I felt empty inside delivering them. I no longer had the zeal. I wanted to be behind the pulpit, but not without conviction, and mostly, not without the Spirit of the Most High. Because I had backslid, my own conscience told me I had to leave the ministry, and Alabama.

The pastor in Brooklyn called me and asked me to come back up to his church to preach for Sabbath Divine Service. I told him the truth: I couldn't. I told him that I was struggling spiritually. He said to come anyway, I didn't have to preach. He purchased me a ticket and I flew to New York. On the way up, I had a connecting flight in Atlanta; I flirted with the ticket lady at the counter, and she gave me her number and upgraded my seat to first class.

I arrived in New York on Friday and attended church on Sabbath, but for the rest of the weekend, I gallivanted through the boroughs and drank beer and liquor.

I was in a convenience store on Flatbush Avenue in Brooklyn buying some beers, when I heard a man shout my name. He yelled "Junia! Junia!" so loud, I wouldn't be surprised if the entire state of New York heard him. I looked toward the familiar voice and saw Richie standing by the entrance of the store, ecstatic. He shouted my name again before telling everyone in the convenience store, "This is my best friend from Canada. I haven't seen this motherf*cker in years."

That night Richie took me club hopping all over Brooklyn. We got back to his place at about five in the morning, and I got a few hours' sleep on the bed in his basement. I was awakened by what felt like four fingers pressing down on the side of my leg on top of the single sheet that I was under. It was Richie trying to wake me up for breakfast – I thought. I was wrong. I hadn't seen many rats in my life, but this must have been the biggest sewer rat in New York City. It casually walked over me, across the bed and onto the floor with its eight-inch tail dragging behind. I froze. When I mustered enough courage to reach for my pants on the floor, I went upstairs and woke up Richie. Embarrassed, he apologized. I walked the fifteen-minute route to my host's house, completely disgusted.

My return flight back to Alabama was scheduled for Monday evening. Richie picked me up and we drove around Times Square. I sat in the passenger's side in my black undervest. I had taken off my multicoloured polo shirt because it was hot, but not only because of the weather: I'd been working out all semester. I noticed a well-dressed Caucasian cutie on the busy corner with another girl, waiting to cross the street.

"What's up?" I hollered at her out the window.

"What's up?" She threw up a sign with her fingers, pretending to be gangster.

I told Richie to pull over. I startled her when I popped up behind her. "So, what's up?"

"Holy shit. My mouth is always getting me in trouble," she said.

I crossed the street with her and her business partner. She liked my style and my Canadian accent. I told her I was going back to Alabama that night, but I would rather hang out with her. It only took one block to convince her to let me stay at her place. I called my new friend in Atlanta, and she switched my flight to the next day.

There was nothing left for me in Alabama. Every experience up to September 11th was a blessing. Four years had transformed my life; one *day* had damaged it. After that fateful day, I was ready to go to war. I was prepared to fight for a country that wasn't even mine. I loved the United States. I loved Alabama and the southern hospitality. Most of all, I loved Oakwood College, but the joy I experienced when I arrived had now been replaced with sadness, partly brought about by my own actions. By the grace of God, I did a lot of good, but it wasn't as easy to escape the habits of my past.

I had my struggles and made mistakes, but I was resilient. I was going to bounce back. Other than my mom, I was the strongest person I knew. I would use that strength and make a difference in the world. I knew how to move on, but I never knew how to quit. I wasn't dropping out of school; I was beginning a new chapter: *For a just man falleth seven times, and riseth up again.* Proverbs 24:16. I would get back up, lead the people as I was called to do, and fight for the oppressed. But not here; not in Alabama. My time had expired. Although it was time to go, I never stopped believing in the Most High. *He* brought me, a little brown boy, born into a dysfunctional family, raised by a young mother in the projects, and delivered me from the valley of the shadow of death. After everything I had experienced in life, after everything I had seen, done, and learned, I went back to Toronto, not knowing which direction my life would go. The only thing I know for certain now, is that my *redemption draweth nigh*.

To God be the glory, great things He has done.

THE END

ACKNOWLEDGEMENTS

A huge shout out and much love is extended to those who supported me, helped me, believed in me, and contributed to the process of me completing *Memoirs of a Bad Boy*. To my mom, who has always believed in me. Even when I had the craziest ideas, she was still there and supported me to the end. Mom, you were a huge encouragement to me during the final lap of writing this memoir. Thank you for answering the phone when I was pestering you every two to three minutes with questions about the past that you would have much rather have forgotten about. I'd like to thank my dad for his participation and input as well; he too had to suffer through my intense questioning, which I'm sure seemed interrogative at times. He even asked me (jokingly, I think) if I was an investigator.

In the beginning I couldn't bear to read my own writing, but through the years it became more tolerable due to the help of a chosen few who educated, guided, and advised me throughout the process. The first person to read and edit the first few pages (which I'm sure were a task to get through) was Craig Samuel. I'd like to thank him for his insight and help in paving the way for me to become a better writer. A special thanks to Cameron McCloud, a former staff at Bronson Detention Centre, where I spent too much of my time as a teenager. Cameron's words of encouragement and wisdom pushed me through the first few years of this journey. He has been there to help with the beginning stages of editing, and it was his motivation that got me through that part.

I owe a special thanks to Andrea, the mother of my kids, for taking care of our three children while I travelled for work and spent time in different countries writing parts of my memoir. My kids, Israel, Josiah, and Semaiah were an inspiration to me as well; they gave me the desire to finish this project and do great things. I know they will do even greater things. One specific time stands out when I saw Josiah lying on the living room floor when he was only eight or nine years old, reading my manuscript page by page for about half an hour. I thought to myself, if my story can hold a child's attention for that long, I really got a story to tell the world.

Marina Nemat, my professor at the University of Toronto, *Writing the Memoir*, has influenced me greatly. She is the author of the best seller *Prisoner of Tehran*. I found her class to be extremely informative and educational. Her style of teaching, her love for writing, and her genuine care for the students, pushed me to rise to the next level. I want to thank my former classmates from Marina's class as well for their honest feedback and words of encouragement.

Finally, Chris Cameron, my editor, author of *Dr. Bartolo's Umbrella and Other Tales from my Surprising Operatic Life*. He is a large part of the reason why you are holding this book in your hand. He guided, taught, and mentored me from the first sentence all the way to the last. I enjoyed working with Chris throughout the years. His insight and feedback inspired me to keep going, even when I was discouraged and ready to put the project off. I knew I'd never quit, but at times I was drained, but after reading his detailed notes and how much he had invested in my story, it motivated me to continue. Thank you, Chris, we are finally at the finish line.

The back of a building in South Regent Park

My little brother, Andrew, and my mom visiting me in the Bronson Detention Centre when I was 15 years old.

My former school Regent Park/Duke of York

Store clerk charged in teenager's slaying

By John Duncanson
TORONTO STAR

An 18-year-old store clerk was to appear in court today charged with second-degree murder in the fatal stabbing of a teenager during a Victoria Day fireworks display at Ontario Place.

"We got a lot of help on this one," said Detective Sergeant Tom McNamara of the homicide squad, the lead investigator on the Mathew Smith slaying.

McNamara thanked the slain teenager's family for calming Smith's friends, who had vowed revenge for his slaying and had set out looking for the killer.

The family's help bought police time to put the case together and find the suspect, he said. No weapon has been recovered.

According to friends, Smith, 18, of Flemington Rd., North York, was trying to break up a fight in the crowded parking lot of Ontario Place on May 24 when he was stabbed in the chest.

One of Smith's friends accidentally bumped someone in the holiday weekend crowd of

FATAL FIGHT: Reginald Tull, left, is charged in Mathew Smith slaying.

700 that had gathered in the Ontario Place parking lot to watch the annual fireworks display, and an argument ensued, friends said.

Smith, a weightlifter who was almost 6 feet tall and weighed 190 pounds, wasn't carrying any weapon.

McNamara said yesterday's arrest was the culmination of numerous interviews with witnesses who were at the fireworks display that night.

Reginald Junior Tull, 18, of Kingston Rd. in Toronto was arrested yesterday at the store where he works as a clerk. He is scheduled to appear today in court at old city hall.

Quartermen cleaning the range during locukup

Quartermen serving the evening Jug Up

The yard

Segregation (the hole)

Manufactured by Amazon.ca
Bolton, ON

33399583R00150